Advance Praise for

The NEXT Sustainability Wave

The Next Sustainability Wave provides valuable insight into communicating with corporate leaders in their own language to bring about "enlightened self-interest." We can all expect to become better sustainability change agents by reading and applying the lessons found here.
— Karl-Henrik Robèrt, founder of the Natural Step and author of
The Natural Step Story: Seeding a Quiet Revolution

This highly informative and thoroughly researched book presents a wealth of data, ideas, and insights drawn from a vast array of sources and the first-hand experience of practitioners. Bob Willard's genius is finding the gems, presenting them in plain language, and building a strong case that corporate sustainability is approaching the tipping point.
— Dr. Brian Nattrass, Managing Partner, Sustainability Partners, co-author of
The Natural Step for Business: Wealth, Ecology and the Evolutionary Corporation
and *Dancing With the Tiger: Learning Sustainability Step by Natural Step*

If you are going to read one reference book on corporate social responsibility this year, this is the book. Bob Willard takes complex and often ill-defined ideas and distills them into bite-sized chunks that can be easily understood and acted on.
— Adine Mees, President and CEO, Canadian Business
for Social Responsibility

Bob Willard has done a great service for all of us with an interest in the future of business by synthesizing a vast literature into a strategic roadmap that lights the way ahead for those who pull the levers of power. *The Next Sustainability Wave* bridges the gap that has too long separated strategic management and sustainability — this is a book that both sharpens the mind and catalyzes action.
— Robert M. Abbott, CMC, Founder & Chief Strategist,
ABBOTT STRATEGIES, author of *Uncommon Cents:
Henry David Thoreau and the Nature of Business*

The Next Sustainability Wave heralds a new era in which sustainability strategies help business leaders to pursue competitive advantage in a complex global environment.
— Dr. Chris Laszlo, co-founder, Sustainable Value Partners, and author of
*The Sustainable Company: How to Create Lasting Value through
Social and Environmental Performance*

With *The Next Sustainability Wave*, Bob Willard has utilized a particularly effective structure, combining the fresh ideas of a host of leading edge experts with his own unique insights.
— Bruce Sampson, Vice President Sustainability, British Columbia
Hydro and Power Authority

Bob Willard's *The Next Sustainability Wave* is a strategy guide, encyclopedia, and compelling collection of stories and anecdotes — all in one volume. It belongs on the desk of every executive who cares about the future.
— David Ticoll, co-author of *The Naked Corporation: How the Age of Transparency will Revolutionize Business* and *Digital Capital: Harnessing the Power of Business Webs*

The Next Sustainability Wave is a must-read for any business, government, or non-profit leader concerned with high performance today and survival in the future. It provides a clear, step-by-step approach for analyzing how sustainability can assist an organization to thrive in rapidly changing times.
— Bob Doppelt, director, Program in Watershed and Community Health, and academic coordinator, Sustainability Leadership Academy, University of Oregon

No other author has drawn on anywhere near the depth of experience from such a range of practitioners as Bob Willard has with *The Next Sustainability Wave*. He provides a robust framework that both highlights his insights and lets the voices of many others add color and perspective.
— Don Reed and Paul Gilding, Ecos Corporation, authors of the paper "Single Bottom Line Sustainability"

Thoroughly researched and packed with lots of great come backs for all the "yeah-but" responses you're likely to encounter, *The Next Sustainability Wave* offers great insights on why sustainability makes good, practical, and strategic business sense.
— Ronald Nielsen, Director, Sustainability and Strategic Partnerships, Alcan Inc.

The data, information, stories and personal perspectives contained in *The Next Sustainability Wave* provide a clear and compelling vision of a new way of doing business. Bob Willard shows us in clear terms how and why sustainability should be the core strategy of business in the 21st Century.
— Kevin Brady, Director, Five Winds International and co-author of *Mapping the Journey: Case Studies in Strategy and Action toward Sustainable Development*

The Next Sustainability Wave captures from all perspectives the best current thinking on the business case for sustainability, in an accessible, practical, and balanced manner. Bob Willard makes it clear — there is no longer a valid reason for companies not to pursue environmental and social sustainability.
— Dr. Marlo Raynolds, Executive Director, Pembina Institute for Appropriate Development

The NEXT Sustainability Wave

BUILDING BOARDROOM BUY-IN

BOB WILLARD

foreword by L. Hunter Lovins

NEW SOCIETY PUBLISHERS

To Sherrill,
my inspiration and partner in life,
with love.

Cataloging in Publication Data:
A catalog record for this publication is available from the National Library of Canada.

Cover design by Diane McIntosh. Cover Image: Photodisc Blue.

Printed in Canada. First Printing February 2005.

New Society Publishers acknowledges the support of the Government of Canada through the Book Publishing Industry Development Program (BPIDP) for our publishing activities.

Paperback ISBN: 0-86571-532-7

Inquiries regarding requests to reprint all or part of *The NEXT Sustainability Wave* should be addressed to New Society Publishers at the address below.

To order directly from the publishers, contact:

New Society Publishers
P.O. Box 189, Gabriola Island, BC V0R 1X0, Canada
1-800-567-6772

New Society Publishers' mission is to publish books that contribute in fundamental ways to building an ecologically sustainable and just society, and to do so with the least possible impact on the environment, in a manner that models this vision. We are committed to doing this not just through education, but through action. We are acting on our commitment to the world's remaining ancient forests by phasing out our paper supply from ancient forests worldwide. This book is one step towards ending global deforestation and climate change. It is printed on acid-free paper that is **100% old growth forest-free** (100% post-consumer recycled), processed chlorine free, and printed with vegetable based, low VOC inks. For further information, or to browse our full list of books and purchase securely, visit our website at: www.newsociety.com

NEW SOCIETY PUBLISHERS   www.newsociety.com

CONTENTS

ACKNOWLEDGMENTS

My formal and informal study during the 1990s awoke me to the pressing need for sustainable development. My objective is to harness resources of the global business community in the race toward sustainability before it is too late.

Several early influences shaped my crusade. Dana Meadows' two books, *Limits to Growth* and *Beyond the Limits,* contributed to my wake-up call. Her weekly columns were an amazing blend of wisdom, passion, and humor. Her unique ability to connect events and her self-effacing style made her premature passing all the more tragic.

Bill Alexander, my supervisor and mentor during my master's program at the Ontario Institute for Studies in Education at the University of Toronto, first seeded the idea to write a book and to use a doctorate as a vehicle for research. Despite my initial dismissal of both ideas out of hand, his discerning questions and friendly encouragement started me down the path to my graduation/second book publication milestone this year. He was a kindred spirit whose counsel I miss.

The experts who graciously agreed to be interviewed and quoted were essential to this work. Between January 2002 and March 2004, I interviewed 43 sustainability experts, listed on the next pages. They represent a mix of sustainability consultants (17), senior corporate leaders (13), NGO representatives (7), and academics (6). Geographically, most were from Canada (27). Others were from the US (12) and the UK/Europe (4). Interviews with the experts yielded 278 single-spaced pages of transcribed material. Ideas from all of them were a wonderful catalyst to my thinking, especially about drivers of sustainability, and I use quotations from many to reinforce points made throughout the book. I sincerely thank them for their time and assistance. Thanks also to the hundreds of authors, researchers, academics, activists, consultants, conference speakers, and reporters who provide a rich reservoir of material for sustainability champions.

Another incarnation of this book is my doctoral thesis. Gary Knowles' editing, supervision, and guidance has enlivened its content and supported a much more dynamic design than I would otherwise have the courage to use. Marilyn Laiken's and Rodney White's insightful suggestions improved both the thesis and the book versions.

Thank you all.

LIST OF EXPERTS INTERVIEWED

Experts are listed alphabetically by surname. Pseudonyms for those preferring to remain anonymous are listed at the end.

- Mark Anielski: Adjunct Professor, Corporate Social Responsibility & Social Entrepreneurship, School of Business, University of Alberta

- William R. Blackburn: President, William Blackburn Consulting, Ltd.; former Vice President and Chief Counsel, Corporate Environment, Health, and Safety, Baxter International Inc.

- Kevin Brady: Director, Five Winds International

- Susan Burns: Principal, Natural Strategies LLC; Managing Director, Global Footprint Network

- Professor Martin Charter: Director, The Centre for Sustainable Design, UK

- Louise Comeau: Former Director, Federation of Canadian Municipalities

- Neil Cooney: Former Vice President, Human Resources, IBM Canada Ltd.

- Devin Crago: Senior Analyst, Innovest Strategic Value Advisors

- Steven Cross: President, Threads Lifestyle

- Steve Elbert: Senior Vice President, Remediation Management, BP America Inc.

- Claude Fussler: Director, World Business Council for Sustainable Development (WBCSD); Special Advisor to the UN Global Compact

- Greg Gulyas: Vice President, Sales & Marketing, IBM Global Services

- Mitch Gold: Vice President, North American Affairs, International Association of Educators for World Peace

- Gib Hedstrom: President, Hedstrom Associates; former Vice President, Environmental Management, Arthur D. Little

- Stephen Hill: Assistant Professor, Environmental & Resource Studies, Trent University

- George Khoury: Director, Conference Board of Canada
- Laurent Leduc: Principal, Leadership Horizons
- Amory Lovins: CEO, Rocky Mountain Institute
- Antony Marcil: Former President and CEO, World Environment Center; behavioral economist
- Bill McClean: Vice President, IBM Canada Ltd.
- Mark Milstein: Post-Doctoral Fellow, Johnson Graduate School of Management, Cornell University; Business Research Director, Sustainable Enterprise Program, World Resources Institute
- Richard Mireault: Former Environmental Manager, IBM Canada Ltd.
- Sam Moore: Vice President, Burlington Chemical Company
- Paul Muldoon: Executive Director, Canadian Environmental Law Association
- Gerry Pelletier: Transformation Executive, IBM Canada Ltd.
- David Powell: President, Canadian Institute for Environmental Law and Policy; staff, Innis College Environmental Studies Program at the University of Toronto; verifier, Canadian Chemical Producers' Association Responsible Care program
- Marlo Raynolds: Executive Director, Pembina Institute
- Don Reed, CFA: Principal, Ecos Corporation
- Steve Rice: President, Environmental Opportunities
- Nigel Roome: Chair, Sustainable Enterprise and Transformation, Eramsus University Rotterdam, The Netherlands
- Scott Rouse: Managing Partner, Energy @ Work
- Brian Shannon: Former Director, Customer Fulfillment, IBM Canada Ltd.
- Julian Smit: Principal, SOHO/SME
- John Swannick: Manager, Public Affairs, Lloyds TSB Group
- John Szold: Former Vice President of Licensed Brands, Delicious Alternative Desserts (former Canadian licensee of Ben & Jerry's Ice Cream)
- Mark Thomsen: Director, SRI World Group Inc.
- Rodney White: Director, Institute for Environmental Studies, University of Toronto

- Martin Whittaker: Senior Vice President, Swiss Re Financial Service Corporation; former Managing Director, Innovest Strategic Value Advisors

- Alan Willis: President, Alan Willis & Associates; representative, Canadian Institute of Chartered Accountants on Global Reporting Initiative (GRI) founding Steering Committee; Chair, GRI Verification Working Group; collaborator with Stratos Inc. for the "Building Confidence" 2003 survey of corporate sustainability reporting in Canada.

- Mel Wilson: Senior Manager, PricewaterhouseCoopers

- Ron Yachnin: Former Senior Research Associate, Conference Board of Canada

- Expert A: Manager, Environment, Health and Safety, a major Canadian company

- Expert B: Vice President, Marketing, a major Canadian company

FOREWORD

By L. Hunter Lovins

In 2000, as part of rebranding itself as "Beyond Petroleum", British Petroleum announced a corporate commitment to reduce its emissions of greenhouse gasses 10 percent over its 1990 levels by 2010. BP achieved the cuts in only two years and in the process, saved itself $650 million. Rodney Chase, a senior executive at BP, subsequently reflected that even if the program had cost BP money, it would have been worth doing because it made them the kind of company that the best talent wants to work for.

This shouldn't come as a surprise: people like to solve problems — it's one of humanity's most endearing features. Business, at its best, is a rewarding adventure in just such problem solving. It is a sure sign something's wrong when so many talented people express distaste for tackling the typically narrow business agenda. While economists, politicians and business leaders believe that this bottom line mania brings wealth and opportunity, an increasing number of people, particularly those in the next generation of managerial talent, are asking whether there isn't something more to life.

Most managers have not yet recognized that what they seek — greater employee productivity, retention of top talent, easier attraction of capital and profits — are all benefits of sustainability strategies. In fact, sustainable strategies can align an organization with the intrinsic values of its people. Bob Willard's prior book *The Sustainability Advantage* outlined what these benefits are. With this book he describes how to achieve them.

The traditional capitalist approach requires a strange faith: that the system responsible for the decline of all global ecosystems will somehow use its remarkable engineering capacities to restore the systems on which life and thus prosperity depends. As Einstein said, it is folly to expect the same mindset that created the problem will foster its solution.

It is time then to find a new answer. Much of the world's life support system is badly broken. According to a pioneering analysis of the world's ecosystems prepared by the World Resources Institute, United Nations and The World Bank, "There are considerable signs that the capacity of ecosystems, the biological engines of the planet to produce many of the goods and services we depend on, is rapidly declining." According to the report, half the world's wetlands have been lost in the last century, half of the world's forests have been chopped down, 70 percent of the world's major marine fisheries have been depleted, and all of the world's coral reefs are at risk."

This is the context within which business is conducted today. The good news is that much of what is needed to solve the world's challenges represents an enormous business opportunity. Witness the four engineers at DuPont who recently figured out how to spend less than $100,000 to save more than $5 million per year in energy costs. Leading semiconductor maker STMicroelectronics is finding that its commitment to become carbon neutral by 2010 is not only driving its innovation as a company but will save it almost a billion dollars.

Traditional executives, especially in America, would be wise to pay attention. Even if they do not see much interest in sustainability among their peers, their competitors are well along with this strategy. The "European dream" of sustainability is now eclipsing the "Wall Street dream" of instant wealth around the world. Reluctant globalists throughout most of the last century, Americans have believed in an immature capitalism that has ignored the environmental and social realities of a fragile world where humans are altering all ecosystems without the knowledge to competently manage them.

But things are changing fast. The 150 largest companies in the world nearly all have a "sustainability officer" at the VP level or higher. In just the past two years, new MBA programs like Presidio World College that embed sustainability in business training rather than derisively as a single elective have been created — and are flourishing in the United States, Europe and Canada.

In 2003, ten leading banks (now 28, collectively representing over 90 percent of all developing country private finance) initiated the Equator Principles to infuse sustainability principles into such lending. Citibank now states that it sees sustainability as a distinct competitive advantage in the lending marketplace.

In December 2003, The Chicago Climate Exchange (CCX) began trading carbon in North America. When environmentalists bemoaned the failure of the U.S. Senate to ratify the Kyoto Protocol, Exchange founder Richard Sandor responded, "Governments don't make markets, traders do. I'm a trader, let's make a market." Seventy-five companies, state governments and other institutions are now using CCX, and its sister company the European Climate Exchange, to trade "carbon financial instruments" that further support the profitability of opportunities to reduce climate impacts.

Using the whole-system approach of Natural Capitalism, most sustainability challenges can be solved at a profit. Natural Capitalism rests on three principles:

- Using all resources dramatically more efficiently, not only because doing this is profitable, but because it buys time in which to implement more broad-based sustainability practices;

- Redesigning all products and services using innovation inspired by nature (i.e. Biomimicry); and

- Managing all systems to be restorative of human and natural capital.

Taken together, these principles can enable companies to achieve their stated goal of increasing shareholder value, but to do so in ways that are responsible to life on earth.

New tools are emerging to enable businesses to implement Natural Capitalism and other frameworks of sustainability. Natural Capitalism, Inc. recently joined with The Global Academy, and The Natural Edge Project of Australia to develop the Sustainability Helix system. The Helix provides a whole-system menu that enables a business to explore, experiment, implement, and eventually mainstream its choice of sustainability strategies. It offers a sequenced flow of sustainability activities that leads to continual improvement rather than the trial and error approach that necessarily characterized the efforts of the sustainability pioneers.

The Sustainability Helix is an example of the important insights Bob Willard offers into how to bring about the transition to sustainability. *The Next Sustainability Wave* shows business leaders how to use sustainability to bring greater profitability. It can help those in government balance the market's short-term competitive realities with long-term economic health for their community. Sit back and enjoy learning how you can become a partner in making all this happen.

L. Hunter Lovins is the founder and president of Natural Capitalism, Inc. and is a founding faculty member of Presidio World College's Sustainable Management MBA program. She is also co-author of 9 sustainability books including Natural Capitalism: Creating the Next Industrial Revolution *and* Factor Four: Doubling Wealth, Halving Resource Use.

CHAPTER ONE

INTRODUCTION

The goal of corporations is to survive and prosper, to be sustainable enterprises. To achieve this goal, companies must create more value than they consume, maintain their social license to operate with their stakeholders, innovate, and adapt to continual and rapid change, while attracting and retaining customers and employees.[1]

The goal of societies is to survive and prosper, to be sustainable social systems. To achieve this goal, people around the globe must fulfill their present needs within the carrying capacity of the planet, without compromising the ability of future generations to meet their needs.[2]

The goal of the environment is to survive and prosper, to be a sustainable ecological system. If it is to achieve this goal, people cannot keep extracting minerals, heavy metals, oil, and gas from the earth's crust and returning them as garbage faster than nature can absorb them. Similarly, humankind cannot keep generating synthetic materials and toxic substances and throwing them away faster than they can decompose or nature can absorb them. Nor can people increasingly degrade the ability of fish, bird, forest, plant, and animal resources to sustain and regenerate themselves.[3]

Are the sustainability goals of corporations, societies and the environment mutually sustainable? If not, who dominates this complex and dynamic interplay of systems?

Corporations have enormous impact. Business is a direct or indirect contributor to most 21st-century ecological and social challenges. Corporations also have power. It is increasingly evident that corporations, especially multinational ones, are the only institutions on the planet large enough, well-managed enough, and resourceful enough to address global sustainability issues — if they have the will. Groups and individuals championing sustainability can seek to either contain corporate impact and power or harness them to their ends. I prefer the latter course.

Sustainability strategies give corporations the choice of getting ahead of the curve, defining new rules, and being rewarded by their stakeholders for behaving responsibly. This book is about how to engage corporate leaders positively in conversations about sustainability for the benefit of the company, the environment, and society.

Enlightened managers must use business language if they are to be effective when lobbying hard-nosed business colleagues. They have to show the relevance of sustainability to day-to-day business priorities. If it doesn't help the business, it's not on business leaders' radar screens (Expert A)

Setting the Stage

My primary audiences are sustainability champions and chief executive officers (CEOs), followed closely by those people working with them on sustainability issues — board members, senior executive colleagues, nongovernmental organization (NGO) representatives, sustainability consultants, policy makers, and academics. That is, the book is intended for anyone who wants to learn how to engage senior leaders of more companies in sustainability initiatives.

The language of the book honors that audience. It is deliberately direct, conversational, and brief. Metaphors and phraseology are intended to appeal to executives and engage them in the content.

You may have noticed the unusual format of this book. On each right-hand page is a self-contained topic with a bold heading, which helps busy executives quickly grasp the essence of the content in concise nuggets. Since the table of contents lists main headings on right-hand pages, readers can quickly get a sense of the flow by browsing the table of contents and directly accessing topics of most interest.

All left-hand pages hold "sidebars" — quotes from experts interviewed, quotes from the literature, cartoons, tables, or charts that supplement the point being made on the facing right-hand page. The reader can choose either to read the backup material on left-hand pages or to skim the book reading only right-hand pages. The intent is to enable busy business readers to quickly and comfortably access sections that are most useful.

For brevity, quotes on left-hand pages from interviews with experts are cited with their names or pseudonyms. Further information about their positions and organizations is available in the "List of Experts Interviewed," at the front of the book.

Having set the stage with this audience and format context, on with the show.

There are exemplary individual citizens, there are others who just make do, and there are others who are criminal. Why should corporations be any different from individuals? You would expect it to be much more difficult for businesses to be criminal unless they happen to be a criminal fraternity like the Mafia which does operate quite a successful business from what I understand. But in the main, legitimate organizations only have pockets of bad doing. So the first inhibitor is lack of awareness or lack of appreciation that it matters — they are doing successfully without it. (Nigel Roome)

I see three reasons companies focus on sustainability:
• The companies that have made serious commitment and progress can be described as well-managed and well-run companies — well-run businesses with a fairly consistent earning stream. They would generally be in the top half of their industry or higher.
• The nature of their business requires a longish-term horizon. In companies like BP [British Petroleum] or Shell, the investments they make in pipelines or refineries are likely to last for 50 years. Therefore, the basic nature of their business and investment decisions is such that the decisions they make today are going to be around for a while.
• The third important ingredient is being global. If companies are operating in multiple countries around the world, especially if they are looking for growth outside the US, a strong green positioning is imperative. (Gib Hedstrom)

Early Thoughts on Inhibiters

Corporations are only interested in undertaking challenges that make business sense. In my first book, *The Sustainability Advantage*, I outlined a quantified financial business case for sustainability. I felt good that I had nailed how to accelerate a corporation's commitment to sustainability principles and practices for the benefit of the firm, the environment, and society. Almost as an afterthought, I included a subsection in the concluding chapter entitled "Yeah, but ... " It began with the question "If the business case is so good, why are smart executives not taking advantage of it?" I went on to propose four possible answers:

1. They are not aware of the business case.

2. They are aware of the business case but don't believe it.

3. They believe the business case but are uneasy about setting themselves up for accusations of "green-washing."

4. Their entrenched mental model dismisses sustainability as irrelevant to business.

As I learned more about how financially beneficial it is for companies to commit to sustainability, I was intrigued by the question of why more companies have not done so. After all, if sustainability champions are going to build a critical mass of companies that are committed to operating sustainably, they need to be more effective in convincing them to do so. Do the observations on the opposite page about successful, well-managed, global, long-horizon companies being the best candidates for responsible social and environmental strategies imply others are not?

I decided to learn from experts and the latest literature, to discover what motivated companies that already "get it," to identify additional emerging drivers, to understand objections companies have to sustainability agendas, and to explore effective counterarguments to objections.

That is, this book is about the "whys" and "why nots" of companies' commitment to sustainability, with particular attention to the supportive role played by a compelling financial business case to justify sustainability initiatives for the next wave of companies.

Sometimes people stumble into it.

For example, the green real estate developer Stanley Selengut, who did the Maho Bay and Harmony Studio projects in the US Virgin Islands, didn't start off green. He started off realizing that were he to clear the site in Maho and build a resort on the wooded hillside conventionally, the wooded hillside would end up on top of his coral reef and there would go his main asset for attracting tourists. So he improvised this odd-looking thing you can hardly see from the ocean side, with platforms and walkways up on stilts so that the ground would be undisturbed. That caused him to invent a kind of eco-resort based on tents instead of cabins.

Then he found it resisted hurricane damage. People really like being up in the treetops, so he ended up with very high occupancy, making a lot more money, and yet he had much lower construction and operating costs. Then he realized he was onto a good thing.

He is now a committed eco-resort developer, but not because he started off green at all. (Amory Lovins)

6

Who is in the Next Sustainability Wave?

Most companies. There are about 73 million legally constituted firms in the world.[4] Try naming 10 that are leaders in environmental and social responsibility. Okay, now try 100.

Organizers of conferences on sustainability find they repeatedly go to the same shortlist of executive spokespersons as keynote speakers. Even if 1% of companies were on the sustainability bandwagon, there would be 730,000 companies to choose from. There are not. What companies are in the next wave, and how do sustainability champions breach the dam holding them back?

Companies in the next wave fit loosely into four categories:

1. *Leaders:* They are doing good things, and know they are, but are deliberately not talking about them. They need to be convinced to tell their good stories and lead by example.

2. *Coincidental Leaders:* They are exemplary sustainability companies, but they do not think of themselves as such. If their social and environmental accomplishments were reframed using sustainability concepts, they would have an impressive sustainability track record. They just never thought of describing their accomplishments using sustainability language.

3. *Too-Tiny-To-Toot Leaders:* As discussed in the appendix, over 99% of companies in Europe, Canada, and the United States are small and medium-sized enterprises (SMEs) with fewer than 500 employees — 75% to 92% of them have fewer than five employees. They have neither the money, resources, time, or interest to tell the world their sustainability stories, even if they are exemplary. They need help.

4. *Laggards:* These companies don't "get it" or are only giving lip service to sustainability. Some are quite proud of this position. They need encouragement ... or enlightenment ... or awakening.

How many companies are in each category is anyone's guess. The good news is there are thousands of potential candidates for the next wave. The bad news is there are many obstacles to convincing enough of them to get on board to achieve the "tipping point" in corporate environmental and social stewardship. The intent of this book is to help identify and overcome those inhibiters.

"

The business case/value is starting to emerge a little bit more, given the latest information we are seeing on the link to shareholder value, works such as you've done, and others. Companies are starting to see this, but I think there is still a long road to a critical mass of companies that think of sustainable development or corporate social responsibility as a value driver. (George Khoury)

When we are trying to make an idea or attitude or product "tip," we're trying to change our audience in some small yet critical respect; we're trying to infect them, sweep them up in our epidemic, convert them from hostility to acceptance. That can be done though the influence of special kinds of people, people with extraordinary personal connection. That's the Law of the Few. It can be done by changing the content of communications, by making a message so memorable that it sticks in someone's mind and compels them to action. That is the Stickiness Factor. I think both of those laws make intuitive sense. But we need to remember that small changes in context can be just as important in tipping epidemics, even though that fact seems to violate some of our most deeply held assumptions about human nature.

Once we're part of a group, we're all susceptible to peer pressure and social norms and any number of other kinds of influence that can play a critical role in sweeping us up in the beginning of an epidemic .... The spread of any new and contagious ideology also has a lot to do with the skillful use of group power .... [John Wesley, founder of the Methodist religious movement,] realized that if you wanted to bring about a fundamental change in people's belief and behavior, a change that would persist and serve as an example to others, you needed to create a community around them, where those new beliefs could be practiced and expressed and nurtured.
— Malcolm Gladwell, The Tipping Point[5]

"

The Sustainability "Tipping Point"

What is the big deal about getting coincidental leaders, silent leaders, and too-tiny-to-toot leaders to speak out? Why nudge laggards forward? To make real progress on sustainability, sustainability champions need a critical mass of companies that embrace environmental and social strategies. They need enough to get to the threshold described by Malcolm Gladwell in *The Tipping Point*.

It is a numbers game. It takes about 20% of a community to adopt a new idea or trend before it "tips" and becomes the norm. But it is not just any 20%. It must be the right 20%. According to Gladwell, some must be Connectors, people with influence who are good at using word-of-mouth epidemics to spread the word in their extensive networks of friends, using their social power rather than position power. Some must be Mavens, respected for who and what they know, especially how to get things done and how to help solve other people's problems. Some need to be Salesmen, who enthusiastically but subtly persuade others and are trusted, listened to, and respected by their "clients."[6]

Some sustainability champions are combinations of Connectors, Mavens, and Salesmen. Although I use the term "sales call" throughout this book, I am assuming the salesperson has some of the other attributes, as well.

An optimistic, powerful message in *The Tipping Point* is the hopefulness that small things can make a big difference. Language, packaging, timing, location, gestures — they can all have a multiplier effect on the outcome.

Gladwell uses terms like "epidemic" and "infection" as value-neutral descriptors. They are the metaphorical medical mechanisms that enable new ideas, whether positive or negative, to catch on rapidly. This book is about how to make positive sustainability contagious. If the critical mass required to reach the tipping point is 20%, I estimate about 1% to 5% of corporations buy into the concept now. The good news is that many of them are high-profile, influential Connectors within the corporate community. Sustainability champions just need more of them, and more corporate-responsibility Mavens and Salesmen.

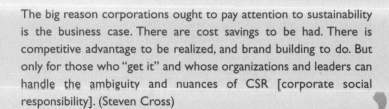

> The big reason corporations ought to pay attention to sustainability is the business case. There are cost savings to be had. There is competitive advantage to be realized, and brand building to do. But only for those who "get it" and whose organizations and leaders can handle the ambiguity and nuances of CSR [corporate social responsibility]. (Steven Cross)

Figure 1.1: *Pardon My Planet* on terminology

Pardon My Planet reprinted by permission of King Features Syndicate

The Squeeze on Boards

Boards are being squeezed between commercial pressures and societal pressures. Commercial pressures include institutional shareholder demands, threats of hostile mergers and acquisitions, competitive innovators, customer service challenges, attrition of highly qualified people at all levels, governance issues, and global market fluctuations. Societal pressures, driven by nongovernmental organizations (NGOs), consumers, and governments, are relentlessly raising the bar of expectations for socially and environmentally responsible behavior. The commercial-societal vice is tightening, and boards are caught in the middle.[7]

Boards are proactive custodians of corporate values and value creation. They monitor management's internal alignment with overarching corporate goals and principles; they shape accountability and risk-management frameworks to align with external public policies; and they select and reward CEOs who produce good results.[8] Should they dig in their heels and resist efforts to expand the role of business in society? Would that position protect shareholder interests or jeopardize them? How real is the business case for sustainability and, more importantly, how real is it for their company?

Sustainability champions must recognize one barrier to working together is the tribal jargon both sides proudly, and perhaps unconsciously, use. People from not-for-profit, nongovernmental organization (NGO) cultures need to learn to "talk suit," and people from for-profit cultures need to learn to "talk NGO." I will suggest common terms to bridge the divide and to help for-profit and not-for-profit organizations recognize that they are in a collaborative three-legged race together for the same finish line.

In this book I explore drivers of sustainable behavior that are relevant to senior executives and to boards of directors. I use governance considerations to ground hypothetical conversations with senior executives in order to align motivators, arguments, and terminology with the fiduciary responsibilities of corporate leaders. Using the language of the cartoon opposite, I will talk about their "cotton candy" rather than my "insulation on a stick."

The terminology is messy. You just need to find the one that gets the least wrinkles in their face and go with that one. (Marlo Raynolds)

Much of the language used on the advocacy side is from the NGO world. When it doesn't work, much of the reaction is, "Well, these people don't get it. Maybe they're just stupid or just jerks." There is a need for significant translation, and it is striking how few people speak both dialects well. (Don Reed)

The issues have to be translated into business language, have to be translated into the language of the different business functions. You have to scale the "green wall." Often people come into the environment side from an environmental science background and they don't have a strong knowledge of the business or marketing side. (Martin Charter)

A Sustainability Sales Call

Suppose you care about the state of the world, but you are not sure if your executive colleagues share your values. You are uneasy about being dismissed as a tree-hugging environmentalist if you suggest the company should pay more attention to its ecological and social responsibilities. Your colleagues and manager might pat you condescendingly on the head, applaud your worthy though naïve convictions, and suggest you work with like-minded NGOs in your spare time. Just broaching the subject risks your credibility as a corporate leader who has the best interests of the bottom line at heart. It could be a career-limiting conversation. Not good.

Then an opportune moment arises. It may be a chance meeting in an elevator, at a reception, at a conference, or during a break at an annual general meeting. Sustainability evangelist meets corporate nonbeliever. How does a sustainability champion start the conversation in such a way that it continues excitedly instead of being quickly terminated and awkward, like a Saturday-morning doorway conversation with Jehovah's Witnesses? How can sustainability champions appeal to corporate leaders' critical priorities, handle likely objections, and use serendipitous opportunities to engage their interest?

That is, how would a sustainability champion have a "sales call" with an executive or director that builds to boardroom buy-in on sustainability strategies? This book is intended to prepare courageous champions with the arguments, facts, credibility, and confidence to capitalize on such opportunities in a win/win way. It uses proven marketing and sales techniques to frame the material. That is, it suggests that you know your executive "customers," their needs, and their business priorities; you understand why others in your industry, including competitors, have "bought" sustainability and whether similar drivers apply to your company; you know the features and business benefits of your sustainability "product"; you anticipate typical objections and know how to handle them; and you frame sustainability as a "solution" to existing problems, rather than just one more thing they should worry about.

You don't evangelize corporate social responsibility (CSR) for its own sake.[9] You sell CSR for the sake of the firm. To do this, you have to use language that sticks, that sinks in, that is relevant.

Sustainable Development: Meeting the needs of the present without compromising the ability of future generations to meet their own needs.
— Brundtland Commission, 1987[10]

Corporate Social Responsibility: The overall relationship of the corporation with its stakeholders. Elements of social responsibility include financial performance, creation and maintenance of employment, environmental stewardship, employee relations, and investment in community outreach.
— Conference Board of Canada[11]

Corporate Social Responsibility: The commitment of business to contribute to sustainable economic development — working with employees, their families, the local community and society at large to improve their quality of life.
— World Business Council for Sustainable Development (WBCSD)[12]

Corporate Social Responsibility: A concept whereby companies integrate social and environmental concerns in their business operations and in their interactions with stakeholders on a voluntary basis.
— European Union Multi Stakeholder Forum on Social Responsibility[13]

Four Systems Conditions for a Sustainable World: In a sustainable society, nature is not subject to systematically increasing ...
1. concentrations of substances extracted from the earth's crust
2. concentrations of substances produced by society
3. degradation by physical means
... and people are not subjected to conditions that systematically . . .
4. undermine their capacity to meet their needs.
— The Natural Step[14]

The Terminology Swamp

The definitions on the opposite page all describe a future as well as a present state and include multiple, holistic dimensions. The Brundtland Commission and the Natural Step definitions refer to people's "needs." Canadian Business for Social Responsibility (CBSR) outlines the needs of present and future generations:

- *Economic well-being:* Job security, decent wages, safe and healthy work environments

- *Environmental health:* Clean air, clean water, diverse ecosystems, safe and reliable food sources

- *Social equity:* Equal access to opportunities, freedom from discrimination, poverty, and homelessness; protection from terrorism and wars; assistance after natural disasters[15]

Eco-effective design guru William McDonough's hope for a sustainable world is "a delightful, safe and healthy world, with clean water and renewable power, economically, equitably, ecologically and elegantly enjoyed."[16] John Ehrenfeld at MIT describes sustainability as "the possibility that we all flourish forever"[17] — "all" being all living things, not just us humans. These definitions evoke a bit more enthusiasm than the others. As William McDonough says, if you ask someone how their marriage is going and they say, "Sustainably," it doesn't have quite the same zing as "Flourishing!"[18]

Although they have become increasingly synonymous, the labels and embedded ideas in the definitions have different origins. "Sustainable Development" evolved from economic, ecological, and social justice disciplines. It is development that does not breach ecological limits or destroy social cohesion.[19] "Corporate Social Responsibility" evolved from a moral philosophy discipline. The stakeholder theory, implied by references to community, employees, environment, and society, comes from strategic management. The notion of corporate accountability evolved from business law.[20]

These are noble notions. However, it is time I acknowledged a significant speed bump on the road to corporate sustainability: the terminology is not helpful. It needs to be more focused so that business executives can see the relevance of sustainability to their companies. Otherwise the sustainability message will not be memorable. It will not stick.

"There has been some evolution towards "CSR." It has become the standard term .... I think "sustainability" by itself does work very well. The word sustainability embodies a number of ideas and principles, all of which are intuitive objectives for any company. Consider some synonyms of "sustain": maintain, nourish, prolong, support, feed, experience. These all make for natural corporate strategies. To commit to sustainability is to commit to long-term thinking and the active pursuit of long-term gain for your company. I think it works well as language. (Julian Smit)

I personally prefer the word "sustainability" more than "sustainable development." SD has an implicit or explicit assumption about growth. In the context of the third world that might be appropriate, but corporations tend to have focused on the development part much more than the sustainable part. Sustainability embraces more than development. It includes a restorative component as well as steady state where the latter is appropriate. (David Powell)

We use "sustainability" with the immediate caveat that it has many stigmas and has been overused. (Marlo Raynolds)

"Sustainability" in North America, if not elsewhere, is a vague and misleading term having multiple meanings in different circles and contexts. And I don't much like "triple bottom line." So I end up thinking in terms of "corporate responsibility to investors and other stakeholders" — not very catchy or simple, but then the concept of sustainable development is neither catchy nor simple. (Alan Willis)

I expect a "corporate responsibility" conference will draw anywhere from the general counsel of the company, who is looking at governance and ethics, to the other groups within the corporation, including the environmental and social sides. (George Khoury)"

Pick a Label, Any Label

Everyone agrees the legs of the three-legged stool of sustainability are economic, environmental, and social responsibilities that contribute to public good and quality of life. Expressed as groupings of capital assets, the economic leg is about sustaining financial, structural, and manufactured capitals; the environmental leg is about protecting and restoring natural capital and living off its interest instead of its principal; and the social leg is about nurturing human, intellectual, and knowledge capitals within the company and fostering social/relationship capital with the local community and the rest of global society.

The three legs are inclusive. For example, the five dimensions rated by the Corporate Responsibility Assessment Tool used by the Conference Board of Canada can be mapped against them: governance and management practices (economic); human resource management practices (social); community investment and involvement (social); environment, health, and safety (environmental and social); and human rights (social).[21]

The issue is what to call the stool supported by the three legs. The definitions on page 14 have different labels: Sustainable Development, Corporate Social Responsibility and Sustainable World. There are at least a dozen such umbrella nouns, adjectives, and phrases in the running, including sustainability, corporate social responsibility (CSR), corporate responsibility (CR), corporate sustainability (CS), triple bottom line (TBL), sustainable development (SD), sustainable growth, natural capitalism, corporate stewardship, corporate citizenship, conscientious commerce, 3 Es (Economics, Environment, Equity), and 3 Ps (Profits, Planet, People). Each has different origins and nuances, but all have evolved to be interchangeable.

"Corporate social responsibility (CSR)" is a popular term. It is comfortably used by many practitioners and is echoed in names of organizations like Canadian Business for Social Responsibility (CBSR), Business for Social Responsibility (BSR) in the US, and CSR Europe. Both "corporate responsibility (CR)," gaining currency in Europe, and "sustainability" are more inclusive umbrella terms because neither of them uses one of the sustainability trinity — economic, environmental, or social — as a limiting adjective. To be fair, CSR advocates say that environmental and economic dimensions are implied in CSR.

I will primarily use "sustainability," "CSR," and "corporate responsibility (CR)" as interchangeable, inclusive terms denoting all three dimensions of sustainability.

In the States, the words "sustainability" and "sustainable development" are not something that they are happy to fill their literature with yet. They talk about "environmental leadership," "community or social activism" in a philanthropic sense, "environmental excellence," or "operating excellence" ....

We've talked to thousands of companies all over the world. If you really get to the bottom of it, there is a deep mistrust of UN lingo. Some oil companies I have spoken with just do not believe that anything coming out of the Rio conference, or a UN-associated gathering, or even the World Bank, can be trusted. (Martin Whittaker)

I wonder if there is a difference between "sustainable development" versus "CSR" to the people you are trying to sell the message. "Sustainable development" is a phrase like "church." As soon as you say it, half the people say, "Oh, yeah," and they are onside right away with you, and the other half of the people turn off and say, "Forget about it. I'm not interested." As a phrase, it can be a big stumbling block.

I don't know how you preach to the unconverted. Some of these phrases can be a danger. As soon as you say Sustainable Development, half the corporate audience is going to say, "Forget it," no matter how compelling the case that follows is. (Stephen Hill)

Language Matters. Talk Theirs.

Terminology matters. Colonel Sanders understood. He instinctively knew that "finger-licking-good chicken" would attract more customers to KFC than "fried dead bird." Both are descriptive. Our mental baggage of associations makes the latter phrase fundamentally repugnant.

Effective marketing requires getting inside customers' heads, understanding their wants and needs, and positioning your product so that they see how it helps them satisfy their wants and needs. Features and characteristics of the product that are unrelated to a particular customer's needs are unlikely to grab that customer's interest.

Language comes with baggage — value-laden, subconscious associations formed by years of random experiences. Choice of language is one of the biggest challenges faced by sustainability champions attempting to gain the attention of busy, preoccupied executives. Sustainability champions have to talk the customer's language, not their own. A sustainability champion's preferred terminology is interesting, but irrelevant. From a marketing perspective, the executive's response to the terminology is more important than its "correctness" or the sustainability advocate's personal preferences.

So what is the best umbrella term to use with businesspeople? When discussing the issues with a single business leader, the decision is easy: ask him or her. Most will not be shy about telling you which term they prefer and why. It's more challenging with a larger audience. "Sustainable development" might raise UN associated mixed feelings, especially with Americans, while others might feel it is an oxymoron. And so on.

Perhaps sustainability champions should be less preoccupied with the completeness, depth, and breadth of whatever sustainability label they prefer and be more attentive to the usefulness of the concept in the world of harried business executives. Convincing executives to embrace "sustainable development" is no different than marketing any product to them. If the customer wants a hammer and you have a rock, then you had better re-label your rock a "stone hammer" or you risk losing your customer. If the customers need bottom-line results to save their jobs, bonuses, or the company, using language suggesting that they save the world is not an effective sales technique, as I found out when I wrote Lou Gerstner.

To: Lou Gerstner [Chairman and CEO of IBM Corporation]
From: Bob Willard
Date: October 10, 1997
Subject: IBM Sustainability Leadership Opportunity

I was impacted by your introduction to the 1996 IBM Environment Report where you state IBM feels a stewardship for "the well-being of the Earth and the life it supports." This suggests a leadership opportunity for IBM: "sustainability leadership."

Sustainability leadership includes the use of our leadership and ingenuity in leading the world toward a sustainable global economy ... an economy that meets our ongoing needs without compromising the ability of future generations to meet their needs. The attached articles elaborate on reasons for this concern ....

Many other business leaders agree that global corporations hold the future of our planet in their hands .... Sustainable development is not only good sense, it is also good business. IBM could grow and excel by offering leading-edge sustainability solutions for a small planet .... Global sustainability is good for IBM, our customers, our communities, the world, and future generations.

IBM is well-positioned to seize sustainability leadership .... What would IBM's sustainability leadership look like? Whatever we decide it should ... partnering with our customers, other corporations and governments on sustainability initiatives ... unleashing the creativity and commitment of IBM leaders on sustainability issues would identify many more IBM sustainability leadership opportunities.

You joined IBM to help save one of America's greatest companies. You have. Now, would you be willing to apply your leadership to help save our future?

Bob Willard
IBM colleague

Letter to Lou

In the early 1990s, my involvement in a three-year campaign about a proposed water treatment plant in my Ontario community awoke me to ecological issues. I became convinced that global corporations are critical actors in the planet's socio-ecological play and decided to explore if my employer, IBM, could become more strategically committed to sustainable development, building on its award-winning track record in environmental affairs.

So in 1997 I wrote a letter to Lou Gerstner, CEO and president of IBM Corporation at the time, asking him to embed sustainable development principles into IBM's business strategies for the good of the company and the planet. It took me six months and reviews by 18 people to craft the page-and-a-half letter, excerpts from which are opposite. I thought it was pretty good. I included statements from other business leaders, attached *Harvard Business Review* articles about sustainability being relevant to business, made suggestions about what sustainability strategies at IBM might include, and appealed to his desire to show leadership in our industry.

It failed. My proposal was treated as a philanthropic request, not as a strategic business suggestion. The reply encouraged me to discuss my ideas with IBM's corporate community affairs director. I did. He reassured me that the leadership role I was suggesting in the area of sustainability was exactly what IBM was doing in the area of public education with its "Reinventing Education" philanthropic program. They obviously did not "get it."

Or maybe I did not. Beyond the excerpts opposite, my letter also included phrases like "business will play a vital role in the health of our planet," "more sustainable forms of consumption," and "funding research on causes of environmental issues." I intended these good-for-the-world notions to support my case for strategic sustainability initiatives being good for IBM. Instead, they were interpreted as an appeal for IBM to support more worthy causes. They were intended as icing on the cake. Instead, they were seen as the cake.

This frustrating experience reminded me that it is important to speak executives' language and relate any proposition to their current business challenges. Maybe a better letter would have been: "Dear Lou: I have some thoughts on how IBM could increase its profit by 38%. Interested? Yours truly ... "

Appeal to their self-interest. Find out their driving forces and appeal to them. (Stephen Hill)

Your job is not to tell them why they should do something for your sake. Your job is to tell them why they should do something for their sake. You position it as a way to solve their problem. The biggest key to our success is that we actually try to listen to what their real problem is. "What is it that is bugging you? What's in your way?" We simply position it as solving those problems. It may have long-term benefits, but it has to be about solving current issues for them. You have to be malleable in the way you present it so that it is always reflecting priorities that they have said they have in the short term. It's not about you at all. (Louise Comeau)

We have a lot more success when we make the argument that all these social and environmental trends are market forces. Couching it in those terms does a lot to move people into the mindset that this is a real business issue, that they have value at stake on these issues, and that this is about business strategy. They deal with changes in their operating environment and business strategy all the time, so they are comfortable dealing with it. You are not relegating this to someone in charge of sustainability over there in the corner. You are doing it in a way that looks at how this affects your whole business. (Don Reed)

The compelling business case has to be translated, company by company, to the agenda of the CEO. Whatever terminology is used, if it is separate from the top three things on the CEO's agenda, it will go nowhere. Find out whatever the CEO's agenda is — whether it is customer focus or growth or low-cost provider or Six Sigma, whatever it is — and ingrain the relevant aspects of sustainability directly into that agenda. That agenda exists and defines how people get measured, managed, and incented. (Gib Hedstrom)

Sustainability Is a Means to Their Ends

What results drive company executives these days? Boardroom and senior executive meetings will be focused on some subset of typical business priorities:

- Revenue improvement, expense reduction, and profit
- Share price, growth and market share
- Leadership, vision, mission, purpose, and values
- Governance and ethics
- Productivity, healthy workers, absenteeism
- Risk management, emerging market forces
- Security of supply, price, and availability of raw materials, energy, and water
- Beating competitors to market
- Attracting and retaining good customers
- Attracting and retaining top talent
- Regulatory compliance
- Quality of products and services
- Teamwork, learning, and innovation

Unfortunately, "saving the world" does not make the list. Sustainability champions should not push sustainability, per se. They should solve business problems. If they talk about sustainability rather than issues like the above, executives may hear them talking about "fried dead bird" instead of "finger-licking-good chicken." They need to help executives tune into WII-FM (What's In It — For Me?), instead of WII-FW (What's In It — For the World?). They need to channel their passion and commitment to sustainability and focus on how sustainability strategies get traction in the boardroom as an irresistible means to achieve executives' already existing goals. Sustainability champions' ends need to be reframed as executives' means.

Experts agree that companies are at different stages of integrating sustainability factors into their business strategies. The benefits of sustainability that sustainability champions cite should be governed by the stage the company is at in its sustainability efforts, and the broad generalities of CR should be translated into relevant strategies and goals.[22]

CEO and the top management team
Focus: Issues that pertain to the whole corporation, such as strategy, financial performance, mergers and acquisitions, and governance.
Corporate Responsibility (CR) Interest: The above issues, and how increased CR can help improve stock price, financial performance, corporate reputation, and risk management.

Head of Marketing and Sales
Focus: Increased sales, product differentiation, and customer loyalty.
CR Interest: How CR combined with marketing tools and techniques in cause-related marketing boosts action/sales versus opinion/intent to buy.

Head of Human Resources
Focus: Issues of workforce development, recruitment, and retention.
CR Interest: How CR helps increase employee satisfaction and loyalty, improves recruitment and retention, and builds the long-term pipeline of employees.

Heads of Operations
Focus: Production of products and services in a timely, cost-effective way; beating competitors on price, innovation, and quality.
CR Interest: How CR helps improve the company's ability to innovate, helps it be efficient and cost-effective, and helps make its products and services more attractive through the use of a diverse set of suppliers.
— Conversation with Disbelievers, "Methodology"[23]

Different Strokes for Different Folks

All executives are not the same. Therefore, their hot buttons from the preceding list will be different depending on their roles in the company. The sidebar, opposite, outlines different priorities for different executives, as reinforcement that sustainability champions are well-advised to relate their arguments to the focus of the particular executive in the conversation.

Specifically, a report, news item, survey, or case study about sustainability needs to score high in four areas to be convincing to an executive.[24]

- *Information type:* The least credible is data about opinion or intention, unless it is opinion of peers. Convincing data shows cause-and-effect action, especially evidence about CR's impact on business functions and finances that the skeptical executive deems critical to success. For example, a study that shows people actually buy more from companies after reading about their CR deeds is better than a survey that shows people say they will.

- *Relevance of the data:* First, are the data accurate — does the study have sufficient methodological rigor and validity? Second, is it material — are the business effects significant, relative to other ways to achieve similar ends? Third, is it applicable — will it work for this company, in this industry, now?

- *Source of the data:* People believe people, not data. Most managers have a "hierarchy of belief." Most trusted is a peer businessperson who has tried CR and found that it "really does work"; well-respected consultants or vendors are next; and after that, industry trade associations. Information from most academics, foundations, advocacy groups, companies outside the mainstream, and much of the media is believed less.

- *Alignment with attitudes:* Strong evidence may be rejected because it is contrary to deeply held beliefs, mindsets, or political agendas. Usually internal CR advocates must rationalize their propositions using typical business reasons rather than moral or ethical arguments.

Sustainability advocates gain the trust of skeptics by acknowledging these credibility attributes, being more skeptical than the skeptics, filtering studies cited, and influencing executives through their trusted influencers.

25

Figure 1.2: Sustainability Continuums

Source	Stage 1: Pre-Compliance	Stage 2: Compliance	Stage 3: Beyond Compliance	Stage 4: Integrated Strategy	Stage 5: Purpose & Passion
Mark Schacter *Altruism, Opportunism and Points in Between*[25]	Fundamentalism		Self-Interest & Social Contract Theory	Stakeholder Management	Stewardship
Forum for the Future *Just Values*[26]	Outlaws	Compliers	Case-Makers	Innovators	Trailblazers
Coro Strandberg *The Future of Corporate Social Responsibility*[27]	CSR Lite	CSR Compliant	CSR Strategic	CSR Integrated	Deep CSR
Carl Frankel *In Earth's Company*[28]		Regulatory Compliance	Public Disclosure & Beyond Compliance	Corporate SD	Global SD
European Corporate Sustainability Framework[29]	Pre-CS	Compliance-Driven CS	Profit-Driven CS	Caring CS & Synergistic CS	Holistic CS
Mark Goyder *Redefining CSR*[30]		Compliance CSR		Conviction CSR	
Natural Capitalism Sustainability Helix Framework[31]		Exploring the Sustainability Opportunity	On the Road with Traction	Sustainability Leadership	The Restorative Company

Sustainability Stages

In PricewaterhouseCoopers' "2002 Sustainability Survey Report," 89% of respondents from 140 large US companies believe there will be more emphasis on sustainability in 2006 than in 2002.[32] The increased emphasis anticipated in the PwC survey will move the next wave of organizations from wherever they are today on the five-stage sustainability continuum (Figure 1.2) to the next stage. Authors of continuums use different labels and language to describe "shades of green" at each stage, but the overall concepts are similar.

- *Stage 1:* The company feels no obligation beyond profits. It cuts corners and tries not to get caught if it breaks the law or uses exploitative practices that cheat the system. It ignores sustainability and actively fights against related regulations.

- *Stage 2:* The business manages its liabilities by obeying the law and all labor, environmental, health, and safety regulations. It reactively does what it legally has to do and does it well. Emerging environmental and philanthropic social actions are treated as costs, projects are end-of-pipe retrofits, and CSR is given lip service.

- *Stage 3:* The company moves from defense to offense. It realizes it can save expenses with proactive and incremental operational eco-efficiencies, cleaner processes, and better waste management. It recognizes community investment and social marketing can minimize uncertainty, enhance its reputation, and help maximize shareholder value.[33] However, sustainability initiatives are still marginalized in specialized departments — they are tacked on as "green housekeeping," not built in and institutionalized.

- *Stage 4:* The firm transforms itself. It re-brands itself as a company committed to sustainability and integrates sustainability with key business strategies. It captures added value from breakthrough sustainability initiatives that benefit all stakeholders. Instead of costs and risks, it sees investments and opportunities. It makes cleaner products, applies eco-effectiveness and life-cycle stewardship, and enjoys competitive advantages from sustainability initiatives.

- *Stage 5:* Driven by a passionate, values-based commitment to improving the well-being of the company, society, and the environment, the company helps build a better world because it is the right thing to do.[34]

> For some early adopters, it is what they do. They were founded on certain ethical principles and they live them. It is the way they operate. (Mark Thomsen)

Figure 1.3: The Five Sustainability Stages

Stage 1: Pre-Compliance	Stage 2: Compliance	Stage 3: Beyond Compliance	Stage 4: Integrated Strategy	Stage 5: Purpose & Passion

The Stage 3 to Stage 4 Transformation and the Stage 5 Difference

The leap from Stage 3 to Stage 4 on the sustainability journey requires linking market opportunities with corporate responsibilities: creating positives like innovative products and services for the world's poor while eliminating negatives like pollution, waste, and child labor; creating new value like sanitation, health, safe food, clean water, and new jobs while eliminating non-value; seeing partnerships with diverse stakeholders in the market as a source of innovative solutions; seeing sustainability as an engine for growth as well as risk mitigation.[35]

Stage 3 is about incremental, continuous improvements in eco-efficiency. Stage 4 is about discontinuous, leapfrogging breakthroughs. It is about creative destruction of existing manufacturing process and product design, and breakthroughs in new products, services, markets, and processes. It is a transformation from Stage 3, not a transition.

Transformations are not trivial. Moving from Stage 3 to Stage 4 requires internalizing sustainability notions in profound ways, both personally and organizationally. Environmental considerations move from the Environmental Affairs or Environment, Health, and Safety (EHS) department into the boardroom. Social considerations move from the Community Relations or Corporate Donations department into the strategy function. Sustainability-based thinking, perspectives, and behaviors are integrated into everyday operating procedures and the culture of the organization.[36] When these migrations happen, the metamorphosis is underway. The payoff is tapping into the revenue, innovation, and productivity side of the sustainability business case rather than just the risk-mitigation and cost-savings side.

What about Stage 5? Stage 5 is very different, but simultaneously very similar. About 90% of what Stage 4 and Stage 5 companies do looks the same. They both deploy business strategies that respect the environment, the community, and the ongoing business health of the firm. Motivations differ. Stage 4 companies "do the right things" *so that* they are successful businesses. Stage 5 companies are successful businesses *so that* they can continue to "do the right things." The line between Stage 4 and Stage 5 in Figure 1.3 denotes this significant difference.

The distinction is not meant to be a value judgment. Frankly, if we got to the tipping point of companies using sustainability as a management discipline at Stage 4, I would be delighted. I am less concerned with the righteousness of motivations than I am with results.

29

Figure 1.4: *Dilbert* on "Locusts"

Dilbert reprinted by permission of United Feature Syndicate, Inc.

Elkington's Insect Metaphors Fit the Stages

Sustainability is described as both a journey and a destination. In John Elkington's *The Chrysalis Economy*, he uses clever biological imagery to classify a corporation's stage on the sustainability journey.[37] His four insect archetypes can be mapped to the five stages of corporate sustainability evolution.

- *Locusts:* These companies have a potentially high negative impact and destroy various kinds of capital. The more they do, the worse it gets. They exploit nonrenewable resources; overwhelm the carrying capacity of social, environmental, and economic systems; and do not heed early warning signals from diverse stakeholders. They believe the short-term interests of shareholders and management are best served by their degenerative activities. Locusts are in Stage 1 or Stage 2.

- *Caterpillars:* These companies are in Stage 3. They have the potential for transformation but are still based on an unsustainable model. They have relatively low impact and are only interested in the short-term benefits of sustainability. They profess to be further ahead than they are, which undermines their capacity to make the jump from Stage 3 to Stage 4.

- *Honeybees:* They have a sustainable business model, based on ethical principles integrated with sound business strategies. They cultivate human, social, and natural capitals, working in an inclusive partnership with key stakeholders for business success. They learn, they network in industrial ecosystems, they cross-pollinate, and they incubate innovative new products and services. They are positive, high-impact actors in the market and are at Stage 4.

- *Butterflies:* These Stage 5 companies generate environmental, social, and economic value. They "get it" for values-based reasons and sometimes publicly chastise locusts for not being on the same wavelength. Unfortunately, although they are beautiful to watch, they are usually smaller, founder-led lightweights in the corporate world and lack economic muscle. Their impact is low.

The world needs more Stage 4 honeybees.

Figure 1.5: Sustainability Drivers Overview

Three First-Wave Drivers	Two Emerging Drivers
1. *Founder's Personal Passion* · Corporate values / "Right thing to do" * 2. *Public Relations Crisis* · Reputation / Brand image* · Relations with stakeholders / Dispute resolution / Issues management* 3. *Regulatory Pressure* (or threat of it) · Compliance with regulations* · Expedited permitting / Relations with regulators* · Regulations / Enforcement** · Legislated product performance standards** · Legislated reporting** · Voluntary agreements** · ISO 14000**	1. *A Perfect Storm of Threats* · Reduced business risk* · Improved reputation with investors, bond agencies, banks* · Social license to operate or grow* · Changing stakeholder expectations* · Economic instruments** 2. *Compelling Business Value* · Improved access to markets / customers* · Cost savings / Improved bottom line* · Attract and maintain skilled employees* · Increased employee morale and productivity* · Stimulate innovation* · Input to strategic planning* · Corporate role models*

* From 2002 Government of Canada CSR cross-industry survey of ten companies
** From 2003 GlobeScan survey of 201 experts in 40 countries

Drivers of Sustainability: Overview

In 2002, the Government of Canada studied ten companies in various industry sectors to determine drivers, implementation approaches, success factors, and challenges facing companies implementing CSR.[38] The companies were: Teck Cominco, DuPont Canada, Husky Injection Molding, Home Depot Canada, Weyerhaeuser Canada, Canadian Pacific Railway, Nutreco Canada, Syncrude, VanCity Credit Union, and TELUS. The ten companies identified 15 drivers/benefits that encouraged their commitment to sustainability initiatives and strategies (the number of companies mentioning each driver is shown in parentheses).[39]

1. Reputation/Brand image (10/10)
2. Corporate values/"Right thing to do" (9/10)
3. Relations with stakeholders/Dispute resolution/Issues management (9/10)
4. Improved access to markets or customers (8/10)
5. Expedited permitting/Relations with regulators (8/10)
6. Compliance with regulations/Environment (8/10)
7. Social license to operate or grow (7/10)
8. Cost savings/Improved bottom line (7/10)
9. Changing stakeholder expectations (6/10)
10. Attracting and maintaining skilled employees (6/10)
11. Increased employee morale and productivity (6/10)
12. Reduced business risk (4/10)
13. Improved reputation with investors, bond agencies, banks (4/10)
14. Stimulate innovation (4/10)
15. Input to strategic planning and understanding sustainable development (4/10)

In 2003, a GlobeScan survey of 201 experts in 40 countries revealed eight predicted drivers of sustainable development.[40] To set the stage for our discussion of historic and emerging drivers of sustainability, Figure 1.5 shows the Government of Canada study's 15 drivers and the GlobeScan experts' 8 drivers arranged under the five categories of drivers used in this book: three drivers that worked for the first wave of companies adopting sustainability practices, and two emerging drivers. The figure reinforces that the five drivers I will be looking at are representative of those at play in the marketplace.

CHAPTER TWO

THREE DRIVERS OF THE FIRST WAVE

What can sustainability champions learn about motivational factors from companies that have already established themselves as leaders in sustainability? Why did they decide to pursue responsible environmental and social agendas, and what rationale sustained their momentum on the journey? Surveys say ...

In PricewaterhouseCoopers' "2002 Sustainability Survey Report," 75% of respondents listed enhanced reputation (90%), competitive advantage (75%), and cost savings (73%) in their top three reasons for adopting sustainability practices.[1] In another 2002 PricewaterhouseCoopers and World Economic Forum survey of 1,200 CEOs worldwide, 68% said that a company's reputation on CSR is important to profitability and can prevent the loss of customers, shareholders, and even employees.[2]

According to a 2002 study published by Springpoint Consultancy in the UK, the main driving forces behind CSR were company culture (51%) and a desire to enhance the brand (29%). Only 11% of managers stated that campaigning by NGOs influenced their company, and 10% cited current or forthcoming legislation as a factor in CSR programs.[3]

A 2003 survey of 277 human resources specialists by the Work Foundation in the UK found that 42% of the organizations surveyed had a strategy for social responsibility or corporate citizenship. Of those with or planning a CSR strategy, 82% said they saw it as important for creating a positive public image, 76% saw CSR as important to building relationships with stakeholders, and 76% wanted to give something back to the community.[4]

Notice how concern for the environmental and social health of the planet is glaringly missing from these surveys of corporate drivers. Image/reputation, competitive advantage, cost savings, stakeholder relations, philanthropy, and customer/shareholder/employee retention all play motivational roles for companies practicing sustainability today. That is what companies are saying now, but were those the original motivators behind their interest in sustainability?

In this section, I dig behind today's rhetoric and examine three primary drivers that caused the first wave of CSR-focused companies to become committed to sustainability strategies: founder's personal passion; public relations (PR) crisis; and regulatory pressure.

But first I explore which companies were early sustainability adopters.

When asked which companies are the very best, I tend to divide them into the high-impact sectors and the low-impact sectors. There is a tendency to not give any credit to the companies in the high-impact sectors — auto, oil and gas, mining, and refining — but in a sense they are, in many cases, doing the most because they have the largest obstacles to overcome and, ultimately, they have the greatest impact on the environment and society. (Devin Crago)

There are fewer companies in the "leading" category than I hoped there would be five years ago. There are two ways of answering this. One: "How ingrained is sustainability in the fiber of every employee, from the boardroom to the shop floor?" A few small companies like Timberland pave the way here. A second way looks at the magnitude of impact you could have on society. BP and DuPont stand out here. [Sir] John Browne had the courage to stand out on climate change in 1997, changing the way a whole industry addressed sustainability. Chad Holliday has been transforming DuPont for several years in a most impressive way. (Gib Hedstrom)

First I should say what I go looking for when looking for sustainability leaders. I look for companies that 1) have changed their mindset from products to services, because that immediately draws in product stewardship and brings in systems thinking about having to understand what's happening upstream and downstream. That leads to having thought through your supply chain and really understanding the value created for the customer; 2) are committed to a zero waste goal and zero emissions; 3) are playing or pushing on renewable energy, either from the commercial use side or investment side; 4) really understand how to engage with their stakeholders. (Marlo Raynolds)

How Would You Know a Leading Sustainability Company If You Saw One?

In the early 1990s, IBM Canada was aggressively pursuing quality programs, as were many companies at that time. In the leadership development department, we decided to benchmark our offerings with other companies' "best of breed" leadership programs. As we began listing companies to visit, we soon realized that we had more questions about criteria by which to select our benchmark companies than we had answers:

- Should we select them on the basis of their external awards for the quality of their programs, or were the awards simply evidence of their prowess in applying for and winning awards?

- Should we develop our own set of rigorous criteria for effective leadership development programs and processes and then see how others' programs measured up, or would they be able to provide the implied data for our criteria?

- Should we just poll our counterparts in other companies about firms they thought had the best leadership development programs? But if we did that, what criteria would they use, and would they have any better insights than we did?

- Should we take into account the financial success of comparison companies to ensure we avoided the irony of benchmarking against great leadership development processes in failing companies?

In short, how would we recognize a leading leadership development process if we saw one?

Selecting leading companies in the sustainability arena presents a similar dilemma. Have some companies simply invested more effort in winning external rewards than others that might actually be better but had decided not to invest considerable time and energy in applying for awards or publicizing their good works? What criteria are being assessed when companies are ranked? Whose opinion is being asked? To what extent will consultants be influenced by their client base when they list leading sustainability companies? And should efforts by companies in "clean" industries be valued over ones in "dirty" industries, or vice versa?

The diversity of lists of leading companies in sustainability is revealing.

There is no single company that is good at all the dimensions of corporate environmental management or sustainability. What you are more likely to find are companies that are advanced in certain areas .... There are a number of companies that do interesting things, but no single company puts the whole thing together into a package. That's why there are not any sustainable companies and there are not likely to be for at least 20 years. (Nigel Roome)

Figure 2.1: Interviewed Experts' Top-10 List of CSR Companies

Top Ten CSR Companies	Number of Mentions in Experts' Top Five Lists
· Royal Dutch / Shell	18
· BP	15
· Interface	16
· Suncor	12
· DuPont	9
· The Body Shop	6
· Alcan	5
· Husky Injection Molding	5
· Mountain Equipment Co-op	5
· Electrolux	5

Experts' Views on Leading Companies in Sustainability

I asked 43 experts around the world which companies they thought were the top five CSR companies. Most experts interviewed readily admitted that their view was limited to companies with which they had firsthand experience. They also struggled to find companies whose corporate responsibility warts did not overshadow their beauty marks. Most had concerns about gaps between what companies professed and their behaviors or products. Several lamented lack of evidence that companies had truly started to rethink their business. They used such a high standard of overall corporate culture supporting corporate responsibility behaviors that they struggled to list even two or three exemplary companies.

Such lists are also moving targets. Things change. Leading companies can become laggards in the blink of a CEO change. One expert cited Exxon as a company he would have included in his list in 1986 but not today. Nortel is another example of a company where sustainability reputation took a sudden downturn after new CEO John Roth took over in 1997. Will today's CSR leaders still be at the top of the list after their inevitable senior management changes?

Ignoring all caveats, Figure 2.1 is the very unscientific top ten list of companies named by sustainability experts I interviewed, derived from their individual top five lists of leading CSR companies. Since most experts were from Canada, it is not surprising that they acknowledged the visibility of Canadian companies (Suncor, Alcan, Husky Injection Molding, and Mountain Equipment Co-op) more than experts in other countries did. What was a surprise was the very wide diversity of companies named by the experts. Beyond those listed in Figure 2.1, 19 companies received three to four votes, and another 66 companies had one or two mentions. All told, the 43 experts generated a list of 95 companies that at least some of them deemed to be among the top five most sustainable companies.

Do more rigorous evaluations done by organizations that make it their business to make these assessments have more consistency? Let's see ...

Figure 2.2: The SustainabilityBusiness.com SB 20 List for 2004 (alphabetical)

- Baldor Electric
- Canon
- Chiquita Brands International*
- East Japan Railway
- Electrolux*
- Green Mountain Coffee Roasters*
- Henkel*
- Herman Miller*
- JM*
- Novozymes*
- Philips Electronics
- STMicroelectronics*
- Svenska Cellulosa
- Swiss Re*
- Timberland*
- Triodos Groenfonds
- United Natural Foods*
- Vestas*
- Wainwright Bank*
- Whole Foods Market*

* Denotes companies on the list in both 2003 and 2004.

SustainableBusiness.com's and PricewaterhouseCoopers' Lists

In 2002, 2003, and 2004, the *Progressive Investor* newsletter, published by SustainableBusiness.com, asked five leading social/environmental investment advisors to recommend companies leading the way to a sustainable society while being strong financially. Figure 2.2 is the SB 20 2004 list of the top 20 companies. Novozymes, Herman Miller, Swiss Re, Electrolux, and Triodos Bank have integrated sustainability into their business models. What sets them further apart, though, is that they each take a public stand for sustainability in their respective industries and are helping their industry as a whole make the transition. United Natural and Whole Foods have business models with a sustainable mission — to integrate natural/organic products into society.[5]

For comparison, here is the list of the top five CSR companies compiled by a 2003 *Financial Times*-PricewaterhouseCoopers survey of 903 CEOs in 20 countries:[6]

- Microsoft
- Toyota
- General Electric (GE)
- International Business Machines (IBM)
- British Petroleum (BP)

None of the FT-PwC most sustainable companies are in the SB 20 list for the same year.

Next, I will look at two more lists compiled by the *Financial Times* and *Business Ethics*.

Figure 2.3: *Financial Times* 2001 rankings

Companies that best manage and affect environmental resources						World's most respected companies		In Media & NGO Top 20 Environ'l List	In CEO Top 30 Environ'l List
Ranked by Media & NGOs		Ranked by CEOs		Ranked by CEOs					
Rank	Name	Rank	Name	Rank	Name				
1	BP	1	BP	1	General Electric				X
2	Body Shop	2	Royal Dutch/Shell	2	Microsoft			X	X
3	Honda	3	Toyota	3	IBM				X
4	Ford	4	Weyerhaeuser*	4	Sony				X
5	Royal Dutch/Shell	5	DuPont*	5	Coca-Cola				
6	Ben & Jerry's (Unilever)	6	General Electric*	6	Toyota			X	X
7	Vivendi Universal	7	Ricoh*	7	Nokia				
8	Toyota	8	DaimlerChrysler*	8	Wal-Mart				
9	Otto-Versand*	9	Microsoft	9	Intel				
10	Siemens	10	IBM*	10	Citigroup				
11	Patagonia*	11	Body Shop	11	General Motors			X	
12	Procter & Gamble	12	Procter & Gamble	12	AIG				
13	Interface*	13	Vivendi Universal	13	Ford			X	X
14	McDonald's*	14	Honda	14	3M				X
15	General Motors	15	Matsushita Electric*	15	Hewlett-Packard				
16	Greenpeace*	16	Ford	16	Daimler Chrysler				X
17	Ikea*	17	Exxon Mobil*	17	Nestlé				
18	Co-operative Group*	18	Sony*	18	Southwest Airlines				
19	GlaxoSmithKline*	19	Siemens	19	Johnson & Johnson				X
20	Microsoft	20	Volkswagen*	20	Berkshire Hathaway				
* Companies not in CEO list		* Companies not in the Media & NGO Top 20 list							

Financial Times' *and* Business Ethics' *Lists of Most Sustainable Companies*

In 2001 the *Financial Times* surveyed the most environmentally responsible and most respected companies.[7] The difference between perceptions of CEOs and the judgment of media/NGOs is what makes this survey especially interesting. Only 11 of the companies in the media/NGO top 20 list were in the CEO top 30 list. Only 55% of the media/NGO list of companies that best manage and affect environmental resources, and 60% of the CEO list, were in the top 50 list of most respected companies. Figure 2.3 shows how the top 20 companies in the various lists compare. The criteria used, and rankers' perceptions, can have a significant influence on which companies appear on these lists.

Figure 2.4, on the next page, lists the first 50 of the top 100 "best corporate citizens" in 2004, as judged by *Business Ethics*.[8] The *Business Ethics* criteria included seven comprehensive factors, only one of which was environmental responsibility, as used by the *Financial Times* survey:

- Returns to stockholders
- Service to non-US stakeholders
- Environment: Pollution reduction, recycling, energy-saving measures, EPA citations, fines, lawsuits
- Community relations: Philanthropy, sponsorships, community service projects, educational outreach, scholarships, employee volunteerism
- Employee relations: Wages relative to the industry, benefits paid, family-friendly policies, parental leave, team management, employee empowerment
- Diversity: Percent of minority groups and women among employees/managers/board members, employee equity complaints, diversity programs in place, lawsuits
- Customer relations: Quality management programs, quality awards won, customer satisfaction measures, lawsuits

You find what you look for. The four official rankings by FT-PwC, the SB 20, FT, and *Business Ethics* are not much more consistent than the list produced by the experts I interviewed. Sustainability is in the eye of the beholder. Recognizing leading corporately responsible companies may still be an art cleverly masquerading as science.

Figure 2.4: First 50 of *Business Ethics'* 100 Best Corporate Citizens of 2004

Rank	Company	Rank	Company
1	Fannie Mae*	26	Northwest Natural Gas Company
2	Procter & Gamble*	27	Cummins Inc.*
3	Intel Corporation*	28	Aetna, Inc.
4	St. Paul Companies*	29	Washington Mutual, Inc.
5	Green Mountain Coffee Roasters	30	The Rouse Company
6	Deere & Company*	31	Adolph Coors Company*
7	Avon Products, Inc.*	32	Modine Manufacturing*
8	Hewlett-Packard Company*	33	Clorox Company
9	Agilent Technologies Inc.	34	Delphi Corporation
10	Ecolab Inc.*	35	FedEx Corporation
11	Imation Corporation	36	Pixar
12	IBM*	37	Dionex Corporation
13	Nuveen Investments	38	Moody's Corporation
14	Herman Miller, Inc.*	39	Wild Oats Markets, Inc.
15	J. M. Smucker Company	40	Texas Industries, Inc.
16	Safeco Corporation	41	Harman International Industries, Inc.
17	The Timberland Company*	42	Deluxe Corporation
18	Zimmer Holdings, Inc.	43	AT&T*
19	Cisco Systems, Inc.*	44	Pitney Bowes Inc.*
20	3M Company	45	Starbucks Coffee Company*
21	Symantec Corporation	46	Doral Financial Corporation
22	Southwest Airlines *	47	Staples, Inc.
23	SLM Corporation	48	Merck & Co., Inc.*
24	Motorola, Inc.*	49	Graco Inc.*
25	Autodesk, Inc.	50	Trex Company, Inc.

* Companies on the list for five years, 2000-2004

First-Wave Drivers

It can be tricky learning from sustainability leaders when there is no consensus about who they are. Rather than creating the definitive list of sustainability leaders, it is more instructive to accept that early adopters, whoever they are, provide helpful insights into what triggers interest in sustainability. These companies are written up in case studies, they appear on multiple lists cited above, their executives are on the shortlist of keynote speakers invited to CSR conferences, and they are the icons of companies publicly embracing more responsible practices. Almost by definition, early adopters are the companies experts think of when asked to list sustainability leaders.

What caused their interest in sustainability? Was it always there or did some event trigger it? Can sustainability champions use what drove the first wave of sustainability leaders as motivators for the next wave?

In the next sections, I examine three drivers that pushed the first wave of companies to adopt responsible social and environmental corporate practices:

1. Founder's personal passion

2. Public relations crisis

3. Regulatory pressures, or the threat of additional regulatory burden

I start with a driver that is among the top three reasons given by almost all observers of the sustainability landscape: the founder's personal passion for environmental and social responsibility in company practices.

Some companies do it for altruistic reasons, usually based on the founder's values and principles. Or a senior executive may have a personal experience that wakes them up to the bigger implications of their company's operations. They become parents or grandparents and they start to think about the world differently, or they experience a serious illness of a loved one. (Rodney White)

The first reason that companies pay attention to CSR is the passion of the individual owner in private companies. The person who says, "This is how I want my company to be." You have to be a private owner or majority owner of a private company — all the way from smaller firms up to companies like Interface — ones that are profiled in *In Business* magazine, or something like that. The owner says, "It's my company and this is how I want to live my life through my company." (Steve Rice)

In the case of Ben & Jerry's, they institutionalized CSR not only by hiring people whose sole job was to make sure it happened and to never stop preaching it, but also by mandating that a social audit would take place. It was more than "I have an opinion and I am going to try and drive decisions that way." It was really part of the framework of how the business was run. (John Szold)

Sustainability has to be sincere. The senior leaders have to get it. You have to have complete buy-in from not only the senior managers, but the board of directors and the shareholders and the employees. Everyone has to understand. It takes leadership. (Julian Smit)

When trying to inject corporate citizenship into a corporate culture, it helps if corporate DNA is predisposed to the values and behavior of the sustainability virus. Whether a corporate culture is shaped by the senior leaders, or vice versa, it is an important element to sustaining the momentum and legitimacy of environmental and social initiatives through an organization. (Susan Burns)

Driver #1: Founder's Personal Passion

It is an axiom of leadership and most organizational change disciplines that worthwhile changes are only successful when supported by the top of the firm. A good idea may percolate up from champions in middle or lower ranks in the organization, but without a CEO "Good Housekeeping seal of approval," sooner or later it will wither and die. In the hierarchical world of business, a lack of CEO-level sponsorship equals no real change.

In a private company, the corporate norms and culture reflect the founder's values. The founder hires employees with similar values and ensures those values are integrated into business decision-making processes. As owner, the CEO/founder does not have to answer to other stockholders/owners. As sole shareholder, if he or she chooses ethical behavior over maximizing profit, so be it. Opinions of financial analysts are not relevant. A privately owned company is wonderfully immune to shareholder pressure for quarterly growth that relentlessly drives executives of public companies. By definition, the company "gets it" on corporate responsibility — CR is central to its purpose as a business.

Examples of leading private companies (and their founders) are Ben & Jerry's Homemade Ice Cream (Ben Cohen and Jerry Greenfield), the Body Shop International (Anita and Gordon Roddick), Smith & Hawken (Paul Hawken), Patagonia (Yvon Chouinard), and Husky Injection Molding (Robert Schad). They are lauded as paragons of corporate ethical and responsible leadership. These founders led their companies with strong personal beliefs about social and environmental values, behaving ethically whether or not it affected business success.[9] Essentially, they started at Stage 5 on the sustainability continuum, skipping the first four stages. Many of these companies do very well, showing that ethical behavior counts, and it also pays.

The challenge comes when such companies go public or are bought out. Now the founder, if still present, is subject to the same shareholder pressure as the leader of any public company. The original culture, values, and ethics may be sacrificed on the altar of maximizing shareholder value. Anita Roddick's despair after the Body Shop went public, and Ben Cohen's less-than-satisfying experience after Ben & Jerry's was bought out by Unilever, are cautionary tales for owners expecting preservation of their values in public incarnations of their companies.[10]

47

Recent scandals notwithstanding, companies overwhelmingly believe they should operate ethically and be good corporate citizens, according to a survey of corporate citizenship released Monday. The survey, conducted for the US Chamber of Commerce, found that 87 percent of those responding felt it was very important to operate ethically (an additional 11 percent felt it was important), 85 percent felt it was very important to treat employees well, and 81 percent felt it was very important to have safe and reliable products or services.

"Corporations view corporate citizenship as a fundamental part of doing business," said Steve Rochlin, research director at the Center for Corporate Citizenship at Boston College, which conducted the study. Many companies have hired ethics officers, who conduct training courses for employees, watch over potential conflicts of interest and work with auditors and boards of directors to make sure the balance sheets are accurate.

Consumer advocate Ralph Nader said the survey was meaningless. "They should have released this self-serving survey for April Fool's Day," Nader said. "It's like asking a company, 'Do you believe in being good?' Who's going to say no?"

The survey of 515 companies had a margin of error of plus or minus four percentage points. It was the first-ever study that looked at both small and large companies. Survey officials said they planned to do similar studies every two years to see how corporate attitudes change. They acknowledged the results contrasted with conventional wisdom in the aftermath of scandals at Enron Corp., WorldCom and other companies. In response, Congress passed legislation to crack down on business fraud, tighten regulation of companies' financial reporting and provide new oversight of independent auditors.

"Certainly there are corporations that have not practiced good corporate citizenship," said Joseph Kasputys, chairman of the Hitachi Foundation, which funded the study. "The corporate scandals have given business generally a bad reputation. But this survey shows most corporations are really doing something positive."

Nader said the US chamber is trying to change the subject away from corporate wrongdoing. "They want to put all these abuses and scandals behind them instead of saying to the companies in the survey, 'Why don't you just obey the law?'" Nader said.
— *Deseret News*[11]

Corporations Want to Behave Ethically

The "CSR at a Crossroads" report by Edelman and the Cranfield School of Management in 2003 reinforced that "the prime driver of CSR programs is the vision and values of the company developed on a normative basis."[12] Values are synonymous with moral principles underpinning ethical behavior, an increased focus for many companies as they revisit their governance in the wake of the Enron, Tyco, and Global Crossing scandals. As the survey described on the opposite page confirms, 98% of US Chamber of Commerce members feel it is either important or very important to operate ethically. Notwithstanding Ralph Nader's question about how they could possibly say otherwise, the survey confirms companies at least profess the importance of behaving in an ethically responsible manner.

Beyond simply encouraging employees to not break the law, some corporations have adopted internal codes of conduct. Guidelines refer to dealings between internal departments, handling of personnel issues, and company relationships with suppliers and customers. These codes are used to entrench company values, and often all employees are required to sign a document pledging they will adhere to the company's ethical standards.[13] The codes' relevance to sustainability is more evident when they include guidelines on how the company should relate to its local community and govern its impact on the environment.

The number of companies voluntarily endorsing international ethical standards is evidence of corporate espousal of ethical labor, human rights, and environmental behavior. Over 1,000 companies have endorsed the ten principles in the United Nations Global Compact on human rights, labor standards, the environment, and anti-corruption.[14] However, there is a danger of "blue-washing," which implies that a firm is passively glossing its image by associating with the blue UN logo without actively aligning its practices accordingly. Some 11,822 organizations have endorsed the Earth Charter, which encourages respect and care for the community of life, ecological integrity, social and economic justice, democracy, nonviolence, and peace.[15] However, overlapping agreements are confusing — should companies be expected to sign both the Earth Charter and the Global Compact?

In any event, most companies are led by CEOs who espouse ethical, values-based behavior. The acid test is how they make the values versus profit trade-off and the extent to which ethical values guide their answer to the question "How much is enough?" A values-driven founder may have a different response than a stockholder-driven CEO.

"Over the years I've seen the sustainability performance of some companies deteriorate. They go from solid performance to questionable performance within a relatively short time frame. In some cases a new CEO comes in with new priorities and cleans house, installs a new group of senior managers, and the whole culture and tone of the company changes. They go from being a very values-oriented kind of company to being a very productivity-driven company. It can really frustrate the staff.

But I've seen the opposite, too. I've seen companies improve their sustainability performance in a short time frame, often because of some precipitating reason. For example, they've had some type of close call or, again, they've had new blood at the top who really believes sustainability performance is important for business success.

So I'm always a bit careful about labeling companies as being "good" or "bad" sustainability performers because it's a transitory situation. (Mel Wilson)

Figure 2.5: *Dilbert* on Ethics

Dilbert reprinted by permission of United Feature Syndicate, Inc.

Enough Passionate, Values-Driven CEOs?

When a CEO with personal passion for sustainability values is brought in to an already-established public company, a sustainability agenda becomes a leadership agenda linked to corporate vision, core values, and core culture. The CEO makes those connections explicit, inspires a shared vision and direction for the company, enables and encourages people throughout the organization to contribute to that quest, challenges institutional processes that get in the way, and models espoused behaviors.[16] Examples of companies with CEOs who are publicly committed to sustainability are Royal Dutch/Shell (Sir Mark Moody-Stuart), Suncor (Rick George), DuPont (Chad Holliday), and BP (Sir John Browne). Leaders of other companies profess similar ethical goals.

Digging deeper, what caused these leaders to embrace sustainability? At Interface, Inc., Ray Anderson had a personal epiphany. For others, it is their upbringing, or a granddaughter's awkward question about what Grandpa's company does, or some other serendipitous event. The good news is, personal conversions happen. The bad news is that the unique combination of circumstances that trigger personal transformation to a heightened commitment to corporate morals and ethics is impossible to replicate and all too rare.

Both morals and ethics involve relationships, so a firm needs to decide how ethically it will treat various stakeholders. The notion that ethics surrounding stockholder relationships supersede ethics surrounding all other stakeholder relationships is supported by the notion that corporations are morally and legally obligated to provide their shareholders with maximum return on their investment. This position is famously attributed to the Nobel Prize-winning economist Milton Friedman, who stated that the only social responsibility of the corporation is to make a profit.[17]

There is growing evidence that if a broader group of stakeholders is treated ethically, profits need not suffer. A 2003 report by the Institute of Business Ethics in the UK found that companies with codes of ethics produced profit/turnover ratios 18% higher than similar-sized companies without codes of ethics over the period 1997–2001.[18] Supporting this finding, the Co-operative Bank claims its profits were 20% higher in 2001 because of its ethical policies.[19] Companies can maximize shareholder value at the same they are values-driven ethical stewards of other stakeholders' interests. For those companies, "ethical business" is not an oxymoron; it is a redundancy.

Q: Has business been laboring under the assumption that as long as the bottom line is strong, public confidence is secondary?

Henry Mintzberg: Corporations exist to serve society, not vice versa. If they don't serve society, they have no reason to exist. The popular argument is that by serving shareholders, they make everyone wealthier, which is fallacious. In the US, the distribution of wealth has tilted completely in one direction, so that ordinary people are no better off, and the very poor are worse off. The US is the wealthiest developed country, and it has the highest poverty rate of the developed countries.

How did all this happen?

Mintzberg: The executives made sure that they got as much money as they could, the corporations were paying off the shareholders, and I don't think they thought much beyond that. What we have is a coalition of corporate greed and economic dogma, and that's the real issue. What justifies the greed is the economic dogma that says that if you get as rich as possible, and if you make as much profit as possible, society will be a better place.

What's good for GM is good for the country.

Mintzberg: Exactly. So corporations didn't have to think about these issues, because the dogma told them that if they made profit, they were doing good. They've been told that for decades, by (economist) Milton Friedman, and others who followed. They didn't have to be socially responsible, because by making money, they assumed they were socially responsible.

That's dead wrong, because you can't separate the economic and social consequences of decisions. You will never find an economist — or any thinking person — who will tell you that social decisions don't have economic consequences. So how can economists argue that economic decisions don't have social consequences? They have all kinds of social consequences, but this dogma has made it convenient for business to ignore them.

— McGill News, Interview With Henry Mintzberg[20]

Shareholder-Owner Is Still God

Corporations have a legal duty to make money for shareholders. Failing in this duty can leave directors and officers open to being sued by shareholders.[21] However, some ethicists suggest that corporations' myopic fixation on the "ethic" of maximizing short-term shareholder profit, versus long-term stakeholder value, is based on false premises rather than legal obligations. In *The Divine Right of Capital*, Marjorie Kelly (co-founder of *Business Ethics*) dissects several corporate myths and contrasts them with her view of corresponding realities:

- *Myth:* Shareholders fund major corporations.

  Reality: Surprisingly, 99% of dollars invested by shareholders in stocks are speculative. Companies only get stockholder's money when they sell new common stock, and only a handful of companies have issued any new stock in 30 years.[22]

- *Myth:* Shareholders are the corporation. They own it.

  Reality: Shareholders contribute almost no value to the corporation. The real value of corporations are its employees. To say that stockholders own the corporation is to say that they own employees, which is feudalism in its worst form.[23]

- *Myth:* Corporations must maximize returns to shareholders.

  Reality: To give unproductive, distant, transient shareholders primacy over all other stakeholders, especially over employees and the community, is to foster a privileged, undemocratic, unethical, and undeserving shareholder aristocracy.[24]

The myth that company profit is automatically good for society is debunked by academic Henry Mintzberg in a *McGill News* interview, excerpted opposite. Profits are good, but excessive greed drives irresponsible behavior.

Debunking these myths is a fun intellectual exercise, but it's unlikely to change a CEO's or board member's mind. CEOs' fixations on maximizing shareholder returns are reinforced by the close link between their remuneration and stock prices.

Historically, heretics pointing out the error of believers' ways have fared poorly. Leading with a "shareholders are not gods" argument has not endeared NGOs to CEOs weaned on a steady diet of Friedman-inspired dogma. Trying to get the attention of senior executives with "you guys are living in a mythical world" arguments is a dubious strategy.

Figure 2.6: Motives vs. Outcomes

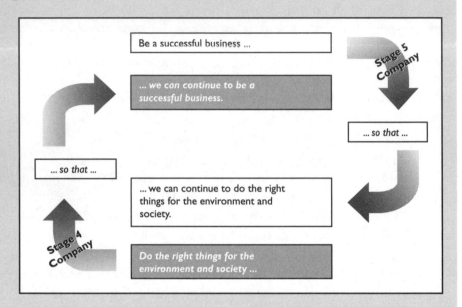

Values or Value?

So is "corporate ethics" an oxymoron? If a passionate founder is not at the company helm, is all lost? Not necessarily. However, it is futile to argue that corporations should do the right thing because corporate charters were originally granted to serve the public good. Further, arguing that corporate responsibility is the right thing to do for ethical/moral/values-based reasons might work with owners of businesses that have not yet gone public. Otherwise, these arguments will be therapeutic for the advocate but ineffective.

Why? People become defensive or irritable when their world view is questioned. Executives are no exception. It is not because they are uncaring, unethical, or stupid. Theirs is not a failure of information, but a difference in ideology. They are immersed in economic doctrine that emphasizes maximizing shareholder value at the expense of all other stakeholders. They feel that is their job. If they fail, they will be fired by shareholders and boards who feel the executives are shirking their fiduciary responsibilities.

However, if it can be shown that acting ethically is better for the bottom line, ethical arguments have a chance to build buy-in within the dominant mindset of today's corporate leaders. As discussed earlier, and as shown in Figure 2.6, the motives of Stage 4 and Stage 5 companies may differ, but outcomes may be similar. Playing to today's business paradigm loop on the left-hand side allows Stage 4 companies to take the first steps that enable executives to explore deeper ethical values rather than instantly and defensively reject them as heresy. It is a subversive rather than marquee strategy.

In summary, it would be rare to win a sustainability argument with a company in the next wave of yet-to-publicly-commit-to-CSR companies using a direct ethical assault. The business case is the Trojan horse of values-based sustainability practiced by Stage 5 companies. It enables the topic to penetrate corporate defenses and mind-sets. Once inside, it can be the catalyst to a deeper and more compelling commitment to a corporate stewardship role in a reinforcing virtuous cycle that simultaneously improves the firm's economic sustainability. Once they twig to its value as a business strategy, CEOs will support corporate responsibility with passion akin to a values-based founder's support.

Bad PR is an attention-getting two-by-four whack on the head of corporate executives. When digging behind what caught the attention of senior executives in the first place, often sustainability initiatives were sparked by an embarrassing wake-up call, by hitting the wall, by trouble that catches them off guard. (Susan Burns)

The company experiences a crisis. This is the number one reason for corporate CSR attention. The classic examples are Shell or Nike. They hit the wall or suffered such bad PR that they decided there had to be a better way. (Marlo Raynolds)

Things like the much more rapid information and communications that we have nowadays will play into that. You used to be able to dump a couple of hundred dozen tons of toxic waste in a jungle in the middle of Burma and no one would know. Now there will be a website up in a couple of days. So the general trend is toward transparency, corporate governance, disclosure, and accountability. (Martin Whittaker)

Driver #2: Public Relations Crisis

There is a story about a grizzled old prospector who sold his unusually obedient mule to a young farmer. However, despite the new owner's best yelling and cussing efforts, the mule stubbornly would not obey his commands. Frustrated, the farmer tracked down the former owner at the local tavern and asked for help. The old man calmly picked up a two-by-four, walked over to the mule, and whammed the board down on the mule's head with all his might. The mule gave a startled shake of its head, and as the prospector casually commanded the mule to move forward, the animal meekly obeyed. "First, you have to get his attention," the prospector drawled. "Then just ask quietly."

Public relations (PR) crises get corporate attention. In 1988, Greenpeace activists scaled the wall of a DuPont plant in New Jersey and hung a big "DuPont Number One Polluter" banner facing the Delaware Memorial Bridge, used by thousands of commuters. TV cameras arrived. DuPont CEO Chad Holliday recalls that as the day DuPont decided to clean up its act.[25]

Between 1991 and 1994, MacMillan Bloedel experienced a relentless Greenpeace campaign that urged customers not to buy MacBlo products made from unsustainably harvested forests. It went from being a hassle to being a life-threatening PR crisis before MacBlo committed to better forest stewardship logging practices.

In 1995, public opposition to the disposal of the Brent Spar oil platform in the North Sea, and the execution of author/activist Ken Saro-Wiwa in Nigeria, were two kicks in the head that woke up Royal Dutch/Shell.[26]

Bad PR works as a CSR trigger. Direct hits get the attention of a corporation. A near miss can be effective too. When rotten things hit the fan, they splatter — a PR crisis might not hit a company directly, but a whole industry's image can be tarnished by fallout from one irresponsible actor. When companies like Nike and Gap have their corporate knuckles rapped by NGOs for human rights and labor abuses in supplier operations in the developing world, other companies with offshore suppliers get sympathy pains. Executives realize how easily the other company's misfortune could have been their own, given their own practices, and are strongly motivated to ensure they mitigate the risk by reforming their practices before their company's reputation suffers a similar PR crisis.

The reason companies pay attention to sustainability is reputation, first and foremost. (Martin Whittaker)

Another reason for growth in corporate sustainable development practices is the increasing recognition of its importance as a key element of reputation management. More organizations are recognizing that sustainable development is an integral part of overall reputation management, market positioning, and brand. Reputation is the broadest of corporate elements — connecting to all drivers — and sustainable development links to many of these. (Ron Yachnin)

The first and foremost reason, maybe not for the long term, is PR. When you've looked at enough companies out there, the top companies have moved beyond PR and are doing it because sustainability, and the notion that sustainability really does add value, has become ingrained in the corporate culture. But a lot of companies that are just starting out are doing it because other companies are doing it — they want to have a good reputation. (Devin Crago)

First, I would say certainly reputation management is a driver of sustainability attention in companies. They are very concerned about that, given the recent scandals. Under reputation management I include preserving the license to operate. (George Khoury)

The second reason for companies to pay attention to sustainability is strictly public relations/image. "This is how we want our company to appear to be." In fact, it may be or it might not be, but "Here it is, and for a low cost can we put a spin on whatever we are already doing and just put a different flag on it? If we are already fairly good on efficiency, how can we spin that to say it's more than just production efficiency but we can help feed the world?" There is nothing inherently bad or evil with it. It is just that it maybe doesn't go quite as deep as some companies might like to suggest. (Steve Rice)

Corporate Reputation Contributes to Brand Value

A company's brand is one of its biggest assets. Stewardship of corporate reputation can make a significant difference in acquisition and retention of talent, revenue, and ultimately share price. Research by Charles Fombrun at the Research Institute at New York University's Stern School of Business found that a 5% change in reputation of a company is equal to a 1% to 5% change in its market value.[27] To maximize shareholder value, companies need to ensure that they and their brands remain unsullied and are viewed in the most positive light possible.

The market capitalization of a company often far exceeds the "property" value of the company. The 2004 World Economic Forum (WEF) "Voice of the Leaders" poll of CEOs from the world's 1,000 leading companies found that, on average, 60% of the market capitalization of corporations is based on "hard" financial data, while 40% is dependent on "reputation."[28] Another WEF study by Arthur D. Little study showed that the proportion of company value derived from intangible assets rose from 17% in 1981 to 71% in 1998.[29] It is helpful to understand the relationship between intangibles and profits. In fact, the real payoff for paying attention to sustainability is that it highlights the relationship between intangibles and tangible company value.

In 2003, the fifth annual global survey of senior executives sponsored by communications consultancy Hill and Knowlton and executive recruitment firm Korn/Ferry International showed that 65% of CEOs accept personal responsibility for their company's reputation. Reflecting a change in attitude from previous surveys, 88% of respondents agree that a company's corporate reputation is more important today than it was five years ago, and 60% believe it is much more important today. CEOs overwhelmingly (78%) point to customers as the external force with the greatest impact on reputation, with print media (48%) and financial analysts (44%) rounding out the top three.[30]

The bank of goodwill accumulated by brand enhancement through CSR initiatives is insurance against a sudden withdrawal triggered by a PR crisis. Reputation tops the intangible asset list of most CEOs.[31] CEOs also agreed that corporate social responsibility initiatives contribute to corporate reputation, as I explore next.

Another reason [companies pay attention to sustainability] would be for perceived competitive advantage. Whether that is legitimate or not is another question. It is a mix of being seen as being green and being able to provide green or sustainable products. Levi Straus is a good example. I would buy their clothes because I knew they had a social contract about where they bought their material. One of the reasons they did that was their headquarters was in San Francisco and they got hit big-time with the AIDS problem. The president was out in front of their offices handing out AIDS information to the employees. That sent a big message when the corporate world was in a panic and did not know what to do.

Pacific Gas and Electric was another one in California who really got on the bandwagon early. Whether it was because of the CEO or whether it shaped the culture or the culture embraced it, they had to deal with it one way or another and they did a good job. I think they recognized that if they wanted to maintain their position, they needed to be out front on the issue.

Look at what happened to Nike when they were not. They really got hammered. (David Powell)

Another reason companies pay attention to sustainability is public relations and ranking. A consulting firm I know has a particular client who is averse to being high on the list of dischargers on the National Pollution Release Inventory. They have done really progressive things to address their ranking on the inventory. They do not want to give the impression that they are a big discharger and polluter. Not only do they want the numbers to go down, but they want recognition that they have put the effort in and not only reduced their numbers but also have done it the right way ....

So the second thing is the whole notion of right to know and public transparency of information. The Internet, the whole right-to-know movement, and the insatiable thirst of the public for information have really created this transparent view of what's going on. The corporate world underestimated the sophistication of the public to use these tools. (Paul Muldoon)

CSR Contributes to Corporate Reputation

What contributes to a good corporate reputation? A 2003 study conducted by Cambridge University's business school asked CEOs from global Fortune 500 companies to rank seven drivers of corporate reputation.[32] Their ranked list is as follows (the six equivalent "reputation dimensions" measured by the Harris-Fombrun Reputation Quotient[33] are in parentheses):

1. Leadership, vision and desire (Vision and Leadership)
2. Quality of products and service (Products and Services)
3. Knowledge and skills of employees (Workplace Environment)
4. Social credibility and valuable corporate citizen (Social Responsibility)
5. Financial credibility and better than average return for shareholders (Financial Performance)
6. Environmental credibility and restorative actions
7. Emotional connections with values and culture of the company (Emotional Appeal)

Each driver corresponds to one of the three legs of the sustainability stool — economic, environmental, and social aspects of a company's performance.

In research by management consulting firm Strategic Asset Management (SAM), 73% of companies listed "reputation enhancement" as a value-adding result of their CSR activities.[34] British Telecom (BT) has the numbers to prove it. Data gathered from thousands of its customers in the UK show that CSR activities account for at least 25% of the basis for the company's image and reputation,[35] and if BT were to lose its positive CSR reputation, its customer satisfaction levels would drop 10%.[36]

A company's geographical location affects its prioritization of reputational risk. A 2004 report by the Conference Board, based on a global survey of 165 company boards, found that US boards are especially motivated by press about governance, corporate scandals, and general legal developments like the Sarbanes-Oxley legislation (created to ensure corporate responsibility and accountability). Reputational risk was of relatively little importance. Only 20% of US survey participants said that it was a most relevant factor, whereas 75% of respondents in India, 62% in the UK, and 46% in Western Europe cited it as a most relevant factor.[37]

An overwhelming majority of business influencers remain confident that companies can restore a damaged reputation, according to new research by global communications consultancy Burson-Marsteller. The 2003 Building CEO Capital study reveals that 97 percent of business influencers believe a company can recover from a tarnished reputation over time. The study shows a surprising level of optimism in corporate America's ability to regain the public trust, as numerous companies work to rebuild their reputations.

While confidence in restoring reputations is good news, the time needed to turn around a company's reputation is not. On average, business influencers surveyed believe it takes nearly four years (3.65 years) for a company to rebuild a blemished reputation. Yet when asked how long it takes for new CEOs to turn a company around, business influencers allow less than two years (22 months).

"CEOs are already under considerable pressure to perform quickly under immense public scrutiny," said Dr. Leslie Gaines-Ross, Chief Knowledge & Research Officer, U.S. at Burson-Marsteller. "Our CEO Capital study findings reinforce the need to give CEOs more time to demonstrate results. With increasingly short CEO tenures averaging four years today, the risk is that new CEOs won't be able to reap the benefits of their reputation-building efforts while in office."

Of all the influencers surveyed, only the business media took exception to the four-year finding, believing that it takes companies slightly less than three years (2.96 years) to rebuild their reputations. Financial analysts and institutional investors hold companies to a higher standard, expecting it to take most companies nearly four years (3.86 years) to rebuild and restore their reputations. Other business influencers surveyed include CEOs, business executives, government officials and board members ....

When Burson-Marsteller first conducted its CEO reputation research in 1997, business influencers estimated that 40 percent of a company's overall reputation was attributable to its CEO. This figure has grown steadily since then, increasing to 45 percent in 1999, 48 percent in 2001 and 50 percent in 2003.

— Burson-Marsteller press release, September 16, 2003[38]

Bad PR Lingers like a Bad Smell

While reputation contributes to brand value, PR crises detract from it and destroy both financial and reputational capital. How long does it take a company to restore a damaged reputation? Up to four years, according to a survey by Burson-Marsteller, the public relations firm (see press release, opposite). That sounds like a stiff penalty, but the reality can be worse. Even today, Barclays Bank is still dogged by memories of the 1970s student campaign to boycott the bank over its operations in apartheid-era South Africa.[39]

When Dow Chemical acquired Union Carbide in 2001, it also acquired the tarnish of the 1984 Bhopal gas leak, which killed 3,800 people immediately and which Greenpeace estimates subsequently killed over 20,000 people from exposure-related illnesses and caused chronic illness in another 120,000 people. Even 20 years after the accident, a 2004 shareholder resolution asked Dow to publish a report on any new initiatives planned to help Bhopal victims and to spell out any risks the disaster's fallout may pose to Dow's finances or reputation.[40]

Bad PR sticks like flypaper. Customer attitudes are influenced by media coverage. As companies struggle to build a credible reputation for being environmentally responsible, a large fine for polluting is a significant setback. A 2003 study by Echo Research found a 52% increase of press articles on corporate social responsibility from 2000 to 2001, and a 401% increase from 2001 to 2002, perhaps fueled by coverage of the World Summit on Sustainable Development (WSSD) in Johannesburg in 2002. Companies that were most often portrayed by media in a positive light for their CSR efforts include the Body Shop, BP, BT, the Co-operative Bank, Shell, and Westpac, whereas Exxon Mobil, The Gap, Telstra, and Wal-Mart received the most unfavorable coverage from media for their CSR efforts.[41]

The danger is to treat CSR as merely a communications exercise, creating the facade of a positive reputation without actually changing business practices. To establish a truly positive reputation, companies have to be responsible, minimizing social, ethical, and environmental risks and maximizing opportunities. Minimizing risks is the foundation of a good reputation — you stop doing things that civil society deems wrong and that attract its criticism.

Bad PR is like corrosion below the waterline. No wonder reputational concerns are shining new light on CSR dimensions of company operations.

Regulations force companies to move. I don't believe many of them would do anything, given a choice. It's compliance. A good example in the US is the exemption of SUVs [sport utility vehicles] from the automobile vehicle emissions standards, which has allowed the auto companies to find this gigantic loophole and produce gas-guzzlers that the public loves. It's not likely it is going to, but if the regulation got changed, compliance would be right there. I don't see any impressive voluntary moves to do the right thing. (John Szold)

In my opinion the Superfund Law in the US was one of the important factors causing US companies to ensure that proper disposition management of hazardous waste was in place before sending any waste off-site for disposal .... I hate to admit it, but environmental sensitizing of the boardroom was mostly driven by regulation. (Richard Mireault)

I think it is kind of a learning curve. You could start the graph with risk management and compliance with environmental laws and regulations, especially in certain industries. They had to start paying attention to certain things just at the compliance level. (Alan Willis)

Compliance as a driver for going beyond compliance is another reason that sustainability has become important. Compliance is a driver in the refining industry, where the bar has been continually raised in the last 20 years in terms of the product itself and the emissions coming from the refinery. (Martin Whittaker)

A lot of lip service is given to the effectiveness of regulations, but I think that regulations are a poor driver of enlightened CSR. Companies will always strive to remain legal, but they do not develop strategy around the fear of regulation. Regulation is important but not the key. (Steven Cross)

I think regulations will be a significant factor, but not one that triggers most companies. It will be for the laggards. (Gib Hedstrom)

Driver #3: Regulatory Pressure

The most basic corporate responsibility motivation is to stay out of jail and avoid fines — that is, to ensure that the company is at least complying with environmental, health, and safety regulations. Compliance is an early rung on the sustainability ladder — Stage 2 in the sustainability continuum. It is as simple as controlling pollution, properly disposing of hazardous waste, and ensuring a safe workplace for employees.

Regulatory compliance motivates laggards who do the bare minimum to maintain their license to operate. Hence, one role of environmental regulations is to raise the bar to a minimum acceptable level and to awaken corporate executives to the issues. Companies understand the value of a clean record and good relationships with regulators who make decisions on regulatory approval, rights-of-way, access easements, land-use permits, and environmental impacts. However, regulations defend against bad practice; they do not promote best practice.

Do regulated approaches work? Yes and no. Strict regulations limiting the manufacture, use, sale, import, and export of ozone-depleting substances worked.[42] The Alien Tort Claims Act (ATCA) of 1789 was virtually dormant until it was resurrected and galvanized corporate attention in a series of court decisions starting in 1980. To date, major brands including Unocal, Chevron Texaco, Union Carbide, Exxon Mobil, Gap, Coca-Cola, Del Monte, Citigroup, Ford, and Nike have been sued in the US under ATCA for complicity in crimes — such as murder, torture, slavery, unlawful detention, and forced labor — committed in developing countries. At the heart of the anti-corporate ATCA cases is the question: How much liability should a multinational have for acts it did not order but that were committed by subsidiaries or by foreign state-controlled entities or their security forces? Defendant corporations cannot argue to limit the act's application without appearing to evade their ethical responsibilities and to be indifferent to human rights, which damages their stakeholder value.[43] It is a Catch-22.

Regulations drive laggards. Lawsuits are the teeth in the regulatory approach.

I hear about corporate social responsibility around governance. Governance is a hot topic, with the Sarbanes-Oxley legislation in the US. That catches people's attention, although at the end of the day, it's the right thing to do. I believe that is preoccupying a lot of the focus on corporate governance. But it will change. It is simply timing. Organizations have to keep reinventing themselves to stay competitive, stay close to what's driving the market and their clients' business. (Expert B)

In Canada, the Bata Shoe environmental case got the attention of CEOs and boards of directors. If you research the Bata Shoe case, you will find that individuals (managers and directors) were personally held accountable and fined for storing chemicals in barrels that eventually leaked and contaminated the environment. That's when environmental issues and reporting got on the boardroom agenda in Canada. Jurisprudence was set. Not only could a company be fined, but there could be personal liability at director and management levels.

The decision to fine individuals in the Bata Shoe case was later reversed. However, I believe that if a company today is in front of a judge regarding an environmental accident or incident and it cannot demonstrate due diligence of industry-acceptable environmental practices and a sound environmental management system, then it has little chance of succeeding in an environmental lawsuit. Due diligence is not just appointing a director or manager to manage environmental affairs. The board of directors must have some skin in it [be personally committed to it] and request that environmental matters be reported to the board so they have a good understanding of the environmental issues and ensure actions are taken to correct these environmental issues.

The Bata Shoe case really got a lot of the CEOs in Canada and their boardrooms interested in environmental matters. It shaped the mentalities of executives and boards. That's when you started to see more and more management and employee education regarding environmental management and regulations, environmental organizations taking shape, management systems being developed, and environmental policies and practices implemented in companies. (Richard Mireault)

The Risk of Lawsuits

On the environmental front, in late 2003 the Climate Justice Programme — an international group of lawyers, scientists, and more than 40 civil groups — was formed to promote the use of law to fight climate change using international and domestic laws covering polluters, product liability, human rights violations, and public nuisance.[44] Governments can prosecute corporate environmental transgressors, holding either the company or its officers and directors criminally liable.

Under US federal security laws, directors are held personally accountable for false or misleading statements made in prospectuses used to sell securities. Investors who are misled by false claims in a prospectus and who suffer losses as a result can sue directors personally to recover the damage.[45] For example, the timing and manner of Royal Dutch/Shell's communications of its downgrading of 20% of its reserves from "proven" to "probable" in early 2004 was a move that wiped £3 billion off the company's value, prompted class action suits from outraged investors, and caused the ouster of chairman Sir Philip Watts.[46]

The real grabber for senior company officers is being personally sued and jailed for allowing their company to commit environmental transgressions. A 1994 KPMG survey found that 69% of Canadian firms cited director liability as a driver for their environmental improvement.[47] The Canadian Environmental Protection Act 1999 has provisions for fines of up to $1 million a day or up to five years' imprisonment for any officer or director who assented to a violation.[48] Although somewhat dated, a 1990 survey of officers and directors from a cross-section of major Canadian corporations agreed that corporate executives would be more likely to take action to have their companies avoid environmental offenses if they could be prosecuted personally for such offenses.[49] In the US, one way to mitigate severe financial penalties is to have an ethics/compliance program already in place, led by a high-level executive.[50] Therefore, some companies have appointed high-level ethics officers almost as insurance policies, should lawsuits arise.[51]

Samuel Johnson's observation that the prospect of hanging in the morning concentrates the mind wonderfully is an apt analogy for the way personal liability focuses the attention of corporate officers and directors on avoiding corporate environmental transgressions. The threat of personal shame, fines, and even imprisonment helps to focus executive attention on due diligence in environmental matters ... wonderfully.

End-of-pipe–based regulation limits a company's vision to compliance and makes it often harder to envisage no pipes for anything to come out of. It traps them into incrementalism rather than radical redesign. Incrementalism tends to have diminishing returns, whereas radical redesign tends to have expanding returns.

Actually the regulators/regulatees have co-evolved in a predator/prey relationship that is an evolutionary blind alley. (Amory Lovins)

Another impediment is regulation, because there are so many regulations that tie people up in how to do things. Your budget of available time is used up responding to ineffective directives from government.

If governments just said, "This is where we want you to get," and left companies to decide how to get there, it would be much better.

A high proportion of the EPA fines in the US are not about harming the environment. They are about not having properly reported that they have protected the environment. That's almost pointless. All the effort that went into those reports could have been directed elsewhere. (Antony Marcil)

Americans in general are much more compliance driven on the environment side, partly because they've had a pretty strong enforcer — the EPA. There is no compliance around sustainable development. There is no requirement that companies be sustainable. (Martin Whittaker)

Good Regulations Are Rare

Sustainability regulations are great attention-getters. They can also get in the way of innovative thinking. The danger of a compliance mentality is that it focuses on the wrong end of the process. It looks at containing pollution instead of eliminating use of polluting chemicals and materials in the process — it looks at the tail end of the pipe instead of the front end.

What are the components of effective regulations? To recognize good regulations, look for five characteristics.

1. Clear jurisdiction between different levels of government ... so that time-wasting and costly legal debates about the validity and relevance of the regulation are avoided.

2. Clear, measurable, and enforceable standards ... so that it is clear when violations occur; mandate the "what/results," not the "how/technique."

3. Mandatory language ... so that it is clear that noncompliance is not an option; "must" is used instead of "may."

4. Effective compliance and enforcement mechanisms, including incentives and penalties ... so that the regulations have teeth and also make it evident that companies doing the right thing will benefit.

5. Adequate resources for implementation and enforcement ... so that the sham of tough laws without a corresponding threat of being caught is avoided.[52]

Unfortunately, this combination of characteristics is rare in environmental law. Many regulations are poorly designed, drafted, implemented, and enforced. A regulation on the books is interesting. Enforcement is compelling. Regulations are only effective if they are enforced and if enforcement leads to court cases. Strong penalties, such as significant fines and jail terms for executives or board members, coupled with rigorous enforcement mechanisms can galvanize management attention.

Government reflects the values of the broader population, so government is lagging those key sustainability leaders in terms of their ability to create the systems and external influences for those companies to be real leaders. But if you look at the innovation curve, government has a role in creating a niche for those leaders to thrive in so the companies that are moving forward in this are able to thrive once they have eked out a little area for themselves. It then drags along the rest of the bunch as the momentum moves forward. I think that for us to see really significant change, we need to have government leadership. (Stephen Hill)

We have a market-based global economy. But that isn't reason enough for governments to neglect bearing some responsibility — particularly when partnership opportunities abound. If you look at the history of the environmental movement, it started before Rio with government-driven regulations, and that was seen as the future of environmentalism. It was expressed in *Our Common Future,* and then we get to Johannesburg and it is all about partnerships — governments partnering with business, business partnering with NGOs, and so on. The business case is motivating, but it needs to go hand in hand with government initiative. (Devin Crago)

In summary, when we are serious that we want to be somewhere other than where we are, we have to first look at where we are, do a rigorous and honest analysis of why we are where we are — the signals that drive us to this spot — and then we have to make an inventory of all the signals we have to destroy and a list of all the signals we have to create that are conducive to moving people to that other spot where we want them to be. When we don't, it is intellectually dishonest. We're kidding ourselves and we're not serious. You can't simply tell people to behave differently and have them do so, but you can sure change the signals. Some will stick to the old behaviors, but most people are pretty damn smart and so are most companies. (Antony Marcil)

Issues with Regulatory Approaches

Legally mandated environmental and social changes will only be effective over the long term if they are supported by sustained political will and public support.[53] A dilemma for governments is deciding whether to be leaders or to await pressure from a critical mass of citizens or companies to implement new policies and incentives. However, that should not discourage governments from institutionalizing already accepted norms of environmental values and also leading with innovative industrial policies and incentives that promote win/win/win market signals for business, the environment, and society. Governments need to be both leaders and followers.

At a more philosophical level, there is a paradox. Regulations are enacted to ensure ethical behavior, but as statutes become increasing explicit about what is forbidden, they imply that what is not forbidden is allowed. Take the standard of proof required in a securities fraud. It is so focused on the minutiae of specific transactions that it is nearly impossible to prove fraud. The overall ethic gets lost in the details. Unless specific violations are proven, behavior is implicitly sanctioned. Though it is obvious the forest has been leveled, prosecutors have to prove each tree was cut down. No wonder so many culpable corporate actors go unpunished.[54]

We need a more compelling governmental and corporate vision of a better quality of life. Rather than just preventing pollution, progress toward sustainability will require the systemic integration of environmental, social, and economic considerations in decision making at all levels in society. Governments need to deploy a much more comprehensive set of policies to bolster efficiencies and productivity, reduce resource use, prevent pollution, eliminate perverse subsidies to polluting industries, foster stronger market incentives for improved processes, and implement an ecological tax shift.[55] Better government regulations are important motivators on this journey. In the end, however, law reform will never be a panacea for a corporate focus on sustainability.

So governments do have an important leadership role to ensure market forces send signals that encourage sustainable corporate behavior and punish the opposite. Some of these motivators will be regulated; some will be voluntary.

A few companies have foresight. They catch things ahead of the cycle. They do not miss silent trends and weak signals.

Examples would be some large players in the cement industry. There is no public campaign against cement companies. Very few people realize that cement production contributes 5% of the total man-made CO_2 emissions. Holcim, Lafarge, and eight other companies said, "We better start to think about this before we get into the public limelight and initiate a deep rethinking about the license of our industry to operate in the next five years." They decided to seize the opportunity without any significant public pressure. Those leaders said, "Look at where the world is going. Climate change is serious. Do we want to be part of the solution or part of the problem?" (Claude Fussler)

There are lots of potential, if not actual, regulatory drivers. You have the voluntary approach — the carrot — or the Association of British Insurers insisting there is a risk-management aspect to CSR, and increasing expectation that it become part of the year-end operating and financial year-end reporting and accounts. So there is that regulatory driver. There is also a realization that the company is going to have to go with the agenda if they want to avoid more draconian regulations. It is the threat of regulation. (John Swannick)

The Threat of Regulations Works

The debate about the wisdom and effectiveness of regulations in promoting environmental stewardship, versus voluntary industry initiatives, has raged for years. Of course, industry groups favor voluntary approaches, lamenting "red tape" and the cost of "command-and-control" regulatory compliance.

The threat of impending regulatory burden may be an even more effective spur for corporate environmental behavior than enforcement of regulations already enacted. Anticipating the cost of the bureaucratic procedures required to demonstrate compliance with new regulations, companies are anxious to show governments they can voluntarily accomplish the objectives of imminent regulations. Companies hope to preempt regulations with voluntary self-regulation and even to become beyond-compliance leaders so they can better influence regulators to institute measures that align with their proactive initiatives.

The ultimate objective of voluntary accords is that companies will self-impose such stringent practices that regulations would be redundant. An oft-cited example of industry self-regulation driven by the specter of impending regulations is the voluntary Responsible Care® initiative, launched first by the Canadian Chemical Producers Association and then adopted by the global chemical sector. Between 1992 and 2002, members reduced their emissions by 72% or 188,000 tonnes. A unit of chemical product is now manufactured with 78% less chemical emissions than in 1992. Associated health and environmental benefits include fewer toxic emissions, less smog, reduced climate change and stratospheric ozone depletion, and improved water quality.[56] If the chemical industry had not taken these voluntary steps, governments would likely have taken regulatory action to accomplish similar emissions reductions.

Much as sustainability champions would like it to happen, few executives wake up one morning and spontaneously decide to improve their environmental track record just because it feels like the right thing to do. The threat of government regulations is a powerful catalyst to voluntary industry action, reinforcing that "voluntary" is a relative term.

In some ways, the threat of new regulations can be as effective as the actual regulations themselves. I heard numerous corporate managers say their companies adopt voluntary standards or participate in voluntary initiatives because they know that if they don't, the regulators will impose the new regulations sooner rather than later. Acting voluntarily rather than under pressure by regulators is often preferable because (a) there is less threat involved if the objectives are not met, and (b) the regulatory regimes often involve greater bureaucracy, resulting in additional cost. (Mel Wilson)

On environmental issues, for example, we are saying it is not just about meeting the latest standard. It's about preventing pollution in the first place. It is trying to be ahead of that curve.

Inco was smart on that with acid rain. They fought it and fought it until they were legislated into doing it. They said, "Well, fine, if we're going to do it, we are not going to let them come and get us every five years to give us more to do. We are going to redesign our production process to really get ahead of the curve." That's where the real competitive advantage is. The companies that will win, and the corporations that will do well, are the ones that have the capacity to do that. (Louise Comeau)

Another reason for corporate CSR attention is fear of new regulation. That is certainly true in the chemical industry. They are very transparent about that. Bhopal scared the heck out of them. Companies fear regulation because they don't get to shape the policy agenda the way they do with a voluntary program. The timing of Responsible Care® was in the mid-1980s, after Bhopal. (David Powell)

How Voluntary Is "Voluntary"?

Corporate volunteerism on sustainability issues is a relative term and perhaps even a misnomer.[57] In North America, a "voluntary initiative" suggested by government may mean "business as usual," whereas in Europe it may mean "do it or we will make you do it."[58] There is little doubt that complying with government regulations is not "voluntary." However, how "voluntary" are the following?

- Compliance with industry environmental codes of practice, with the risk of sanctions by the industry association for failure to comply?

- Publishing annual reports on environmental achievements and transgressions to satisfy investors, neighbors, and NGOs?

- Acceding to customers' demands for more environmentally friendly products and operations to avoid a tarnished reputation or lost business?

- Reducing environmental liabilities and risks to avoid higher premiums from insurers and higher rates from lenders?

- Capitalizing on reduced expenses and increased productivity possible through environmental strategies in order to satisfy shareholder demands for higher profits?

- Paying attention to environmental issues because of the threat of government regulations, in the hope that further regulations are preempted or weakened?[59]

Direct regulatory pressures for environmental improvements have been joined by a host of additional inducements. The point is to acknowledge that few companies altruistically undertake environmental initiatives simply because it is the right thing to do. Out of self-interest, they are responding to, or anticipating, pressure from industry groups, NGOs, customers, the financial sector, shareholders, or drafts of regulations hanging over their heads.[60] A 1997 survey by the European Union found that two thirds of company respondents cited the potential to forgo or postpone regulation as the most important benefit of voluntary environmental regulations.[61] Companies taking early action may help stave off pressure groups' calls for tougher compulsory regulation.

Hard laws are legally binding regulations, while "soft laws" are voluntary codes of conduct adopted under threat of regulations from cooperate-or-else governments.[62] But do voluntary measures work?

One of the more interesting views is the cynical view that the sustainability/CSR field is simply a scam dreamed up by academics, consultants, and NGOs. I have heard some, though, granted, not many, state that companies that believe in all this sustainability stuff are being duped. No doubt much of what has been written about sustainability and CSR was written by consultants, academics, NGOs, and so forth, but a significant amount was issued by major companies too. (Mel Wilson)

It's pretty hard to experience a public outcry or crisis because there isn't even the enforcement staff around. You have voluntary reporting everywhere, and not enough people from the environment department to adequately spot-check corporate operations in one of the wealthiest provinces [Alberta] in the country. That in itself is a bit of a perverse subsidy — lack of enforcement. The companies would never tell you that. (Marlo Raynolds)

One thing that can upset some NGOs is having a senior representative of a company standing up and saying, "We manage sustainability issues because it's good for business." Even though that might be an accurate statement, for a lot of groups it is a very selfish motivation. They view it as basically saying the company cares because it is good for the company, not because it is good for society. That's not what NGOs are fighting for. They don't want more self-serving companies. They want more socially aware companies.

Similarly, if a senior representative says to a group of mainstream investors, "We manage sustainability issues because it's good for society," it is quite likely that some investors will be concerned. They invested to get a return on their investment, and they don't want their investment put at risk. If the company is spending money on social issues rather than making a return, there is a risk of losing their money.

Companies that have most successfully communicated their sustainability policies are those that have successfully linked the two: "We manage sustainability issues because it's good for business *and* good for society." (Mel Wilson)

NGO Issues with Voluntary Agreements

Increasing vehicle fuel efficiency through voluntary efforts of vehicle manufacturers has resulted in the fuel efficiency of new vehicles sold in Canada *worsening* from 8.4 liters/100 kilometers to. 9.5 liters/100 kilometers between 1986 and 1998. A voluntary building code encouraging construction of R-2000 energy-efficient homes in Canada has resulted in only 0.6% of new homes being built to that standard. Voluntary approaches, despite industry lobbyists' claims to the contrary, have had mixed results.[63]

International pacts call on corporate signatories to develop self-monitoring and self-enforcement mechanisms. A complaint from civil-society organizations is the lack of evaluation and follow-up on the effectiveness of voluntary programs, which are characterized by self-selection and voluntary reporting.[64] The United Nations (UN) Global Compact was launched in 2000 and signed by 61 member companies of the World Business Council for Sustainable Development by 2004.[65] Its ten principles call on businesses to take specific actions in the areas of human rights, labor standards, the environment, and anti-corruption. A 2004 McKinsey report, "Assessing the Global Compact's Impact", says the compact has accelerated corporate policy changes and promoted partnership projects.[66] However, it notes there is a lack of international monitoring and enforcement mechanisms to hold companies accountable to their pledges. A critical question is whether voluntary agreements driven by the threat of regulations are appealing to business because they reduce reporting requirements and have greater flexibility or because they have weaker standards and allow companies to sign up to do what they would have done anyway.[67]

The Equator Principles are another example of a voluntary agreement. Among the global banking community, 23 banks signed the International Finance Corporation's (IFC) Equator Principles within a year of their launch in June 2003.[68] These principles commit signatories to apply social and environmental policies in all their project lending.[69] A 2004 report by BankTrack, an NGO whose members include Friends of the Earth, the World Wildlife Fund, and the Rainforest Action Network, says the Equator Principles are having little impact. BankTrack's report claims many controversial pipeline, hydroelectric dam, and oil and gas projects have gone ahead virtually unaltered by the existence of the principles. BankTrack is asking for more transparency, accountability, and stakeholder engagement in the way banks apply the Equator Principles to specific projects.[70]

Folks like Forest Reinhardt at Harvard Business School appear to believe that environmental strategy in business means manipulating the regulatory system to disadvantage your competitor. We think it means designing your business in a much superior way, which happens to make regulation irrelevant to your business and only relevant to your competitor.

One of the elements of natural capitalism is to design out waste and toxicity so there is nothing left in the process that can hurt the workers or the neighbors. So providing you follow normal workplace safety procedures, what's to regulate? Typically your slower competitors won't realize what happened, because they are still in the compliance mindset and can't imagine that anybody would not need to comply. (Amory Lovins)

I think there is a lot to be said for getting ahead of the curve. Think what the world is going to be like 20 years from now, anticipating there could be laws for this and laws for that, or international conventions. If you are smart, you want to get ahead of the curve, so you say, "Let's do it now. Once we are ahead of the curve, let's encourage the legislators to put in the laws that make it really tough for our competitors and laggards." It is Machiavellian, but it gets the job done. (Alan Willis)

Corporate Issues with Voluntary Agreements

Although a number of multinational corporations have voluntarily endorsed international agreements outlining codes of responsible business conduct, a complaint from the business community is the proliferation of codes on human rights and other sustainability issues. In addition to the UN Global Compact and the IFC Equator Principles discussed above, other international compacts and agreements include the Voluntary Principles on Security and Human Rights,[71] Global Sullivan Principles,[72] Universal Declaration of Human Rights,[73] and International Labor Organization (ILO) Declaration on Fundamental Principles and Rights at Work.[74] How many are companies supposed to sign? Which ones are the right ones?

To address this proliferation, a subcommission of the UN Commission on Human Rights (UNCHR) spent four years distilling the social, economical, and environmental obligations of transnational companies outlined in existing international declarations into a single statement of "Norms on Business and Human Rights," unveiled in 2004. While confirming that states have the main responsibility to protect human rights, the norms oblige businesses to refrain from activities that directly or indirectly violate human rights and suggest that breaches can result in compensation to the victims. Because the proposal moves beyond pure voluntarism, it is strongly opposed by the International Chamber of Commerce, the International Employers Organization, and the US Council for International Business. They claim that voluntary industry initiatives are sufficient to protect human rights.[75]

Finally, there is an important distinction between company-led voluntary approaches and industry-led voluntary approaches. Some company-led voluntary corporate responsibility approaches are criticized by sector colleagues as thinly veiled divide-and-conquer attempts that would give leaders in sustainability a competitive advantage. How? Leaders could lobby governments to pass new regulations that would give them an advantage over rivals forced to implement costly catch-up pollution-abatement measures. Well-coordinated industry lobbies do just the opposite — fend off regulatory threats with promises of self-regulation.[76]

A deeper partnership implies a medium-term relationship, with both parties contributing skills, resources and expertise, and sharing the risks. It should help the business achieve something it otherwise couldn't, and the NGO should get a change of business practice, not just project funding .... NGOs risk jeopardizing their legitimacy. Businesses risk wasting resources. But there are also risks for the partnership — that the business simply reaps the reputational reward without making serious efforts to achieve progress. That could backfire on both partners ....

[The UK sustainability consulting company] SustainAbility identified some key success factors:

- The company must be serious about changing its behavior, and should be able to drive change in its own sector and across the business community more generally.
- The NGO must be able to maintain clear accountability to its own key stakeholders, and must maintain its independence from the business partner.
- Each partner needs to benefit directly, and to understand the other's benefits.
- The "rules of engagement" need to be clearly agreed at the outset.
- Individual participants must be sufficiently senior to have their organization's mandate and be able to take difficult decisions without constantly having to refer back.
- The people involved must trust each other.

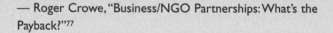

— Roger Crowe, "Business/NGO Partnerships: What's the Payback?"[77]

Blended Responsibilities

It may have occurred to you, as I considered the three legs of the sustainability stool, that there is an intuitive division of traditional institutional roles and responsibilities: corporate institutions are primarily responsible for the economic leg, while nongovernmental organizations (NGOs) and governments are responsible for the environmental and social legs. To that end, corporations support NGOs and local communities with charitable donations and sponsorships, using external benchmarks such as donating 1% of pretax profits, as suggested by the Canadian Centre for Philanthropy's Imagine Program,[78] or adhering to company-unique internal philanthropic guidelines. As well, corporations support various levels of governments with taxes. Case closed?

Well, not quite, not any longer. For-profit corporations can no longer assume that their donations to NGOs and taxes paid to governments adequately protect their social license to operate or offset environmental and social damage caused by making their profits in the first place. Nor can not-for-profit NGOs and the public sector still assume that they can survive without business plans or without tracking the economic value of their social performance or by working in the margins. Both private-sector corporations on one hand, and NGOs and governments on the other hand, are now expected to directly maximize economic, social, and environmental value from their respective capital. Their responsibilities are blended, as is the economic/environmental/social value they create.[79]

NGO/corporate partnerships, as encouraged by the 2002 World Summit on Sustainable Development in Johannesburg, are challenging for both parties. As they work from the inside rather than the outside on corporate responsibility, NGOs risk being co-opted by the corporate agenda and losing their credibility, independence, or capacity to criticize as the company exploits the partnership for reputational advantage. For corporations, partnerships may appear to be just another device to pry open their sponsorship pocketbooks to philanthropically fund NGO projects in exchange for enhanced corporate citizenship reputations. A meaningful, ongoing relationship requires trust, a challenge for traditionally adversarial organizations leery of being contaminated or exploited by the other. Partnerships are a source of cautious optimism.

The US has something called Federal Sentencing Guidelines. If a company is brought into the courts for something, if they can show that they have a program in ethics or CSR, the fines are a lot less. From a risk-management standpoint, there is a huge growth in ethics officers In companies because of legislation. In Canada that isn't the case, so ethics is less important to many executives. (Laurent Leduc)

Communities and corporations that have environmental management systems in place are considered to have exercised due diligence in the courts in terms of complying with legislation like the Canadian Environmental Protection Act. Environmental management systems, even though not required by law, end up being a very important part of your compliance regime. (Louise Comeau)

Regulations are typically a second-order priority. They can contribute to creating value, but mainly in combination with the other activities. There is a huge amount of denial about public policy. Companies tend to think of market forces first and "that damned regulations stuff" second. It doesn't tend to be as strong a motivator by itself. That's not to say that it is not important. Its importance is a bit lower in the hierarchy from a company's internal perspective, but from an outside world perspective it is pivotal and essential. (Don Reed)

The threat of regulations is a motivator .... I think some companies are a bit nervous that the government is going to come down and regulate all sorts of things. The threat of that regulation is pushing them to look more closely at voluntary initiatives. (George Khoury)

As we see environmental regulations grow, a lot of companies are getting involved because they want to try to preempt new regulations. They want to either be ahead of the curve on new environmental regulations so they don't get punished by them, or they want to help develop them so that, when they do become law, the company will be in a favorable position. (Devin Crago)

Regulations are Necessary but Not Sufficient

As mentioned earlier, a 2003 GlobeScan survey of 201 experts in 40 countries revealed eight predicted drivers of sustainable development: economic instruments like ecological taxes and emissions trading (69%); corporate role models (69%); regulations/enforcement (62%); legislated product performance standards (61%); legislated reporting (53%); green consumerism (51%); voluntary agreements (48%) and ISO 14000 (32%).[80] Clearly the respondents foresee a significant continued role for regulations as drivers of corporate environmental attention.

Regulations require stringent levels of accountability, verifiable objectives, and transparent public reporting that voluntary initiatives seldom match. Regulations also create a more level playing field for all companies than voluntary measures ever could, providing a competitive advantage opportunity for companies that innovatively solve environmental problems sooner and more smartly than their competitors.[81]

The effectiveness of regulations as a credible motivator of better business environmental practices depends on the size of the company, the industry sector, the mindset and beliefs of the company senior executives, the perceived teeth in enacted and pending regulations, and how proactive industry associations are. "Command-and-control" regulations are a necessary, but not sufficient, condition for sustainability progress. We need more "command-and-prevent"[82] and "command-and-incent" policies and regulations to achieve real progress on sustainability by capitalizing on market-driven approaches.

There is a false dichotomy between regulations and voluntary corporate environmental initiatives. These should be complementary, not adversarial, approaches. Voluntary initiatives are not justification for dismantling regulatory capacity or for government shirking its role as regulator and becoming an industry stakeholder. Long-term strategies for environmental protection require cooperation among governments, businesses, and citizens' organizations with shared visions. Combinations of voluntary and regulatory measures are needed to make corporate environmental responsibility mandatory, increasingly habitual, and ultimately profitable.[83]

After compliance, risk management kicks in, whether it is risk of being caught out or risk of a disaster or risk of a mess or risk of the community, customers, or employees coming after you. There is a risk-management component in there. (Alan Willis)

A big driver of CSR attention is managing environmental and social risks. One of the big reasons for Suncor getting into this was the realization that they were at risk, particularly with respect to climate change. They had to be in a leadership role to try to shape the issue, manage it, and be sure they were well positioned to deal with it. I think they recognized in the early 1990s that they had terrible stakeholder relationships and were widely seen as an appalling company. Few stakeholders thought anything nice about them, and no one wanted to work for them. Then they embraced the idea of stakeholders and became more open and reasonably transparent compared to most corporations .... There seems to have been a big shift. I think it is related to how they want to manage social and environmental risks to their business. (Stephen Hill)

Two Emerging Drivers

The three drivers of sustainability discussed in this section obviously worked for leaders in the first wave of sustainability companies. Otherwise, they would not be leaders. The companies had founders who had a values-based passion for sustainability and/or they suffered a PR crisis and determined they would never allow that to happen again and/or they were triggered by complying with regulations and decided to go beyond compliance.

Executives sometimes use a "SWOT" analysis to assess how best to deal with a pressing business issue. They look at company Strengths to handle the issue, company Weaknesses in handling the issue, Opportunities presented by the issue, and Threats associated with the issue. If CSR were the issue being considered in a SWOT analysis, two emerging sustainability drivers would be categorized in the last two quadrants: a "perfect storm" of risks would be in the Threat category, and enhanced business value from sustainability initiatives would be in the Opportunity quadrant. In some ways they are two sides of the same coin, as we will see.

Starting with threats, some companies are motivated to pay attention to sustainability because of risks and potential liabilities associated with unacceptable environmental and social practices. In fact, before "sustainability" and "CSR" gained currency in the lexicon of business, many CSR initiatives were categorized as risk-management programs. Social, cultural, demographic, and technological changes mean that social and environmental risk management is more important than ever to brand value.

Risk of what, exactly? For openers, risk of losing market value because financial analysts deem the company has environmental exposures. Then there is risk of losing revenue as fallout from bad press, risk of being blindsided by pollution control regulations requiring costly end-of-pipe filters or retrofits, and risk of fines. The ultimate company risk is losing its social license to operate. Although this sounds drastic, the legitimacy slope is slippery. It is not so much that the government will step in and close the company down. It is that a bad press report, beyond normal damage control measures, causes panic in the marketplace, affecting customers and investors and creating an irreversible downward spiral.

CHAPTER THREE

FIRST EMERGING DRIVER — A PERFECT
STORM OF THREATS

The change literature is unanimous on one premise: a "burning platform" causes change. The "burning platform" expression comes from a story told by Daryl Conner in *Managing at the Speed of Change*.[1] He tells of a nighttime explosion and fire on the Piper Alfa oil platform in the North Sea off the coast of Scotland on July 6, 1988. It was the worst catastrophe in 25 years of North Sea exploration: 167 people died, 61 survived.[2] One of the survivors, Andy Mochan, plunged 150 feet (15 stories) into a burning sea of oil and debris, knowing he could survive only 20 minutes in the freezing water.

Why did Andy jump? When interviewed in the hospital later, he said he had chosen uncertain death over certain death — he knew that if he stayed in the inferno on the platform, he would die. The pain of the "status quo" was too great. He jumped because he had to, not because he was attracted by a personal growth opportunity.

Personal and organizational change is often precipitated by a real or perceived "burning platform." The push of a problem or crisis is sometimes supplemented by the pull of an attractive "shared vision" of what it will be like after the change is complete, but most of the time the will to change is driven by discomfort with the status quo or unease about what might happen if a change is not undertaken. We need to be driven by a personal desire to change, based on self-interest or self-preservation.

So what is the burning platform encouraging sustainability? For sustainability champions, the imminent crisis that gets their attention is ecological or socially based. Their burning platform for sustainability might be that humankind is accelerating an ecological catastrophe that will destroy the earth's ability to heal itself, and that it may be impossible to adapt our socioeconomic systems to reverse the process before it is too late for life as we know it to continue.[3] Not a pleasant thought, especially for those of us with children or grandchildren.

For executives, the burning platform it is more likely to be business-oriented risks from a "perfect storm" of market forces that might directly or indirectly blindside them.

"

Sustainability is a change-management issue. It is about moving people and companies off their status quo patterns of behavior, which is never easy. People and organizations resist change. There has to be a compelling reason to overcome the inertia. Sometimes it takes a crisis. (Kevin Brady)

Between October 27 and 29, 1991, Hurricane Grace formed over the warm waters of the Atlantic Ocean off the east coast of Florida. In the next two days it swept north, pushing 10- to 15-foot swells toward the coast of the southeastern United States.[4] By October 29 it was downgraded by meteorologists from a hurricane to a tropical storm and lay just off the coast of Bermuda.[5] It was no longer considered a threat.

About the same time, an extratropical cyclone was moving across the Great Lakes, and an old warm front was swirling off the coast of the Atlantic provinces and New England states. These two weather systems suddenly joined with Hurricane Grace on October 30 and 31, causing the old hurricane to regenerate itself into a new monster hurricane that came to be known as the "Halloween Storm" or the "Perfect Storm." With average waves 40 to 80 feet high, and some waves recorded at 101 feet high (higher than a 10-story building), some meteorologists say it was the worst storm in history.[6]

Hybrid storms such as this are rare, but can be particularly dangerous. Sometimes storm systems cancel each other out. Sometimes they feed on each other. Only because the Perfect Storm occurred in the mid-Atlantic were horrendous property damage and casualties avoided. Devastation did happen, though. The *Perfect Storm* movie and book chronicle the experiences of the ill-fated *Andrea Gail*, a fishing boat caught in the full force of the storm in the mid-Atlantic.[7]

— The "Perfect Storm" story

A "Perfect Storm" of Market Forces

Like the real meteorological event, a "perfect storm" of market forces is brewing on the horizon for unsuspecting companies. Some forces may initially appear irrelevant to the organization. However, if these separate market forces synergistically cluster together, their combined impact on unprepared companies could be devastating. Wise business strategists tracking emerging market forces will react to early blips on their environmental-scan radar screens and ensure their companies are ready to pragmatically respond to them and capitalize on them, rather than be blindsided by them.

The 1991 perfect storm resulted when three weather fronts suddenly converged and fed on each other's energy. The potential perfect storm for businesses consists of threatening market forces, five of which are demanding stakeholder groups.

1. "Green" consumers
2. Activist shareholders
3. Civil-society sector/nongovernmental organizations (NGOs)
4. Governments, both national and international
5. The financial sector

Each stakeholder group is powerful. However, they are not discrete; the same individual might be a consumer, a shareholder, and an NGO member. As overlap among these market forces becomes more pronounced, the chance they will merge to become a unified tidal wave of rising expectations about corporate citizenship also increases.

What mega-issues are turning up the heat under simmering, demanding stakeholders? From dozens of global market forces, I will consider the impact of five:

1. Climate change
2. Pollution and its effect on health
3. Globalization backlash
4. The energy crunch
5. Erosion of trust in institutions

Figure 3.1: Mega-Issues + Demanding Stakeholders ➤ Business Risks

Ten Market Forces		Five Categories of Business Risk
Five Mega-Issues	Five Demanding Stakeholders	
1. Climate Change	1. "Green" Consumers	1. Market risks · Regulatory bans or restrictions on sales · Reduced market demand for products · Degradation of product quality by environmental factors · Customer boycotts or reduced acceptance
2. Pollution / Health	2. Activist Shareholders	2. Balance-sheet risks · Remediation liabilities · Insurance underwriting losses · Impairment of real property values · Damage assessments · Toxic torts
3. Globalization Backlash	3. Civil Society / NGOs	3. Operating risks · Costs of cleaning up spills and accidents · Risk to worker safety from handling hazardous materials · Expensive regulation-driven process changes · Reduced process yields · Rise in prices of materials or energy
4. The Energy Crunch	4. Governments	4. Capital cost risks · Product redesign to meet new industry standards or regulations · Costly input substitutions to meet new industry standards or regulations · Pollution and waste treatment upgrades
5. Erosion of Trust	5. Financial Sector	5. Sustainability risks · Competitive disadvantage from energy or material inefficiencies · Impact of mandatory take-back rules · Exposure to future taxes and regulatory restrictions
		+ More difficult access to capital

Mega-Issues + Demanding Stakeholders ➤ Business Risks

In combination with five demanding stakeholder groups, the five mega-issues generate ten threatening market forces. In turn, these market forces contribute to five categories of business risk.[8]

1. Market risks

2. Balance-sheet risks

3. Operating risks

4. Capital cost risks

5. Sustainability risks

In Figure 3.1, the labels for the mega-issues, demanding stakeholders, and business risks in the three columns are deliberately offset, signifying they are not uniquely associated with neighboring factors. Some mega-issues fuel several stakeholder groups, others only one. In turn, some demanding stakeholders contribute to several business risks, others to only one. There can be no greater business risk than the whole company going under. This threat is a powerful driver of sustainability strategies.[9]

Stakeholders are groups or individuals who are affected by an organization's actions, products, or services, or who can affect the company's operations or image. Demanding stakeholders may overlap incestuously. So may mega-issues. Worries about climate change may intersect with concerns about pollution and a destabilizing energy crunch. Concerns about the impact of global trade may also erode trust in corporations. The five mega-issues swirl around each other, feeding off each other's momentum. They fan the flames of demanding stakeholders and present direct threats to corporations. No one knows how, or if, the ten market forces will coalesce. This uncertainty means their potential impact on an industry sector or individual corporation is unpredictable. As with any business risk, the potential of a perfect storm makes anticipation and preparation wise.

I will examine each of the ten market forces, outlining the "what?" and the "so what?" of each. First I will consider the five mega-issues and then the five demanding stakeholder groups. Finally, I will explore business opportunities that arise from this potential storm of market forces. Smart executives can use aikido-like strategies to transform the energy of threatening market forces into impetus for business opportunities.

"What is the relationship between corporate strategy and societal issues such as the environment, poverty, health, population, and international development? Business leaders have a tendency to see "social" concerns as having little relevance to competing. Instead, these fall under the headings of corporate citizenship or corporate philanthropy, or are left to managers to address as matters of individual conscience.

It is becoming more and more apparent, however, that treating broader social issues and corporate strategy as separate and distinct has long been unwise, never more so than today. Seeing strategy narrowly leads to missed opportunities and bad competitive choices. It can also cause managers to overlook potential competitive advantages.
— Michael Porter, preface to *Tomorrow's Markets*[10]

For me, it seems sometimes that to capture the collective interest of the general public, there may have to be some major environmental problem or disaster. We've seen this with Bhopal, Hurricane Andrew and a couple of other big headliners. These events seem to raise collective awareness for a while, but it doesn't seem to have resulted in a sea change. Certainly I wouldn't want to wave my magic wand to have that kind of thing happen, but I wonder if there is going to have to be something that severe. Recent research on climate change is saying maybe the impact of this will come fast and furious, not just over the long term, and by then it might be too late. I don't know. (Devin Crago)

We need a crisis. I'm not being cynical. We are muddling through the issues of sustainable development. Some people take a leap, but not many and not enough. Voluntary initiatives are tremendous sources of innovation. But there are not many volunteers, and in the absence of adequate public policies, nothing except your own foresight and values compels you to move. So there is a bit of talk but not much movement, and things are not likely to shape up fast enough; we'll have rather more social tension and more environmental breakdowns. Sooner or later we will have a crisis. People will then adjust, hopefully just in the nick of time. (Claude Fussler)

Mega-Issues

Traditional business risks have been fires, floods, and dangers related to employee health and safety — risks to tangibles. There is a growing, daunting list of mega-issues that threaten both tangible assets and intangible assets like reputation. I have chosen a shortlist of five for discussion. Beyond those considered in this section, several deserve to be included as mega-issues potentially affecting particular companies.[11]

- Physical risks to supply of materials and energy
- AIDS and other threats to workers' health
- Terrorism and security
- Global connectivity
- Population explosion
- Urbanization
- Obesity
- Genetically modified organisms
- Water rights and security of water supply
- Privatization
- Intellectual property implications
- Offshoring of jobs
- Poverty and global inequities

And so on. As executives carry out environmental scans during strategic planning sessions, they need to assess the implication of these issues to the business, both now and in the future. The issue is not whether executives think a company should have to worry about these social, political, or environmental threats to its tangible or intangible value. The issue is whether other stakeholders do.

A new survey of the world's largest companies reveals that companies are paying increasing attention to climate change. The report also unveils a new Climate Leadership Index, comprising the 50 companies "whose responses best addressed the breadth of climate change issues."

The report, from the Carbon Disclosure Project (CDP), a group of institutional investors representing assets in excess of US$10 trillion, and Innovest Strategic Value Advisors, is based on responses to CDP's second information request to the FT500 Global Index of companies.

"The number of leading institutions backing CDP demonstrates that the mainstream investment community is now seriously engaging with the strategic and financial implications of responding to climate change," says the carbon group. "Over the last year the number of participating institutions nearly tripled to 95 from 35, and represented assets more than doubled to over US$10 trillion from US$4.5 trillion."

The report found that responses from the FT500 were up sharply, from 47% for during the first survey to 59% for in the current one. A clear majority of those responding consider climate change to present risks and opportunities to their business. "However, the percentage of corporations that failed to respond to the disclosure request remains large, including a dozen companies of whose common stock the CDP signatories own more than 10%," reports CDP.

"Companies failing to respond or providing weak responses to those that own a significant share of their business will invite particular scrutiny from the investment community," said James Cameron. "Investors now have ample understanding and opportunity to reallocate assets to reduce climate change risk and invest in companies offering solutions to accelerated global warming."
— News item about the Carbon Disclosure Project's second report[12]

Mega-Issue #1: Climate Change

The Intergovernmental Panel on Climate Change (IPCC), the world's most authoritative body of climate scientists, issued its third report in September 2001. It confirmed that human activity is contributing to a rise in concentrations of the six greenhouse gases.[13] Despite the US government's rejection of the Kyoto Protocol, the US National Academy of Sciences agreed with the IPCC report in June 2001. The Kyoto Protocol requires a 5% reduction below 1990 carbon dioxide concentration levels by 2010–12. Burning fossil fuels accounts for 80% to 85% of human-made carbon dioxide emissions.[14]

The fallout from climate change could be disastrous for the environment, society, and the economy. Business would get a triple hit. First, there is the direct financial risk to companies, their customers, and their suppliers of damages from and remediation for severe weather events and other physical risks. Secondly, there are regulation-related risks: the threat of carbon taxes imposed by trading partners or local governments; the risk of greater regulation of greenhouse gas emissions; and the risk of energy inefficiency regulations or penalties.[15] Thirdly, there is the risk of reputational damage that could affect revenue, stakeholder relations, and employee productivity if the company is perceived as a contributor to the problem.

Equity markets are investigating the implications of global warming on their investments. The Carbon Disclosure Project (CDP) report quantified the potential financial impact on companies in various sectors.[16] In its 2003 report, the CDP estimated that the discounted present value of potential carbon liabilities within a single carbon-intensive manufacturing firm could represent as much as 40% of its entire market capitalization,[17] driven by increases in fossil fuel prices and the potential imposition of carbon taxes and other regulations. The 2004 report suggested that even a 5% shift in energy prices could affect per-share earnings by 15%.[18] As China industrializes, its demand for fossil fuels is forecasted to drive energy prices up elsewhere. More sobering, if China's industrialization generates anywhere close to a similar ratio of greenhouse gases per unit of gross domestic product experienced in Europe and North America in the last century, we are all cooked ... literally.[19]

Climate change has become a real market force. More on this later.

In Eastern Europe, there's hardly a river, stream, or brook that isn't contaminated with the runoff from human misuse, whether industrial effluents, agricultural pesticides and herbicides, or worse. (The "worse" could be bacterial contamination — the river as disease vector — or the dumping of radioactive wastes.) A recent Czech study commissioned by the government found that three-quarters of the surface water in the country was "severely polluted," and almost one-third was so badly contaminated it couldn't support fish at all ....

In China, 80 percent of the country's 50,000 kilometres of major rivers are so degraded they no longer support any fish. Seventy percent of China's catch once came from the Yangtze, but it has declined by more than half since the 1960s. In the Yellow River, discharge from paper mills, tanneries, oil refineries, and chemical plants has poured into the water, which is now laced with heavy metals and other toxins that make it unfit even for irrigation. Traces of lead, chromium, and cadmium have been found in vegetables sold in city markets, and so have concentrations of arsenic .... A World Bank study in 1997 put the cost of air and water pollution in China at $54 billion a year, equivalent to an astonishing 8 percent of the country's gross domestic product ....

There are more than 8,000 kilometres of shoreline on the US side of the Great Lakes, but only 3 percent are fit for swimming, for supplying drinking water, or for supporting aquatic life. In 1993, two-thirds of US "fish advisories" were issued in the Great Lakes region, most of them having to do with excessive amounts of mercury, PCBs, chlordane, dioxins, and DDT. Each year 50-100 million tons of hazardous waste is generated in the watershed for the lakes, 25 million tons of pesticides alone .... The 1998 International Joint Commission, in the same report that declared the Great Lakes cleaner than ever before, tracked the accumulation of a dozen or so noxious chemicals and found, to its dismay, a "buildup of radioactive contaminants in the lakes from nuclear power plant discharges. The evidence is overwhelming," the report said. "Certain persistent toxic substances impair human intellectual capacity, change behavior, damage the immune system, and compromise reproductive capacity." Anyone relying on fish or wildlife for food was at risk.
— Marq de Villiers, Water[20]

Mega-Issue #2: Pollution/Health

Climate change concerns focus on one form of industrial pollution — the discharge of greenhouse gases into the air. Pollution and health concerns are about other industrial pollution — the discharge of toxic emissions and hazardous waste into air, water, and soil, directly or indirectly affecting our health. Marq de Villiers chronicles the sobering dangers of water pollution in *Water*, opposite. Air pollution is worse.

Smog is an example of air pollution from industrial sources. Ground-level ozone, a major ingredient in smog, is formed when fumes from automobiles, factories, and other fossil fuel burners react with sunlight. It is linked to respiratory problems including emphysema and bronchitis. About 159 million Americans are breathing unhealthy air according to new, tighter ozone rules the Environmental Protection Agency unveiled in 2004.[21]

The World Health Organization (WHO) reported in 2002 that three million people die annually from the effects of air pollution, three times the number of people who die from car accidents. In the US, air pollution claims 70,000 lives per year, equal to the combined total of deaths from prostate and breast cancer, compared to 40,000 traffic fatalities[22] or 3,000 fatalities on 9/11.

The Ontario Medical Association (OMA) reports that there are 1,900 premature deaths in Ontario each year due to cardio-respiratory illnesses resulting from air pollution, and the number could rise to 2,600 per year by 2015.[23] Air pollution costs Ontario more than $1 billion a year in hospital admissions, emergency room visits, and absenteeism — $600 million in direct medical costs and $560 in indirect costs to employers and employees for lost time — according to the OMA. If one uses conservative estimates of the cost of pain and suffering, and loss of life, these add a staggering $5 billion and $4 billion respectively to the total. This gives a total annual economic loss of $10 billion in 2000, rising to $12 billion by 2015.[24] And that is just in one province in Canada.

Waste and emissions represent lost value, business costs, and a threat to present and future human generations.[25] Backlash from the public as it connects the dots between illness and industrial pollution can erode a carefully earned corporate reputation if a company or its industry sector is seen as being responsible for smog-related emissions. When our children's health is in jeopardy, we demand aggressive action against polluters. It is personal.

The demonstrations against free trade and market globalization have thrown down a challenge for those who believe firmly that markets offer the most promising means to achieve global sustainability. Protestors have leveled varied, often colorful and, we believe, mostly misinformed criticisms at multinational companies and international organizations such as the WTO [World Trade Organization]. Among these concerns are legitimate concerns that must be tackled if markets are to succeed in helping deliver social and environmental progress.

It is clear that today's rough approximation of a global market has some significant limitations[, as] the [World Business Council on Sustainable Development's "Sustainability through the Market, 2001"] report argued. In particular, inadequate framework conditions, exacerbated by persistent trade barriers, perverse subsidies, corruption, monopolies, and deficient property rights serve to perpetuate unsustainable practices ....

Losers in the market globalization process tend to be the low-skilled workers in industrial and developing countries and, in the developing world, farmers who must compete against subsidized farm goods from wealthier countries .... The very structure of the global trading regime itself also limits poorer countries' abilities to benefit from world trade ... Moreover, OECD countries are almost always at a negotiating advantage at trade negotiation forums — perpetuating an imbalance that undermines these institutions' credibility and effectiveness .... The result is that industry sectors in which the South holds a clear competitive advantage — agriculture and textiles, for example — remain among the least liberalized and are characterized by persistent high and price-distorting subsidies ....

So, building a better global market is not only about fairness but also about the well being of global civilization. Many business people do not like the expression "fair market." They assume that this refers to a market burdened with rules attempting to create a better environment and better conditions for everyone: labor, women, minorities, poor countries, etc. The freer the market, they argue, the fairer. But the present market is largely unfair because it is "unfree," burdened by policies and conditions that hinder the poor from freely competing in it.
— Charles O. Holliday Jr., Stephen Schmidheiny, and Philip Watts, *Walking the Talk*[26]

Mega-Issue #3: Globalization Backlash

The World Trade Organization (WTO) was founded during the Uruguay round of the General Agreement on Tariffs and Trade (GATT) talks in 1995. It joined the World Bank and the International Monetary Fund (IMF), two multilateral institutions established largely by the United States and Great Britain after World War II.[27] The stated goal of the WTO is "to improve the welfare of the peoples of the member countries .... The WTO is the only international organization dealing with the global rules of trade between nations. Its main function is to ensure that trade flows as smoothly, predictably and freely as possible."[28]

The goals of the WTO are worthy. However, one contentious issue is the unlevel playing field of trade subsidies and trade barriers that put poorer nations at a disadvantage, as described opposite. Another issue is WTO accountability. Critics describe the WTO as "a global parliament composed of unelected bureaucrats with the power to amend its own charter without referral to national legislative bodies."[29] It also has the power to decide that a country's domestic law violates WTO rules and to recommend that the offending country change its law or face financial penalties, trade sanctions, or both.[30] A third issue is patent protection, especially as it restricts access in less-developed nations to essential medicines.[31]

Beyond these issues related to globalization are concerns about the degree of corporate influence on and within the WTO. For example, when the US Congress debated the inclusion of China in the WTO, "top business leaders issued a stern warning to federal lawmakers: vote against the deal with China and we will hold it against you when it comes time to write checks for your campaigns."[32] This blatant coercion of elected officials casts doubts on WTO integrity.

The primary mandate of WTO national representatives, many of whom are from big business, is to open other markets to exports from their own countries. They tend to give trade goals precedence over public policies like full employment, health and safety regulations, environmental standards, and protecting the democratic rights of citizens to determine the use of their part of the global commons.[33] It is small wonder that many people equate globalization with corporate desire to expand into new markets more for their own benefit than the benefit of citizens in recipient countries, causing a backlash of resentment against global corporations.

Talisman's experience in the Sudan had a ripple effect through the whole oil industry. It brought to everyone's attention that there are as many risks above ground as there are below ground when looking for oil internationally, and that Canadian oil companies are not immune from campaigns by NGOs and other stakeholders. (Mel Wilson)

Subsidies and tax loopholes keep the price of fossil fuels artificially low, making it hard for renewable energy to compete. The fossil fuel companies gave big-time campaign donations and political action committee contributions to encourage politicians to keep the subsidies in place and the special program subsidies flowing. From 1993-1999, Southern Company, Chevron, General Electric, ARCO, Texaco, and 121 other companies that benefited from federal energy subsidy programs gave $39 million in campaign donations and received $7.3 billion in government grants ... a 186:1 return on their investments.[34]

The oil companies are enormously rich .... The average effective federal tax rate paid by oil companies in the US fell from 21.9% in 1981 to 11.9% in 1995; and it's not just the oil companies. Coal companies are required to reclaim mining areas after a mine is depleted, but they can deduct the cost before they do the work. They can also treat income from royalties as capital gains, paying a reduced rate of tax. Taken together, the fossil fuel and nuclear producers gain $14.7 billion a year from various tax loopholes, which contributed to a net profit in 1997 of $29.8 billion.[35]

— Guy Dauncey, *Stormy Weather: 101 Solutions to Global Climate Change*

Mega-Issue #4: The Energy Crunch

Dwindling fossil fuel resources, the escalating cost of their retrieval and refinement, and the pollution they cause are ever-increasing concerns. World energy consumption demand will grow between 150% and 230% by 2050.[36] Unfortunately, research by the University of Uppsala in Sweden predicts world oil and gas supplies will be unable to meet demand sometime between 2010 and 2020, decades sooner than previously predicted, because global reserves are 80% smaller than was optimistically estimated.[37]

The United States consumes 19.5 million barrels of oil a day and has to import half of it — 9.8 million barrels a day. Its daily imports are trending toward 17 million barrels by 2020. The ramifications of US dependence on foreign oil are economic, environmental, and military: Would the US be as consumed with Iraq if Iraq grew radishes instead of sitting on the second-largest oil reserves in the world? Would it be as interested in Afghanistan if a one-million-barrel-a-day oil pipeline from the Caspian basin to the Pakistan coast did not have to go through territory ruled by unpredictable Taliban "warlords"?[38]

Alternative energy options are discouraged by "perverse subsidies" to the nuclear and fossil fuel industries. Industrial countries annually subsidize the fossil fuel industry with $200 billion.[39] Between $29 and $46 billion of that goes to the US fossil fuel industry alone. These are called "perverse subsidies" because they subsidize environmentally destructive behavior. Citizens are billed twice for them: once when their taxes pay for the subsidies and again when they bear the direct and indirect costs of environmental restoration and health care costs. Between 1948 and 1998, the US federal government spent $111.5 billion on research and development (R&D) for the energy industry: $66 billion on nuclear energy R&D, $26 billion for fossil fuels R&D, but only $12 billion on R&D for renewable energy and $8 billion for R&D on energy efficiency.[40]

There is nothing like a brownout or blackout to bring home our dependence on electricity, or a sudden spike in gasoline prices at the local pump to wake us up to our dependence on foreign oil. Whatever the root cause, both governments and corporations are subjected to additional scrutiny when citizens are personally deprived of resources (energy, water, food) that they have taken for granted. As they come to realize how their tax dollars are funding an energy crunch of unsustainable solutions, they will demand a transition to fiscal incentives for renewable energy ... and expect companies to support that demand.

Methodology

The 2004 Edelman Trust Study was fielded in December 2003 and January 2004. It did 400 interviews in the US, 200 interviews in China (Shanghai, Beijing and Guangzhou only), and 50 interviews each in the UK, Germany, France and Brazil.

Trust in Institutions

- Trust in business is trending higher vs. January 2003 (US: 51% vs. 48% and Europe: 40% vs. 35%).
- There is a significant rise in trust in government in general vs. January 2003 (US: 48% vs. 39% and Europe: 31% vs. 25%).
- Trust in media is continuing to decline vs. January 2003 (US: 24% vs. 28% and Europe: 28% vs. 32%).
- Trust in NGOs, which had been growing steadily in previous years, is down slightly vs. January 2003. (US: 47% vs. 49% and Europe: 41% vs. 45%).

Trust in Leading Corporations

- Opinion leaders apply a significant "trust discount" for major US brands operating in Europe, such as Coca-Cola (66% in the US vs. 40% in Europe); McDonald's (53% vs. 27%); P&G (70% vs. 49%); and Citicorp (47% vs. 26%).
- Most trusted brands in the US are UPS (81%); Johnson & Johnson (75%); Procter & Gamble (70%); IBM (68%); Michelin (66%); Heinz (67%); and Coca-Cola (66%).
- Most trusted brands in Europe are Michelin (61%); Amnesty International (63%); World Wildlife Fund (59%); Microsoft (57%); IBM (55%); and Danone (54%). In January 2003, Greenpeace and Oxfam were in the top five.
- Most trusted brands in Brazil are Johnson & Johnson (86%); Danone (82%); Ford (78%); Greenpeace (73%); and Michelin (73%).
- Most trusted brands in China are Coca-Cola (85%); Samsung (82%); HSBC (82%); Microsoft (80%); and IBM (77%)

— 2004 Edelman Fifth Annual Trust Barometer[41]

Mega-Issue #5: Erosion of Trust

The residual effect of corporate scandals is eroding public trust in the business community. Trust is the essential enabler that allows the wheels of commerce to glide smoothly.[42] It is also at the core of its reputation.[43] The value of trust becomes obvious to skeptics when they experience its absence.[44]

The fallout from the unethical activities of Enron, WorldCom, Qwest, Tyco, and Global Crossing is reflected in a Gallup International and Environics International "Voice of the People" poll commissioned by the World Economic Forum (WEF).[45] It surveyed 36,000 people in 47 countries between July and December 2002 and found a dramatic lack of trust in organizations, especially global and large national companies. Asked to rate their level of trust in 17 institutions to operate in the best interests of society, respondents ranked global companies and large domestic companies last. Following up on the "trust" theme of its annual meeting 2003 in Davos, the WEF resurveyed 19,000 individuals across 20 countries between November 2003 and February 2004. Companies continued to be the least trusted of the seven institutions tested, while NGOs remain the most credible in the eyes of respondents.[46] The results of the 2004 Edelman survey, opposite, show slight recent improvement in trust in institutions, but a survey reported in *The Wirthlin Report* in April 2004 indicated that 71% of adult Americans say that only some of the top 1,000 companies operate in a fair and honest manner.[47] Research released in early 2004 by Harris Interactive and the Reputation Institute found 74% of American respondents described corporate America's reputation as either "not good" or "terrible."[48]

It is difficult to measure the precise economic impact of trust. However, lack of trust leads to weaker business partnerships, higher risks, higher interest rates, and lower profit margins.[49] No wonder trust and corporate citizenship were themes of the World Economic Forum in Davos, Switzerland, in January 2003.

The Sarbanes-Oxley Act, passed by the US Congress in July 2002, aims to improve auditor independence, ban loans to company officers and directors, improve corporate responsibility, ensure financial disclosure, and mandate corporate accountability while guarding against conflicts of interest.[50] More needs to be done by corporations to rebuild trust, polish tarnished corporate reputations, and protect social licenses to operate.

How to Boycott a Global Bully

In the face of intense opposition at home and abroad, the US government is determined to fight a war that will be felt around the world. It's a slap in the face to democracy, a cold shoulder to liberty — and it's time to make a visible statement against American power gone wrong.

Here is the one and only rule for the Brand America Boycott: this action belongs to you. You decide what brands and products stand as symbols of America's new empire-building project, and you decide how you'll make your statement. Above all else, this is a culture jam — personal, spontaneous, unpredictable.

Some people are planning a total Made-in-America boycott. Some will boycott oil for the duration of the war. Others are planning public activism against the greatest symbols of the Brand America warriors: McDonald's, Philip Morris, Exxon Mobil, Texaco, the major automakers, Tommy Hilfiger, Gap, Starbucks, Nike, Disneyland, the Hollywood cinemas. Media activists can launch TV Turnoff campaigns against Fox, CNN, ABC, NBC, CBS and MTV. The limits to your participation are the limits of imagination .... Imagine a global action against American oil corporations, or a day when McDonald's restaurants stand empty from Tokyo to Toronto, from Berlin to Chicago. Imagine a 24-hour blackout of America's "big five" media cheerleaders .... We'll post regular updates and spread the word. It's a consumer strike against a corrupted American dream. One final warning: be prepared to change the world! ....

Petition

Because I am one of the millions of people against the war;

And because the American government has made it clear that it won't listen to world opinion;

And because the symbols of American power are its corporations and their brands;

I hereby pledge to boycott Brand America, from the moment the war begins and to the best of my ability until the empire learns to listen.

— Adbusters' "Boycott America" campaign[51]

Wild Card Mega-Issues

Among climatologists, a huge concern is the "discontinuity scenario" — a potentially catastrophic, sudden, and irreversible shift in global climate patterns, such as the erasure of the Atlantic "conveyor belt" of currents, described in Chapter 6. Similarly, "discontinuity threats" to business can come from any direction, suddenly and unexpectedly.

Suppose you are a successful company. You are big, you have excellent brand recognition, you have expanded internationally, you have captured the majority of market share in your industry, and you are still growing impressively. You are also headquartered in the US. Suddenly, the 9/11 terrorist attack occurs, the Enron scandals erupt, and the war against Iraq is launched. As the economy suffers, so do you.

Then a Boycott America campaign is launched (see opposite page) and millions of people are invited to sign its petition against your company. If you are a proud executive in a large, successful American corporation, you may feel a wave of fury as you read the petition and the website information. Nobody said the world would be fair. Discontinuous market forces happen. They are wild cards in the game of commerce. The important question is not what your reaction is after the fact, but how effectively you anticipated and mitigated this wild card.

Wild card mega-issues do not start from scratch. They build on existing platforms of issues, engage stakeholders who are already organized, and can spread like wildfire. For example, the Boycott America campaign could be a magnet for civil-society stakeholders angered by corporate globalization and erosion of trust.

Wild card risks are just that — wild. They are difficult to tame with defensive strategies hastily crafted after the crisis has arisen. The best defense is a good offense — a solid, hard-earned corporate reputation for environmental stewardship, social responsibility, and ethical behavior. Smart companies begin by understanding how business risks are changing and how traditional defensive or dismissive responses to those risks are no longer adequate or appropriate. They engage with stakeholders rather than jeopardizing financial goals by ignoring or overlooking risks associated with environmental and social responsibilities.

Solid financial performance is bound to nonfinancial measures.[52] Wild card risks are "intangible" risks that can torpedo your company.

Stakeholders are those who have an interest or "stake" of some sort in the company and, traditionally, they include primary stakeholders, such as customers, employees, and investors, and secondary stakeholders, such as government and the wider community — though each business needs to determine which is which depending on the nature of the business and the level of "stake" in the company.

In considering potential stakeholder-related triggers, it is helpful to consider stakeholders' needs and motivations, the expectations they have traditionally had of business and then the more contemporary expectations with a CSR Agenda. It is the contemporary expectations that prompt potential triggers.

Such stakeholder expectations, and how they are expressed, will depend on the business sector, the history and success or otherwise of the company and so on. To help the reader with a start in considering how they affect their business, we have mapped generic corporate responsibility concerns, likely stakeholder expectations and possible triggers that might emerge.

We have mapped out stakeholder triggers under the following headings:

- Employees
- Investors
- Consumers
- Business partners and suppliers
- Nongovernmental organizations and media campaigns
- Governmental, intergovernmental and regulatory pressures
- Community and society

— David Grayson and Adrian Hodges, *Corporate Social Opportunity!*[53]

Demanding Stakeholders

Note that the heading is "demanding stakeholders," not "demanding *stock*holders." A significant characteristic of companies with a strong focus on sustainability is the degree to which they engage with, listen to, and partner with diverse groups who are affected by company operations. Why? Because those groups can adversely affect a company's operations and its legal and social license to operate if they decide to take action against it.

Who are the potential stakeholders who should be at the table? They could include:

- Employees/Labor unions
- Government ministries
- Suppliers/Partners
- Consumers/Customers/Clients
- Insurers/Re-insurers
- Banks/Rating agencies
- Media
- Institutional investors/Pension fund managers
- Private investors
- Nongovernmental associations
- First Nations
- Trade associations
- Competitors
- Local community
- The environment, usually represented by NGOs, government, or the community.

Understandably, executives tend to pay attention to relationships with stakeholders who have power, legitimacy, and urgency. They build social capital by developing organizational culture and capabilities to dialogue with an inclusive network of key stakeholders, recognizing that building social capital simultaneously builds financial capital.

They treat stakeholders as important, respected contributors to strategic decisions.[54]

I have chosen to discuss five generic groups of demanding stakeholders, covering most of the above list.

"

Green Consumers [22%] are the most environmentally committed group and they are the key market for green products and services. People in this segment are most likely to disagree that we worry too much about the future of the environment and not enough about the economy. They feel empowered when it comes to environmental pollution and strongly believe in the effectiveness of collective action. They do not believe that industry is working hard to ensure a clean environment and they give the poorest ratings of all the segments to private industry for its environmental performance. Green Consumers are most willing to pay a premium for green products. Green consumers may be a harbinger segment in that they have bridged the gap between their values as citizens and their behavior as consumers, a gap that continues to exist for other segments.

Satisfied Greens [18%], like Green Consumers, accord a lot of importance to the environment. They are second most likely to disagree that the economy is more important than the environment and they feel empowered when it comes to environmental pollution in that they believe that individuals and people acting together can improve the environment. They are more likely than the average consumer to be willing to pay a premium for green products. Unlike Green Consumers, Satisfied Greens believe that industry is currently working hard to ensure a clean environment. They are also one of the groups most likely to give high ratings to private industry for its performance in addressing environmental problems. However, findings suggest that if ever there was a decline in trust (e.g., resulting from a series of environmental catastrophes), the Satisfied Greens could become a swing market for green consumerism, because of the high importance they place on the environment.
— GlobeScan on Green Behavior Segments[55]

"

Demanding Stakeholder Group #1: "Green" Consumers

Despite their environmentally resonant label, "green" consumers are concerned about both social and environmental issues. The driving mega-issues that concern them are climate change, pollution/health, and depletion of resources such as forests and fish stocks. They are concerned that greenhouse gases from industry contribute to climate change. They are concerned about immediate and long-term socio-environmental impacts of hazardous waste and smog-producing pollution. They are concerned about corporate responsibility.

And they are voting with their wallets. As explained in the sidebar on the opposite page, GlobeScan's "Environmental Monitor 2002" survey found that 22% of people in G7 countries are "Green Consumers," willing to pay a premium for green products, but unhappy about corporate commitment to the environment, while another 18% are "Satisfied Greens," who are happier about corporate CSR behavior. In Australia, the US, Canada, and Great Britain, 77%, 69%, 66%, and 61% respectively said they had punished or rewarded companies in the previous year because of their social performance.[56] "Rewarded" means buying products or speaking positively about the company; "punished" means refusing to buy products or speaking critically about the company. It is interesting that higher punishment tendencies came from Internet users, people with a higher education, and people over 24 years old. Forest Reinhardt's analysis of survey data suggests that green goods and luxury goods seem to attract similar buyers: better-educated and wealthier consumers.[57] If those demographics describe a company's leading customers, its green consumer risk is greatest.

There is evidence that environmental considerations have settled into the public consciousness as a second-tier concern for everyday consumers. John Elkington warns that what seems like a soft, spongy consumer shift in values can turn almost overnight into concrete-hard opposition — "soft" values like concern for future generations are superseding traditional "hard" values like the paramount concern for the financial bottom line.[58] Carl Frankel graphically describes green consumers as the superficial whitecaps on a powerful sea change in environmental consumer power.[59] He points to the growing interest in alternative therapies, organic food, and "natural" products as evidence of the growing green consumer movement. Is it "buyer beware" or "producer beware"?

Corporate social responsibility (CSR) can help companies gain a competitive advantage in attracting investors and offer excellent risk management strategies, say a majority of investor relations professionals at Europe's leading companies. A new CSR Europe/INSEAD study, carried out in cooperation with the Investor Relations Society, also suggests that the interest in social and environmental issues has risen significantly over recent years and that investors are beginning to ask more informed and detailed questions about companies' corporate social responsibility performance.

The study, entitled "Corporate social responsibility and the role of investor relations — from switchboard to catalyst," features interviews with investor relations and corporate social responsibility experts from twenty leading European companies. It reveals that the awareness of social and environmental issues among investor relations professionals (IROs) is much higher than previously thought....

Interviewees also predicted that the traditional financial community (in particular the pension fund industry) is likely to come under more pressure to recognize the impact of social and environmental issues on the company value. Almost all IROs said they expect mainstream investors and analysts to increasingly integrate social and environmental criteria into their assessments — but only gradually. Some were looking at a timeline of four to five years.

— CSR Europe news item about CSR and the role of investor relations[60]

Demanding Stakeholder Group #2: Activist Shareholders

As indicated in the news item on the opposite page, investor relations officers are playing a pivotal role in helping investors appreciate the business case for social responsibility and its practical effect on firms' performance. In addition, sustainable development, corporate social responsibility, and climate change are the fastest-growing categories of shareholder-initiated resolutions. Shareholder waters are becoming choppy.

As investors stand up to be counted, using their voices and votes to call for strengthened corporate governance and solid corporate citizenship, they move from passive holders of stock to active and responsible owners. They understand the leverage they have as individuals and institutions who have invested their capital and faith in companies.[61] Using dialogue, proposals, campaigns, and strategic shareholder resolutions, they rattle the corporate cage. Out of 862 resolutions filed in 2003 at AGMs for publicly traded US companies, 237 were on social or environmental issues.[62]

Shareholder campaigns led to Coca-Cola and Pepsi agreeing to use some recycled plastic in their bottles; Staples and Office Depot increasing the amount of recycled content in the paper they sell; and McDonald's and Walt Disney increasing internal monitoring of labor practices at overseas vendors. Many issues don't become resolutions. The hint of a resolution usually inspires corporations to come to the negotiating table rather than hashing out sensitive issues in the public forum of an annual meeting.[63]

What were easily dismissed efforts by marginal investors in the 1970s and 1980s are gaining legitimacy in the investment and NGO community. Now faith-based investment groups are joined by Amnesty International, Friends of the Earth, Sierra Club, and labor unions in using shareholder tactics to pressure corporations. Sustainability-related resolutions are being introduced and supported by mainstream investors at annual general meetings. The actions of giant institutional index-fund managers are increasingly transparent. These institutions have traditionally been secretive about how they cast their proxy votes in order to avoid upsetting potential corporate clients of their pension fund management services. A new Securities and Exchange Commission (SEC) rule in 2004 requires fund managers to reveal their proxy-vote policies and how they actually voted on resolutions. Now everyone will know how fund managers' governance and sustainability rhetoric aligns with how they voted on relevant resolutions.[64]

"

Lester Salamon, director of the Center for Civil Society at John Hopkins University, has undertaken a massive study of the nonprofit sector in forty-two countries around the world .... The world, he reports, is experiencing a rise in the nonprofit sector unprecedented in modern history. So fast is this sector growing in size and importance that it will appear in retrospect as significant an historical development as the creation of the nation-state in the last part of the nineteenth century.

According to early reports prepared as part of Salamon's study, in nine large countries, the nonprofit sector is growing four times the rate of the economy. In fact, Salamon says, with global expenditures of well over one trillion dollars, if all the third-sector groups were amalgamated in one country, they would form the eighth largest economy in the world. Nongovernmental organizations (NGOs) also employ more people than the private sector by a margin of six to one ....

For a growing number of people, particularly young people, governments around the world, including our own in Canada, were no longer carrying out the mandate they had been elected to fulfill .... Unprecedented numbers of young people stopped voting. For them, politicians, political parties, and elections became irrelevant. Citizen groups, particularly those with young members ... began to advocate a more effective form of civil society politics.

The tactics were direct and confrontational — nonviolent civil disobedience. The communications tool was the Internet, which gave enormous power to the grassroots and created what some are calling "globalization from below." The goal was to build an independent international citizens' movement with the power to directly confront not only transnational corporate rule, but also the global institutions that serve it.

The first victory was the defeat of the global investment treaty called the Multinational Agreement on Investment (MAI) — an advance that sent shock waves through the halls of power around the world. By the time the WTO officials admitted defeat in Seattle a year later, the world was put on notice that a new force had emerged on the international scene — one that would change the nature of politics forever.

— Maude Barlow and Tony Clark, *Global Showdown*[65]

"

Demanding Stakeholder Group #3: Civil Society/NGOs

Globescan's "Environmental Monitor 2002" survey, referenced earlier, determined that 17% of people are "Social Activists," with high expectations that companies will solve social problems and act ethically. Another 26% are "Latent Activists," who may soon become Social Activists, bringing the combined total to 43% of the population who are, or may soon be, actively challenging companies to assume greater social and environmental responsibility.[66] They protest, lobby, boycott, and campaign. To many corporations, an activist NGO is like a mosquito in their tent — they know it is there and lie awake wondering where and when it will bite.

Many activists could be described as members of "civil society." They belong to nongovernmental organizations like labor movements, youth-led networks, women's networks, farmers' associations, environmental groups, religious organizations, civil rights organizations, and peace networks.[67] There are more than one million nonprofit organizations registered in India, 300,000 in Brazil, and 180,000 in Canada. As indicated in the sidebar opposite, the civil-society sector represents the eighth-largest sector in the global economy.[68] It is a formidable force and becoming better organized with each new public demonstration.

The claim-to-fame issue for converging NGOs was anti-corporate globalization, with environmental and public health concerns embedded within that cause. The "Battle of Seattle," which disrupted the November 1999 proceedings of the World Trade Organization, included protestors from environmental-protection NGOs, civil rights groups, and a wide range of other platforms.[69]

Civil society is a "naming and shaming" market force to be reckoned with and should be included when corporations are engaging with influential stakeholders. Nurturing stakeholder relationships contributes to learning, innovation, reputation, and competitive advantage. Failure to do so may create adversarial relationships that consume significantly more time and resources than a collaborative partnership relationship, regardless of how challenging that may seem at first.

The February [2003] edition of the Columbia Journal of Environmental Law published an article by Yale Law School graduate David Grossman demonstrating the legal feasibility of lawsuits holding companies accountable for climate change ....

"This litigation could be a catalyst or a trigger for markets to really look at climate change issues, not only with respect to the expected costs of litigation, but also in terms of a general economic assessment," said Henrik Garz, director of equity strategy research at WestLB Panmure, a Germany-based technology investment bank .... Although such lawsuits pose significant challenges and obstacles, climate change litigation against companies in carbon-intensive industries such as oil and gas, electric utilities, and automobile manufacturing seems inevitable .... "It is only a matter of time before companies like Exxon Mobil or General Motors will be facing litigation," said Jon Sohn of Friends of the Earth (FoE), a nonprofit environmental advocacy organization.

FoE, in conjunction with Greenpeace and several western cities, filed one of the first climate change lawsuits last year. The suit charges two US government agencies with failing to comply with National Environmental Policy Act (NEPA) requirements to assess the environmental impact of projects they financed over the past decade. The Export Import Bank and the Overseas Private Investment Corporation provided over $32 billion in loans and funding to US corporations for overseas projects without gauging the potential contributions to global warming, the suit contends.

The states of Connecticut, Massachusetts, and Maine have also filed a climate change lawsuit against another US government bureau, the Environmental Protection Agency, for failing to regulate carbon dioxide emissions under the Clean Air Act.

The blueprint for climate change litigation was drawn by the 1998 Master Settlement Agreement that required tobacco companies to pay states hundreds of billions of dollars in fines. "One similarity between tobacco and climate change litigation might be the consistent patterns of denial and deception by various companies," Mr. Sohn told SocialFunds.com. "The big difference is that the financial liability is going to be much greater for climate change."
— William Baue, article in *SocialFunds.com*[70]

Demanding Stakeholder Group #4: Government Regulations

As previously discussed, when companies miss early market signals, regulations are a wake-up call. Government policies and regulations control pollution and hazardous waste and ensure a safe and healthy workplace for employees. Legislated compliance is the first license-to-operate rung on the sustainability ladder.

What's new? Government regulations are creeping into new areas. The global mega-issue of climate change is addressed in the Kyoto Protocol. As signatory countries enact regulations to comply with the protocol, companies will be required to mitigate their greenhouse gas emissions. Even though the US has not ratified the protocol, US companies are not off the hook. Broad class-action lawsuits — such as the climate change lawsuits filed by some US states, described opposite — have been spurred on by the US Environmental Protection Agency's (EPA) 2003 declaration that carbon dioxide was not a pollutant and therefore need not be regulated under the Clean Air Act. California and a coalition of 11 other US states, three US cities, and three NGOs are suing the EPA to force it to regulate CO_2 emissions.[71] Going even further, in July 2004, New York City and eight states, including New York, California, Iowa, and Wisconsin, sued five major US energy companies for causing a "public nuisance" by contributing 10% of US carbon dioxide emissions. The suit alleges that Cinergy Corp., Southern Company, Xcel Energy, American Electric Power Company, and the Tennessee Valley Authority are among the biggest global-warming culprits in the nation.[72] These class-action suits may prove to have a trickle-down impact on corporate indifference to greenhouse gas emissions from their operations.

The European Union (EU) continues to be the bellwether for aggressive CR initiatives. In 2002, the EU adopted the precautionary principle for regulating the introduction of new products to the marketplace. This means new products cannot be sold until the manufacturer can show they are not harmful. Further, under proposed EU regulations — Registration, Evaluation and Authorization of Chemicals (REACH) — chemical companies would be required to register and test the safety of more than 30,000 chemicals at an estimated cost of nearly six billion Euros. The new regulations could also threaten the import of over $20 billion of chemicals from the US to Europe each year.[73]

The spectre of similar legislation in the United States highlights how globalization can be a double-edged sword for some industries.

Figure 3.2: Innovest on the Iceberg of Intangible Value Drivers

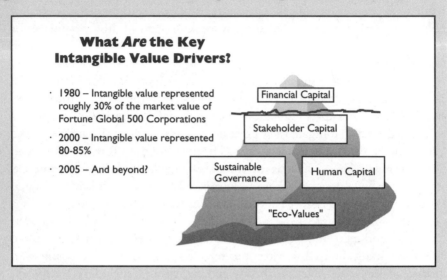

Demanding Stakeholder Group #5: Financial Sector

According to Echo Research, 88% of US financial institutions do not take socially responsible investing into account in their investment decisions.[74] In contrast, over 70% of CEOs surveyed by the World Economic Forum in 2003 believe mainstream investors will have an increased interest in corporate social responsibility in the future.[75] Investment fund managers agree. In a 2003 survey of 388 fund managers, financial analysts, and corporate investment relations officers across nine European countries, 52% of fund managers believed that social and environmental considerations will become a significant aspect of mainstream investment decisions over the next two years.[76] Interest in patient, long-term investments is balancing interest in instant-gratification, short-term investments.

A wry employee expression I picked up in my years at IBM is "What interests my manager fascinates me." A CEO version might be "What interests financial markets fascinates me." The financial sector includes financial services advisors, insurers, re-insurers, asset managers, pension fund managers, financial analysts, investment banks, commercial banks, venture capital companies, project financers, investment advisors and brokers, and rating agencies.[77] If companies were patients, financial analysts would be doctors poking, prodding, and diagnosing their short- and long-term financial health. Corporate patients want clean bills of health from their financial analyst doctors.

Financial markets focus on financial capital, the tip of the value iceberg shown in Figure 3.2.[78] However, according to a 2003 poll conducted by GlobeScan, 84% of Canadian shareholders think that the investment and financial communities should pay more attention to environmental and social performance when valuating companies.[79]

Financial analysts increasingly recognize that financial capital rides on a base of so-called intangibles that represent 50% to 90% of a firm's market value.[80] On average, 35% of the information used to justify investment decisions and predict share price is nonfinancial.[81] To avoid a *Titanic*-like encounter with the value iceberg, analysts' sonars must recognize the materiality of invisible intangibles below the surface, most of which are sustainability-related risks or value-driving sustainability opportunities.[82]

Figure 3.3: Roger Martin's Virtue Matrix, Adapted

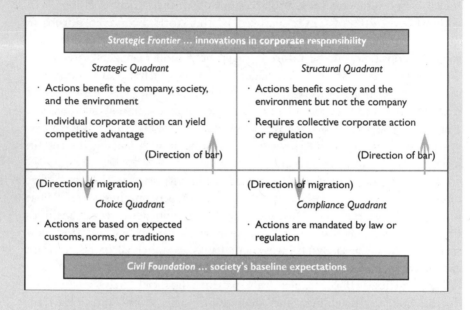

Rising Expectations

Rather than remaining as marginalized considerations, social and environmental topics have crept into mainstream business discourse. *Harvard Business Review* has included articles with titles like "What's a Business For?"[83] "The Competitive Advantage of Corporate Philanthropy,"[84] and "The Virtue Matrix."[85] These articles show the relevance of smart social and environmental strategies to corporate financial performance. Managing key stakeholder relationships and expectations is not "being nice"; it is central to competitive advantage. Companies need to decide whether they will manage stakeholders reactively, defensively, accommodatingly, or proactively.[86] That is, do they want to defensively minimize stakeholders' impact to protect their license to operate or do they want to offensively enter into collaborative relationships with stakeholders to create value for all parties?

Consumers, shareholders, NGOs, the financial sector, and governments are demanding more and more information about corporate social and environmental performance. As companies become more open and transparent, market forces keep pushing for improved performance. There is a growing emphasis on the quality of CSR management, not just on whether companies do it at all. It doesn't stop — continuous improvement applies as much to sustainability as it does to quality.

Companies' social and environmental responsibilities will be viewed very differently a decade from now, as society's expectations change.[87] Roger Martin points out in his *Harvard Business Review* article that the public is continuously ratcheting up the bar on the civil foundation to which corporations are expected to contribute (see Figure 3.3).[88] What used to be considered leading and enlightened social or environmental practices — supporting worthy causes in the community, fostering diversity in the workforce, making workplaces family-friendly, and going beyond the minimum safeguards required by environmental regulations — are now considered to be the entry-level ante for a social license to operate.

New benchmarks of corporate CSR commitment are being used. To maintain a license to operate, a company must be able to predict what will be acceptable. Otherwise it faces hitting a wall and having to adjust course in a very public, often very expensive manner. Might your product become the next "asbestos" or "tobacco?"

Over the past 50 years, the share of tax revenue coming to the federal government from business has collapsed, causing Warren Buffett to declare that "if class warfare is being waged in America, my class is clearly winning." In fiscal 2003 corporate taxes represented just 7.4 percent of federal revenue, down from 32 percent in 1952. The 2003 figure was especially low because of depressed corporate profits, but other measures paint a similar picture of a declining contribution. Corporate taxes as a percentage of our gross domestic product dropped to 1.2 percent in 2003, compared with as high as 6 percent in the early 1950s ....

The question of whether American business is paying its fair share is particularly relevant at the moment. Corporate profits are booming — in part because of lower tax rates — and a higher share of the benefits of this recovery has gone to business (as opposed to workers) than in any recovery since World War II, according to a recent Northeastern University study.

Like anything that has to do with taxes, the reasons for this dramatic decline are complex and multifaceted. At the top of the list: the increasing sophistication of large multinational corporations in managing their tax obligations, particularly by shifting profits to countries with lower tax rates. Companies employ mechanisms for moving these profits, particularly within the murky zone of "transfer prices," the rates at which the various subsidiaries of a company exchange goods and services around the world. By keeping these transfer prices high in low-tax countries and low in high-tax countries, companies can generate more of their profit in places with lower taxes.

One recent study by Tax Notes found that subsidiaries of U.S. corporations operating in the top four tax havens (the Netherlands, Ireland, Bermuda and Luxembourg) had 46.3 percent of their profits in those countries in 2001, but only 9 percent of their employees and 12.6 percent of their plant and equipment.

Companies have become emboldened to push the edges of the tax system in part because enforcement has become lax. According to a recent study by a Syracuse University research organization, the audit rate for the 11,200 largest corporations has fallen by nearly half over the past decade.

— Steven Rattner, "Why Companies Pay Less"[89]

The Corporate Tax Cut Boomerang

With tax breaks, deferred taxes, offshore havens, and other tax-reduction tactics, corporate taxes are dropping like a stone, at least in the US and Canada. As indicated in the sidebar, American corporate taxes in 2003 were 7.4% of total federal taxes, down from 32% in 1954. The stated federal tax rate is 35%, but many large corporations pride themselves on paying nowhere close to that. Between 1989 and 1995, nearly a third of large companies operating in the US paid no US income tax. More than six out of ten large companies paid less than $1 million in federal taxes in 1995.[90]

In Canada, the nominal federal tax rate for corporations was 21% in 2004.[91] Following the US pattern, corporate taxes fell from contributing 25% of federal revenue in 1955 to just 10% in 1995, while individual taxes rose from 33% to 59% of federal revenues. As of 1994, Statistics Canada reports, 81,469 Canadian corporations with combined profits of $17.1 billion had paid not a cent in income tax, and $40 billion in corporate taxes was owed to the federal government.[92]

In a way, companies have set themselves up for higher expectations: they benefit from increasing privatization of services, previously provided by government, that they now provide for profit; they influence government investment and trade policies through corporate-funded think tanks; and they lobby for government subsidies and corporate tax relief. For example, the Royal Bank of Canada, with 2001 pretax profits of $3.9 billion, will save $500 million per year from a 13-point reduction in federal and provincial income taxes by 2005 — over ten times the $45 million it spent on social responsibility initiatives in 2001.[93] Further, corporations that claim to be socially responsible should not be moving money over borders to avoid paying taxes required to fund national social initiatives. As the role of government recedes, the public expects that corporations with deep pockets will take the dialogue to their major stakeholders, credibly communicate their CSR activities, and exercise more meaningful corporate citizenship to fill the void.

Or at least pay their taxes.

Then, in some businesses like Falconbridge and Noranda, the license-to-operate theme entered. If companies are well-received by the communities in which they operate, that speeds up the time to get the project online, which saves financing costs as they get faster approvals. This is especially true for resource industry companies. They moved from strict and narrow compliance to relationships with constituencies — customers, communities, employees, whatever .... If something bad does happen, your recovery time is faster and your treatment in the newspaper is better. (Alan Willis)

The second driver is license to operate. I guess it is a subset of risk. The community around you, and society, isn't going to let you continue if you are seen as being unacceptable, so you have to be at least as good as everyone else or ideally in the forefront to give them that license to not just operate, but expand, because growth is the mantra of the economy. (Stephen Hill)

Another reason that companies pay attention to CSR is protecting their license to operate, which has been a recurrent theme. Companies see that to stay in business long-term effectively, and without spending huge amounts of money battling communities, they need to have a healthy and robust license to operate. Companies recognize that they need to be in regular dialogue with the communities in which they operate so that when something goes wrong, there is an established relationship that makes a dialogue possible. Companies that stay aloof until something goes wrong and then call up the opinion leaders in the community will find that it doesn't work. This relationship is a sub-element of the license to operate. Resources have to be committed to this. Unless you put money into maintaining this dialogue, it will not work. If you want it, you have to pay for it, fund it, and have someone whose job it is to ensure the dialogue is healthy. That's when you know the company is serious. When there are no resources, consciously or subconsciously they are not serious. They put resources behind the objective and incorporate CSR into the evaluation and incentive systems. (Antony Marcil)

Foundations of Social License to Operate

The history of corporations goes back as far as the 16th century in the United Kingdom, where charters were granted by the state to investors to serve a common purpose. Historically, corporations were chartered to serve the public good, as Marjorie Kelly explains in *The Divine Right of Capital*.[94] They were formed to build bridges, canals, roads, railroads, or other public works requiring coordination of various trades. When the project was completed, the corporate charter was expected to be revoked. Profits were incidental rather than the purpose of the corporation.

A legal mandate to do public good may originally have been in a corporation's genes. However, extensive genetic modifications have occurred over time, mutating the corporate organism into a force for shareholder returns more than a force for public good. Restrictions on corporations faded with the onset of the industrial age and with growing competition among municipalities for corporations to locate within their jurisdictions and provide jobs for their citizens. In return for certain rights and obligations, the charters limited the liability of investors should a catastrophe befall the undertaking, such as a fatal storm devastating a ship's voyage to distant countries for spices.[95]

The addition of limited liability provided enormous protection and benefits for corporations. Realistically, the argument that corporations were chartered to be instruments of public good is a tough one to use effectively today in support of CSR. A typical executive response might be, "That was then. This is now." Things change, and few corporate leaders feel bound by historical roots that have been overgrown by more recent court rulings, practices, and priorities. Given legal precedents over the last hundred years, the threat of having a corporate charter revoked for unethical behavior is too remote to be an effective catalyst for ethical corporate behavior.

Although the legal license to operate may not be a big sustainability trigger, the social license to operate is. Shell's plan to dump its Brent Spar drilling platform in the North Sea was legally acceptable, but not socially acceptable. Using refrigerators with HCFCs to keep Coke cold at the Sydney Olympics was legal, but not socially acceptable at the "green games."[96] The perfect storm of market forces presents a threat to companies' social license to operate.

Figure 3.4: Market Forces ➤ Rising Expectations ➤ Business Risks

Ten Market Forces		Five Categories of Business Risk
Five Mega-Issues	**Five Demanding Stakeholders**	
1. Climate Change		1. Market risks · Regulatory bans or restrictions on sales · Reduced market demand for products · Degradation of product quality by environmental factors · Customer boycotts or reduced acceptance
	1. "Green" Consumers	
2. Pollution / Health		2. Balance-sheet risks · Remediation liabilities · Insurance underwriting losses · Impairment of real property values · Damage assessments · Toxic torts
	2. Activist Shareholders	
3. Globalization Backlash		3. Operating risks · Costs of cleaning up spills and accidents · Risk to worker safety from handling hazardous materials · Expensive regulation-driven process changes · Reduced process yields · Rise in prices of materials or energy
	3. Civil Society / NGOs	
4. The Energy Crunch		4. Capital cost risks · Product redesign to meet new industry standards or regulations · Costly input substitutions to meet new industry standards or regulations · Pollution and waste treatment upgrades
	4. Governments	
5. Erosion of Trust		5. Sustainability risks · Competitive disadvantage from energy or material inefficiencies · Impact of mandatory take-back rules · Exposure to future taxes and regulatory restrictions
	5. Financial Sector	
		+ More difficult access to capital

RISING EXPECTATIONS

Rising Expectations ➤ Business Risks

Rising expectations, the middle column in Figure 3.4, lead to new regulations, tougher criteria for bank loans and insurance, forced redesign of manufacturing and operating processes, lawsuits, new environmental liabilities, and revenue stream exposures. As shown in Figure 3.4, they can be classified as market risks, balance-sheet risks, operating expense risks, capital cost risks, and sustainability risks. Rising expectations and resultant risks are impacting the license to operate.

Most of the "unexpected" crises that buffet companies should have been anticipated — they are "predictable surprises." The bad news is that all companies are vulnerable to potential market upheavals caused by the ten market forces. The good news is that business leaders are trained by MBA schools to continuously scan the environment so they will recognize threats, prioritize risks, and do contingency planning. Alert and forward-thinking executives will anticipate market trends, analyze their potential impact on the firm, and mobilize the company around strategies that capitalize on associated opportunities.

In 2004, Echo Research interviewed 240 business and financial opinion leaders from the United States, France, Germany, the United Kingdom, Australia, and South Africa. It found that only 33% of US companies believe good corporate responsibility can result in better risk management, compared to 68% in Europe.[97] Maybe the Europeans know something Americans do not.

The meteorological perfect storm was unfair to the *Andrea Gail*. Rising expectations about corporations' role in mitigating major issues in the world today may also be unfair. No one promised market forces would be reasonable. Savvy executives concerned with the long-term sustainability of their enterprise will give serious consideration to the market forces discussed in this section when they are planning business strategies.

There is no lessening of stakeholder expectations in times of economic downturn. In fact, a downturn sharpens the message that what happens to business matters to society, so what happens to society should matter to business.[98] Companies unprepared for threatening new market forces could be in for a rough ride. Traditional responses to risks may no longer be adequate or appropriate. However, innovative corporations that anticipate and prepare for market surprises will thrive. They will convert the energy from the perfect storm of coalescing risks and threats to a perfect storm of business opportunities.

One camp is the pragmatic, business camp, where the companies view the sustainability area as a risk area that, if not managed responsibly, could affect their ability to meet their business objectives. These companies see their sustainability performance as having a long-term impact on share value. So the driving force is very much a business case. There is nothing all that philosophical about it. (Mel Wilson)

Another reason for sustainable development, coming from the Natural Step ideas, is the shock. Brian Nattrass and Mary Altomare in their book call it "hitting the wall." It's the idea that something hits you so hard — you get blindsided — that your whole organizational culture flips. You might see some sort of chaotic change in the organization. It could be any kind of things: a bad public relations incident, a huge regulatory shift. Suddenly you realize, "Oh, my god. We are so out to lunch here. We had no idea this was even happening" ....They call it "hitting the wall," but I like the idea of being blindsided by a big bat on the side of the head. (Stephen Hill)

An attention-getter for business might be something cataclysmic, like all of a sudden, "Gee. We really don't have enough water." Or "Gee. We don't have enough wood." Or "Gee. We have too much temperature." Those realizations can happen all of a sudden, within weeks or over months. (Steve Rice)

Transforming Mega-Issues into Mega-Opportunities

I have hinted that threats can be transformed into opportunities. Here is how companies might address the five mega-issues, described earlier, to transform risks into opportunities:

1. *Climate Change.* Reduce company greenhouse gas (GHG) emissions to below regulatory requirements. Go further than required and build carbon credits as a potential source of revenue. Declare zero net GHG emissions as a company goal and inspire employee innovation to help meet that target imaginatively.

2. *Pollution/Health Concerns.* Work on upstream sources of hazardous waste by replacing hazardous materials and chemicals with more benign substitutes. Reduce and recycle, using closed-loop processes. Take back products at the end of their useful lives and reuse components. Move from outright sales to leasing products. Declare zero waste as a company goal.

3. *Globalization Backlash.* Work with industry trade organizations to lobby governments and influential international organizations like the World Trade Organization, the World Economic Forum, the International Monetary Fund, and the World Bank to improve the fairness of international trade rules. Position the company to capitalize on fairer trade regulations.

4. *The Energy Crunch.* Commit to alternative green energy. Work aggressively with NGOs and governments to change perverse subsidies for fossil fuel providers to equitable treatment for alternative renewable-energy providers and users. Consider a company goal of being off the utility grid.

5. *Erosion of Trust.* Recommit to ethical financial, environmental, and social behavior. Use third-party audits to verify that company behaviors are ethical and in the best interests of society. Emphasize the values-to-value connections — values build trust; trust strengthens relationships; relationships produce value.[99]

Companies realize the true benefit of these initiatives when demanding stakeholders see they are sincerely undertaking significant corporate stewardship strategies. Concerned customers, vocal employees, and hard-nosed investors create an exciting storm of opportunities for companies with courage and foresight!

CHAPTER FOUR

SECOND EMERGING DRIVER — COMPELLING
BUSINESS VALUE

Sustainability presents a stick and a carrot. The stick is the need to minimize the storm of risks. The carrot is the possibility of maximizing business opportunities through real social and environmental leadership that exceeds society's expectations. Businesses are discovering that the same forces causing rising stakeholder expectations of social, ethical and environmental behavior are also creating opportunities for business strategies that advance commercial objectives and environmental and social sustainability.

There are benefits to framing environmental issues as opportunities to be sought rather than threats to be averted and to choosing proactive, rather than reactive, environmental strategies. A business is more likely to capitalize on these opportunities if environmental issues are legitimized as part of the corporate identity (as they are in Stage 4 companies) and if managers are allowed discretionary time and resources for creative problem solving.[1]

If a "moral imperative" attracts a company to sustainability, terrific. Driven by the values-based conviction of its leader/founder, it will start at Stage 5 and thrive. For the other 90% of enterprises out there, value creation trumps values. Unless sustainability strategies enhance profits — the single bottom line — growth, and/or cash flow, they will never develop traction in publicly owned companies.[2]

Five Winds International and Pollution Probe identify 11 components of the business case for sustainability in their "Policy Framework for Environmental Sustainability Project."[3] They correspond to the seven business case benefits I outlined in *The Sustainability Advantage*, as shown in Figure 4.1 on the next page. The majority of sustainability case studies quantify potential energy, materials, and waste management savings in manufacturing locations and in the operation of commercial sites. They provide the low-hanging fruit for action in Stage 3. The three human resource co-benefits are usually not factored into the business case, but they should be, as should potential improved revenue and risk management, the last two factors. It is when benefits from those five categories are achieved in Stage 4 that the real business value of corporate responsibility is realized.

Figure 4.1: Comparison of Business Case Elements

Seven Business Case Benefits	Five Winds International and Pollution Probe Sustainability Business Case Components
1. Reduced recruiting costs	· Corporate reputation and enhanced brand image
2. Reduced attrition costs	· Employee morale and productivity / Elevate employee awareness of environmental and sustainable development issues
3. Increased productivity	· Employee morale and productivity / Elevate employee awareness of environmental and sustainable development issues · Stimulate innovation and generate ideas
4. Reduced expenses in manufacturing	· Ensure continual improvement · Cost savings / Improve the bottom line
5. Reduced water, energy, and consumables expenses at commercial sites	· Cost savings / Improve the bottom line
6. Increased revenue and market share	· Access to markets and customers / Customer loyalty · Expedited permitting / Improved relations with regulators
7. Reduced risk / Easier financing	· Reduce and manage business risks · Earn and maintain a social license to operate · Improved relations with stakeholders / Dispute resolution / Issues management · Establish or improve reputation with investors, bond agencies, and banks

Sustainability Lens on a Balanced Scorecard

If the company has already formally or informally adopted a balanced scorecard approach to business measurement, introducing sustainability metrics will reinforce that framework. A balanced scorecard, made famous by the 1992 *Harvard Business Review* article by Robert Kaplan and David Norton, aids comprehensive management decision making by tracking four distinct sets of measurements: financial, customer, internal business processes, and learning and growth.[4] The scorecard is balanced between short- and long-term objectives, between cost and non-cost measures, between lagging and leading indicators, and between external and internal performance perspectives.

Researchers at the European Institute for Business Administration (INSEAD) studied a wide variety of corporate versions of the balanced scorecard and attempts to integrate sustainability factors into the four sets of measurements. They found that effectiveness of the integration was closely associated with the management team's mindset regarding the strategic importance of sustainability.[5] If the management team participated in mapping a coherent set of meaningful nonfinancial environmental and social indicators in a cause-effect relationship in the value-creation process, it worked. Why? Participation in the mapping process heightened their collective commitment to the relevance of environmental and social issues to business strategy, product innovation, competitive differentiation, stakeholder relationships, and risk management.[6]

In other words, merging sustainability indicators with balanced scorecard measurements reinforces their relevance to business success. It does not matter which of the four balanced scorecard categories is chosen for each environmental and social indicator, or even if a fifth category is added to the scorecard for sustainability indicators. What matters is that the management team agrees that the chosen leading and lagging indicators contribute to company success.[7]

I didn't look at waste reduction as an environmental initiative ... overall the whole waste reduction piece of our distribution centre operation was feint-lined by market-driven quality. It was really a number of aspects that fit together .... We focused on how we could drive for environmental efficiencies as we went through .... So you set up processes that drive the initiatives, and when you have people who you reward and recognize who drive these things, it sort of feeds on itself. (Brian Shannon)

At the end of the day, the reason companies pay attention to CSR has got to revolve around the business case. People have got to see there is a reason why you do this and there is a causal connection between doing it and bottom-line results. If there were a good business case, CEOs and the financial community would support it. (John Swannick)

Some companies see sustainability not solely as an environmental policy but as an industrial policy. They see clean production as a means of staying competitive globally, of getting ahead of the curve, and making a better dollar in the longer term .... They don't hinge it on an environmental issue or public health issue. It's just good business. They see clean production as their competitive advantage. It is an industrial strategy. (Paul Muldoon)

In some cases, companies do it out of self-interest. It just makes good business sense. For example, they can enhance their reputation, which acts as a differentiator in the market. (Mark Thomsen)

You have increasing interest from a variety of different financial aspects — banks, insurance companies and pension funds, socially responsible green ethical fund market — acting as a driver for some. (Martin Charter)

By-Product of Good Business Management

Some companies stumbled on fragments of sustainability benefits almost by accident. CSR benefits are by-products of things they were doing for good business reasons anyway. Eco-efficiencies may be accomplished under the mantle of total quality management (TQM) efforts in manufacturing facilities. Reengineering initiatives may have resulted in redesigned processes that reduced water, energy, wasted materials, and especially hazardous waste. Reclassifying quality and reengineering initiatives as CSR initiatives simply reinforces that sustainability strategies make good business sense, whatever they are called.

Some sustainability conversions were a result of customer pressure. If a customer has corporate stewardship as a supplier selection criterion, supplier companies are motivated to pay attention to this dimension of their operations. Even if executives do not yet feel a personal passion for the issues, as businesspeople they are obliged to be responsive to customer questions about the company's environmental and social track record, especially in requests for proposals from important customers in the marketplace. They stumble on the revenue benefits of CSR from their customer service orientation.

It also makes good business sense to keep an eye on what successful leading companies are doing and emulate them. Ikea, the top furniture maker in the world, is committed to the Natural Step, a strategic framework for sustainability. Home Depot, the top supplier of home renovation supplies, has committed to buying all its wood from certified sustainable forestry companies. Electrolux is another major player making higher-than-normal margins from their environmentally friendly product lines. Interface, an icon of CSR companies, is the largest commercial floor-covering company in the world. You would have to have blinkers on to say these companies don't know what they are talking about when they are among the top companies in the world. Jumping onto the sustainability bandwagon puts you in good company. Emulating leaders makes good business sense.

The *Sustainability Advantage* methodology provided a wide net in which to catch and quantify improved business performance from what might have been independent business initiatives. When co-benefits are included in the business case, attention to CSR is surprisingly compelling. The dilemma is that the more integrated sustainability strategies are, the more difficult it is to tease out their business case benefits as a separate entity.

Figure 4.2: Benefits Quantified for SD Inc.

Seven Business Case Benefits	% Improvement
1. Reduced recruiting costs	-1.0%
2. Reduced attrition costs	-2.0%
3. Increased productivity	+10.5%
4. Reduced expenses in manufacturing	-5.0%
5. Reduced water, energy, and consumables expenses at commercial sites	-20.0%
6. Increased revenue and market share	+5.0%
7. Reduced risk / Easier financing	-5.0%
yielding a profit increase of 38.0%	

Seven Bottom-Line Benefits

I have discussed how companies can not only mitigate the ten threatening market forces, but can also capitalize on them. Specifically, they can benefit in seven ways.[8]

1. *Easier hiring of top talent* by attracting people whose values resonate with company sustainability values and who want to work in that kind of company.

2. *Higher retention of top talent* since employees caring about a company's environmental and social good works want to stay with it longer.

3. *Higher productivity from employees* energized by contributing to the success of a firm doing worthwhile work.

4. *Reduced expenses in manufacturing* through eco-efficiencies, dematerialization, recycling, process redesign, and waste reduction.

5. *Reduced expenses at commercial sites* through eco-efficiencies in energy and water usage, and increased employee stewardship of consumables.

6. *Increased revenue* as green consumers are attracted to the company's products, services are expanded, and new markets are opened.

7. *Reduced risk and easier financing* through risk avoidance, lower insurance premiums, better loan rates, and higher attractiveness to investors.

According to a 2003 survey by Business in the Community, 81% of young people have a strong belief in the power of responsible practice to improve profitability over time.[9] It can. For Sustainable Development Inc. (SD Inc.), a composite company based on five real high-tech companies that I used in *The Sustainability Advantage* as a sample company, the potential increase in profit is 38%, using assumptions based on the lower, conservative range of benefits realized by case study companies.[10] The percent improvement in each of the seven benefit areas is shown in Figure 4.2.

Expressed a different way, the value of the company's financial capital will be improved, as will associated values of its manufactured capital and its contribution to natural capital, human capital, intellectual capital, knowledge capital, reputation capital, and social/relationship capital with its important stakeholders.

Figure 4.3: *Dilbert* **on Who Benefits**

Dilbert reprinted by permission of United Feature Syndicate, Inc.

The Seven Benefits Revisited

In *The Sustainability Advantage,* I dedicated a full chapter to each of the seven areas of potential financial benefit if sustainability strategies are embedded in company decision making. Rather than repeat all the survey, case study, and research data that I used to support the assumptions, I will just restate the assumptions and add different support. One page will be used for each benefit area rather than one chapter.

I am occasionally asked where the costs are allowed for in the business case. There is no explicit line item for them. Instead, I assume that no benefit is counted until the cost of obtaining it has been recouped. For example, if a lighting retrofit costs $15,000, and it takes 18 months of energy savings to recover that amount, then the benefit is only counted from the 19th month onward. Because there would obviously be a wide range of start dates and payback periods for sustainability initiatives in various companies, the staggered benefits are allowed for by assuming only 30% of the benefits were realized the first year, 50% in the second, 70% in the third, 90% in the fourth, and 100% in the fifth. Having said that, many sustainability initiatives require no net new spending to achieve the benefit.

The only cost that is different and explicitly included is the expense of educating the whole company about sustainability. The business case allows for the cost of designing, developing, and delivering two days' worth of education to every employee, manager, and executive the first year, and one day's worth in each of the following four years. It can be delivered in classroom settings, via e-learning, as part of normal business meetings, or through a combination of these. This education can be considered an investment, and the benefits can be used to calculate its return on investment (ROI).

An interesting question is "Which stakeholders get the benefits?" Do the stockholders benefit from higher dividends? Do executives benefit from higher compensation packages? Do employees benefit from wages that are higher than industry norms, or do they experience Dilbert's frustration in Figure 4.3? Do productivity benefits enable growth without additional personnel or do they lead to layoffs? Do customers benefit from lower prices? The company can share the financial benefits in a virtuous cycle that does even more, sooner, for the environment, society, and the bottom line than it otherwise could, by rewarding stakeholders who can help widen the company's competitive advantage.

According to a survey out today, an increasing number of young job seekers and older workers are choosing between potential employers because of their record on recycling rather than the pay and benefits package on offer. For employers who are increasingly targeting these two groups in their recruitment, the message is clear.

The Ethical Employee — a survey of 1050 people by The Work Foundation and The Future Foundation — shows that companies could improve their chances of hiring and keeping talented staff if they were supportive of employees' home needs and paid more attention to environmental and community concerns.

The research found that around 10% of the workforce are "ethical enthusiasts" who hold such strong views on corporate social responsibility that it is likely to influence their choice of employer. Ethical enthusiasts are more likely to be young people (18–24) and older people (45 and over) ....

The report also argues that changing demographics mean that a company's ethical reputation is likely to become an even more important consideration in the job market.

"Employers are going to have to wake up the importance of their ethical reputation. The demographics of our labour market and Britain's population show that bright young graduates from certain universities and older people are going to be more in demand by employers. These are precisely the groups that are most concerned with ethical issues" ....

Michael Willmott, co-founder of The Future Foundation, says: "The ability of an organisation to attract people does depend on its stance on ethics and corporate citizenship, and will increasingly do so. But unsurprisingly perceptions about the work itself and importantly, the products, services and "brands" of the organisation are critical too. Flying a plane is seen as more attractive than serving a burger and fries and so companies, like McDonald's for example, are less attractive to work for than their corporate citizenship rating suggests. Employers who can combine all three are likely to be the winners in recruiting and retaining staff in the future."

—The Work Foundation press release, December 19, 2002[11]

1. Easier Hiring of the Best Talent

In *The Sustainability Advantage*, a 5% saving on hiring expenses was assumed for 20% of the top new recruits for an overall savings of 1%. Only a 5% savings of recruiting costs for this group was used, assuming the need for recruiting will be slightly less because retention will be higher, and positive word-of-mouth may also reduce hiring costs. The 20% came from various surveys showing that at least that number of talented recruits care enough about the sustainability reputation of a potential employer to let it influence their decision to accept that company's job offer. Some surveys suggest that number is too low.

A survey reported in *The Wirthlin Report* in April 2004 indicated that 76% of adult Americans say their view of a company's honesty has a direct influence on their willingness to accept a job with the company.[12] A 2001 survey of UK professionals by the Industrial Society found that 82% would not work for an organization whose values they did not believe in, and 52% chose their current organization because they believed in what it did and what it stood for.[13] A Corporate Citizen Poll of 803 citizens by MarketExplorers and the Conference Board of Canada in 2000 found that 71% of employees want to work for companies that commit to social and community concerns.[14] A 1997 Walker Information Survey revealed that 42% of respondents took a company's ethics into account when deciding whether to accept a job.[15] A 2004 survey of MBA students found that 97% said they were willing to forgo 14% of their expected income to work for an organization with a better reputation for corporate social responsibility and ethics.[16]

More conservatively, a 2002 survey by the Work Foundation and the Future Foundation found that "around 10% of the workforce are 'ethical enthusiasts' who hold such strong views on corporate social responsibility that it is likely to influence their choice of employer." In addition, a further 10% of the workforce "looks for an employer with employment practices that come under the umbrella of good corporate citizenship — such as flexible working arrangements, compassionate approaches to illness and family crises."[17] Coincidentally, the two groups add up to the 20% assumed in the business case.

Admittedly, 1% is not a big saving for a company the size of SD Inc., with $44 billion revenue, $3 billion profit, and 120,000 employees Consider it a placeholder that can be tuned higher, depending on the company. The real benefits are the increased retention and productivity of these talented employees after they are hired, which are calculated next.

> The personal drivers are interesting. It's about professional development and those innovators who want to do something unique. They love the chance to learn new marketable skills. (Louise Comeau)

If there is no "in loco parentis" now between a company and its employees, then the relationship has to be based on an ongoing mutual dialogue on work, achievement, and rewards ... but there also has to be something greater than that. Business trends may come and go, but a vision that includes the broad concepts of "social responsibility" can be remarkably stable, even if business conditions swing wildly.

If you are in a company that gives great consideration to the most sustainable way of doing things when making decisions, this large vision gives people something to hold onto even when market conditions change. If you stick to your guns and run your organization using this vision as a competitive advantage, stakeholders see this as a constant. Constants are important management tools during times of rapid change.

If stakeholders see behavior consistent with a sustainable vision — that the company is "not going to behave as bad as the law will allow," as Ray Anderson says — then your chances of convincing them you are not going to screw them either is much better. This "trust" is an advantage. We have people who have not had a pay raise since 1997. The top people have taken severe pay cuts. But employees want to stay here. They believe in what the company is doing. A sustainable enterprise can be a stable foundation when the storms of change occur.

That relates back to why sustainability is a competitive advantage. Stakeholders can see that if your goals are lofty enough, that you are including social and ecological footprints, then they can also believe that you are going to look after their concerns. This is especially true in a small company. (Sam Moore)

2. Higher Retention of Top Talent

Hiring top talent is one challenge. Keeping it is another. A detailed accounting of the costs of losing a good person, hiring a replacement, and training that new person showed SD Inc. could save 2% of its attrition costs. The Saratoga Institute, a division of PricewaterhouseCoopers, reports that the standard voluntary and involuntary (firing, death, disability) turnover rates across all industries in Canada are 15% and 5% respectively.[18]

I assume that 10% of SD Inc.'s employee base leaves each year, and 10% of those are top talent that SD Inc. wants to retain. I assume only 20% of the 1% (10% of 10%) it wants to retain care enough about the company's sustainability focus to stay, despite higher salaries and better job opportunities elsewhere.

Retention of top talent is a top priority. In early 2004, Pricewaterhouse-Coopers' "Trendsetter Barometer" interviewed CEOs of 387 privately held product and service companies, identified in the media as the fastest-growing US businesses over the previous five years. Asked the top factors critical for success over the next 12 months, an overwhelming 78 % of "Trendsetter" CEOs pointed to retention of key workers.[19] A 1999 study by Fleishman-Hilliard found that 87% of employees in Europe would be more loyal to a company involved in activities that help improve society.[20] A Market and Opinion Research International/Co-operators Bank poll in the UK found 73% of people would be more loyal to an employer that supports the local community.[21]

According to the Work Foundation and Future Foundation's 2002 "Ethical Employee" survey of 1,050 people in the UK, mentioned earlier, a third of all employees are very likely to be job hunting in the next 12 months because their employers have a poor record on corporate social responsibility. This is particularly true of ethical employees, over half of whom (53%) rate their employing organization as below par in its contribution to the wider community and say they are fairly, very, or extremely likely to leave within the next year.[22] A 2002 Hay Group/Fortune study showed that 15% of employees are thinking of leaving soon, and another 30% plan to stay only a few years. Unfortunately, they follow through. Tracking of survey respondents showed that 8% actually did leave in the short term, and 34% left within five years.[23]

Compared to these surveys, my attrition assumptions look conservative.

Another part of Management 101: people are twice as smart as you think they are. When you operate under the premise that management knows the right road and speed to the destination/objective, you're never bringing enough to the table. You're underestimating them all the time. And they know you are. Employees can see right through you. You may have the big chair, but that doesn't buy you anything but one opinion, and not necessarily the right one. (Brian Shannon)

I've been involved in business and the environment, wearing various hats, since 1988. I know very well, for example, the whole CFC scare with ICI. It actually came down to people getting accosted in pubs if they were employees of ICI. This went down into the whole corporate change within the company.

ICI were a big supplier of CFCs in the late 80s. There was a speech by Margaret Thatcher in the late 80s legitimizing the ozone layer problem. Then there was the connection with some people that the employees of ICI were somehow responsible for the "ozone layer" problem. That led to significant morale problems internally. The interesting point is that they then set up an environmental opportunities team where they started to look at new business opportunities. They ended up setting up a water care business and looking at biodegradable plastics and various things like that.

I've just got back in contact with ICI, and their whole business is totally changed. They seem to have got rid of all their bulk chemicals and they are a totally different business now. Was the CFC thing the catalyzing thing to really lead to a navel-gazing exercise because they were facing some really serious problems? I'm sure it was one of several issues, but maybe it accelerated the process. (Martin Charter)

3. Increased Employee Productivity

Productivity matters. The Work Foundation found that top-performing UK companies were 42% more productive than those at the bottom.[24] In a 2003 survey by Business in the Community, 81% of employees agreed that responsible organizations are more likely to be creative and innovative.[25] Innovation usually translates into productivity.

In *The Sustainability Advantage*, I assumed the personal values of 20% of employees resonate with a sustainable development vision. Conservatively assuming these employees would then be 25% more productive, this worked out to an average 5% (25% of 20%) increase in individual productivity averaged over the whole workforce. An additional 2% in productivity was added to acknowledge productivity from improved company-wide teaming around common sustainability issues that transcend departmental boundaries. Another 3.5% productivity improvement came from improved workplace conditions (especially daylighting) as a surprise by-product of eco-efficiency building retrofits for 50% of SD Inc. employees.

To reinforce the latter productivity contributor, West Bend Mutual Insurance Co. reduced energy costs by 40% in the early 1990s following a move into a new 150,000-square-foot green building. However, the real payoff was a 16% productivity gain associated with daylighting, individually controlled workstation environments, connectivity to nature, and improved lighting. Its annual payroll at the time was $13 million; the increased productivity was worth more than $2 million a year.[26] The Rocky Mountain Institute says green buildings can increase occupant productivity by between 6% and 26%.[27] A 2001 study by the Heschong Mahone Group showed that learning rates for elementary school students in classrooms with the most daylight were 21% higher than those of students in classrooms with the least sunlight.[28] Biophilia, a concept first described by Edward O. Wilson in 1984,[29] suggests that humans need to connect to the natural environment, which may partly explain why greater access to daylight and natural ventilation seems to be innately linked to increased human productivity.

That 3.5% workplace contributor to productivity is added to the 2% from teamwork and the 5% gain in individual productivity to yield a 10.5% overall gain in workforce productivity. The power of sustainability initiatives to unleash employee productivity is too big to ignore. Companies ignoring this potential are leaving money on the table.

We have recently, in the last three years, started to track the financial benefits. We put a process in place to do this. In energy, for example, there are tremendous benefits in saving energy by reducing consumption, and we have quantified that. In addition, we have quantified the many benefits of pollution prevention through source reduction.

I remember about five years ago we eliminated a chemical solvent in one of our manufacturing processes by using a new approach that also eliminates a cleaning step in the process. Our mindset was to recycle and reuse the solvent, but that required significant infrastructure. We had to build stills, dilute it, pass it through different passive systems and air-treatment systems, which meant capital investments in equipment, floor space, maintenance on that equipment, and people assigned to recycle the product.

It's nice to recycle. We were proud. We would show our recycling system to anyone who walked into our facility: "See how good we are?"

Then we took a look at it and asked, "Why are we doing all this?" That was the day we realized that if we eliminated this solvent, we'd get rid of buying the solvent, all the cost of recycling, we freed up manufacturing space, freed up air-abatement system space, and we reduced the cycle time to produce the product because we eliminated the cleaning steps — just by changing one small component in the process. The benefit of this was in the millions of dollars in savings.

So there are all sorts of benefits in source reduction. You eliminate waste, you can use your space better, you can reduce your production cycle time and deliver your product faster to your customer. The difficulty in changing any manufacturing process is product reliability. It is not easy to go into any kind of manufacturing process and ask your engineer to change it and convince your customers that by changing this process you're not going to impact the reliability of the product. To change processes or invest in new technology requires capital, and the capital cycle has to be allowed for.

We have quantified good environmental benefits. If you go to IBM's latest environmental report on its Internet site, there is a section in there on benefits. (Richard Mireault)

4. Reduced Expenses for Manufacturing

There are substantial savings to be derived from today's manufacturing operations by substituting less expensive, more environmentally friendly raw materials and energy sources for those currently being used; reducing the amount of material, energy, and water used per product; reducing, reusing, and recycling scrap material and wasted energy, turning them into useful product instead of throwing them away; and reusing and recycling components and materials from returned products that have been designed for disassembly. It pays to replace straight-line "take-make-waste" production systems with circular, closed-loop "borrow-use-return" systems.[30] The low-hanging fruit of eco-efficiency savings excite companies in their first blush of enthusiasm for environmental concerns.

Sales of manufactured goods are assumed to contribute 50% of SD Inc.'s annual revenue, with the remaining revenue generated from software and services. Material, energy, and water costs are assumed to be 30% of product sales, and I assume a very conservative 5% of those are saved. I then assume 50% of the savings is reserved in a capital fund to invest in further sustainability projects, so only 2.5% is added to SD Inc.'s annual profit. The self-financing, rotating capital fund would be used for sustainability-related capital projects that do not meet normal corporate payback period criteria for capital projects.

The Xerox Corporation saved or avoided $2 billion in costs by designing environmentally friendly products and redesigning manufacturing processes over the past ten years. As a result, the equivalent of 1.8 million printers and copiers were reused or recycled, keeping 1.2 billion pounds of electronic waste out of landfills.[31] DuPont set goals of reducing its emissions of greenhouse gases by 65%, and getting 10% of its energy and 25% of its raw materials from renewables, by 2010. STMicroelectronics has announced a goal of zero net CO_2 emissions by 2010, saving almost $1 billion while achieving a 40-fold increase in production. BP reduced its greenhouse gases by 10% by 2002, saving $650 million.[32]

The Rocky Mountain Institute says that industry can save 75% of its energy costs using proven energy-efficiency approaches: 70% to 90% of the energy and costs for lighting, fan, and pumping systems; 50% on electric motors; 20% on steam systems; and 20% to 50% on compressed air systems.[33]

These savings fuel sustainability momentum.

On the staff side, we lead with saving money on the operating budgets, professional development, and getting them excited about innovation and doing something unique. They can take it to council, and council likes to be doing something where there is a lot of citizen support. They end up looking good to the boss(es).

We find that showing the chief administrative officer and council that they are really getting value for money works really well. (Louise Comeau)

5. Reduced Expenses at Commercial Sites

Potential savings at commercial stores, field location office buildings, distribution centers, and storage facilities include savings on employee discretionary consumables, waste handling, energy, water, landscaping, office space, and business travel. I assume the cost of selling, general, and administrative (SG&A) expenses are about 15% of total revenue in SD Inc., and energy costs are 2% of that. I lump water and consumables costs into that amount to be extra conservative. I then assume 20% of this annual expense could be saved by an energized and informed employee population, backed by committed executives.

Using integrated design, many green buildings cost no more to build and may actually cost less due to savings from less costly mechanical, electrical, and structural systems. S.C. Johnson's worldwide headquarters in Racine, Wisconsin, used extensive daylighting and personal environmental systems to save 10% to 15% over traditional construction. If green buildings do cost more, the cost difference is recoverable within the first three to five years of operations — savings in energy costs of 20% to 50% are common.[34] The new eco-designed Internationale Nederlanden (ING) Bank headquarters in Amsterdam uses only 10% of the energy of the building it replaced.[35] Herman Miller estimates it is saving 41% in operating costs of a 100,000-square-foot green-built space the company leases.[36] The Rocky Mountain Institute says energy savings of 60% are possible in areas such as heating, cooling, office equipment, and appliances.[37] According to the National Research Council, 60% to 85% of a building's real costs are related to operations; the initial construction cost is 10% or less.

Engaging employees helps reap short-term savings in the eco-efficiency harvest at commercial sites. Fairmont Hotels found that the majority of usable greening ideas came from Green Teams of non-knowledge workers — frontline people like maids, porters, chefs, banquet managers, security personnel, and service personnel.[38] Between 1975 and 2002, 3M employees voluntarily initiated 4,973 short-term Pollution Prevention Pays (3P) projects, saving the company $894 million.[39] Between 1990 and 2004, a similar Earth Awards program, based on employee team suggestions at Xerox, saved more than $235 million.[40]

Most eco-efficiency savings at commercial sites are not rocket science. They simply require educating, encouraging, and empowering employees working at the sites to unleash their creativity and help capture them.

The second thing I jotted down [as a reason to pay attention to sustainability] is "growth agenda." If you are planning to grow outside Canada or the US, the dynamics of the thinking in global markets is different. The global stand of Bush and the administration on climate change is irrelevant. (Gib Hedstrom)

The opportunity that people miss is that there are these growing green procurement programs. A lot of people, simply because the marketing guys haven't got involved, don't recognize there may be some emerging market opportunities. (Martin Charter)

The US Roper Starch Worldwide Green Gauge Report in 2000 showed a breakdown of consumer attitudes on environmental purchase decisions.

- *11% True-blue Greens:* They recycle, compost, and go out of their way to buy environmentally friendly products, while actively lobbying companies and governments for more action.
- *5% Greenback Greens:* They donate to environmental organizations and pay a premium for green products, but do not consider lifestyle changes.
- *33% Sprouts:* They care, but will pay only slightly more for green products.
- *18% Grousers:* They care about the environment, but view it as someone else's problem. They don't seek green products and won't pay more for them if they find them.
- *33% Basic Browns:* They are essentially unconcerned about the environment.

— Ashok Ranchhod, *Marketing Strategies*[41]

6. Increased Revenue/Market Share

Suppose our hypothetical SD Inc. gains favorable publicity for its environmentally friendly operations, products, and services. More revenue is generated from new "green" customers, and these customers loyally continue to purchase the company's products; the company adds new revenue streams by leasing its products instead of selling them; it opens up whole new markets in the developing world that are good for the company and for needy citizens; the company launches a services business to perform the services of its products; and/or the company charges a premium for its more environmentally friendly products. Given these diverse new revenue opportunities, let us conservatively assume SD Inc. generates just 5% more revenue.

For years, research has shown that consumers are more likely to view brands positively if they know the company behind those brands acts responsibly toward society. Environics' "Millennium Poll" found that a corporation's overall image is most affected by perceptions of how it is fulfilling its social and environmental responsibilities; 49% chose this as the most important factor, ahead of brand quality/reputation (40%) and business fundamentals (32%).[42]

A Weber Shandwick Worldwide survey of 8,000 customers found that 66% of high-education/high-income consumers have considered switching brands because of corporate social responsibility issues.[43] A survey reported in *The Wirthlin Report* in April 2004 indicated that 80% of adult Americans say their view of a company's ethical behavior and practices has a direct influence on their willingness to buy the firm's products.[44]

However, there appears to be a gap between consumers' stated intentions and observed behavior.[45] Other surveys show there is a 30:3 syndrome. While 30% of consumers say they care about sustainability issues, only 3% will pay a "sustainability premium" when they reach the cash register.[46]

I assumed an overall increase in revenue of 5%, which generates a huge top-line benefit amount. So large, in fact, that it risks jeopardizing the credibility of the whole case. However, it is a minor bottom-line contributor, since only 7% of revenue for SD Inc. flows to the bottom line. Even if the assumed revenue were severely cut back, the business case is still robust, as will be shown shortly.

We are also finding, when doing credit analysis for our loans under our investment funds, that those communities that have an EMS [environmental management system] in place have higher credit ratings. We find the same thing for corporations. It is starting to factor into risk assessment. It is happening already in Canada, for both loans and insurance. (Louise Comeau)

7. Reduced Risk, Easier Financing

As discussed in Chapter 3, sustainable approaches to a company's manufacturing processes and operations can:

1. Lower the market risks of regulatory bans on sales, reduced demand, or customer boycotts

2. Lower the balance-sheet risk of remediation liabilities, impairment of property values, damaged assessments, and "toxic torts"

3. Lower the operating expense risk of cleaning up spills, improving worker safety measures, and escalating energy and material costs

4. Lower the capital cost risks of product redesign to meet new regulations and new waste treatment facilities

5. Lower the sustainability risk from energy and material inefficiencies, take-back legislation, and fossil fuel taxes

A derivative of these lower risks is the ability to raise capital in the marketplace more easily, as the impact of these risks spills over into market valuation.

Since risk will ultimately affect either expenses or revenues when and if it happens, I will bundle the financial benefit of reduced risk into savings. Previously I calculated SD Inc.'s selling, general, and administrative (SG&A) expenses to be 15% of total revenue. I assume just 5% of the SG&A expenses are risk-related, such as insurance premiums and allowance for liabilities, or higher interest for loans because the company is a bad environmental or social risk. I then assume 5% of that amount would be reduced by more proactive social and environmental initiatives, so the resulting benefit is negligible.

What is not explicitly allowed for is the perfect storm of risks discussed earlier. Why not? First of all, they are cost-avoidance items, and some companies view such "savings" as suspect. Second, the costs could be so huge they could put the company out of business — how would a business case calculate that sad eventuality? Third, the possibility and potential extent of their impact are so variable that making any assumptions might jeopardize the credibility of the whole case. So they are the icing on the financial case. Not only would a company reap the seven financial benefits, it would also mitigate its particular version of the perfect storm of risks.

151

There was an evolution as we learned, from control to prevention to source reduction. The economic factors started to fall into place, because if you can control waste, you also control costs, and you can leverage good environmental management to get a competitive advantage. (Richard Mireault)

My other hunch is that when companies get into doing this stuff, they find it is not as bad as they thought it was going to be. They actually find it has other spin-off benefits and say, "My goodness! How come we didn't start to do some of these things earlier?" (Alan Willis)

The primary driver for a lot of this is saving money. Once they get beyond the I-don't-understand-it and I-don't-have-the-information point of view, these guys are saving major bucks. [Laughs] It is about the money. There are the co-benefits of meeting community expectations and reducing liabilities, but definitely they are saving money. They don't know that when they start, so they start for other reasons. (Louise Comeau)

We are absolutely convinced that in the long run our posture as a company committed — in the past, present and the future — to SD has added to the value of the enterprise for example in the Brazilian and New York Stock Exchanges. In a market where competitors are increasingly active in the striving to achieve overall excellence, reduction of costs and increases in productivity, Aracruz's well-known option for producing high quality pulp in a sustainable way has become a distinguishing characteristic and a competitive advantage. — Erling S. Lorentzen, chairman of the board, Aracruz Celulose[47]

Overall Recent Studies

Recent studies echo the fact that high-performing businesses show a strong correlation between CSR activities and stronger performance in terms of productivity and profitability than other businesses. A 2004 study released by the United Nations Environment Programme Finance Initiative (UNEPFI) used reports from nine brokerage houses on 11 business sectors and was compiled by 12 fund managers, representing $1.6 trillion in assets. It found that environmental, social, and corporate governance issues affect long-term shareholder value, sometimes greatly. [48]

More specifically, a 2004 report by the Work Foundation and the Virtuous Circle, "Achieving High Performance: CSR at the Heart of Business," argues that there is now a sufficient weight of empirical evidence to indicate that building CSR activities into the heart of business strategy leads to added value — from 19% increase in profitability in one study to outperforming other organizations by more than 40% in another. Reinforcing the human resources aspect of the business case, the study found that employees made a greater contribution toward their organization if they perceived it as a more responsible employer, and this in turn influenced their decision to remain with that employer.[49]

A 2002 survey by the World Economic Forum (WEF) Global Corporate Citizenship Initiative (GCCI) helped reinforce the business value of CSR in executives' minds. CEOs were asked to list the most important factors in making the business case for corporate citizenship activities. Contribution to reputation and brand was in the top three factors for 80% of companies, followed by employee retention (59%), license to operate (49%), competitiveness and market positioning (48%), risk management (28%), operational efficiency (17%), access to capital (12%), and learning and innovation (10%).[50]

According to a 2004 survey of 515 business leaders, conducted by the Center for Corporate Citizenship with the Hitachi Foundation, 53% said that corporate citizenship is important to their customers, and 82% of respondents felt that good corporate citizenship helped their bottom lines.[51] The business case helps verify this claim.

The message to businesses is clear — ethical practice, CSR performance, and the bottom line are more closely linked than ever.

Figure 4.4: Performance of Jantzi Social Index vs. Other Indeces

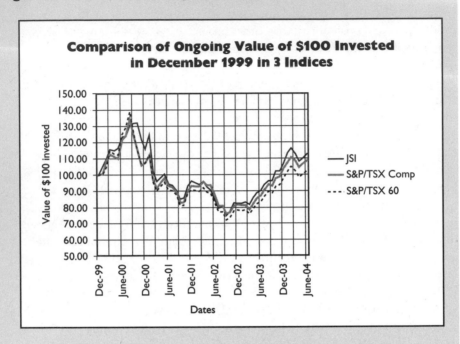

Share-Price Correlations

Does superior corporate social responsibility help a company's shares outperform its competitors' and produce superior returns for investors?

The Forum for the Future examined 30 years' worth of studies — 13 from the 1970s, 16 from the 1980s, 36 from the 1990s and 8 from 2000–2001 — to determine how social, environmental, and ethical screenings of companies correlate to portfolio out-performance. Of the 83 studies reviewed, 60% showed a positive correlation, 27% showed no or inconclusive correlation, and 13% showed a negative correlation. Studies of socially responsible investment (SRI) indices in the late 1990s in the US found significant out-performance. However, some studies suggest that this out-performance may have been based on coincidental reasons, like R&D investment or advertising, and that these indices were biased toward high-tech companies that did particularly well during the late 1990s. While the researchers were hesitant to conclude a cause-and-effect relationship, they conditionally concluded there is growing evidence that, in certain companies and at certain times, improving CSR will lead to financial out-performance.[52]

The Dow Jones Group Sustainability Index (DJSI), FTSE4Good index series, Domini 400 Social Index (DSI), and Jantzi Social Index (JSI) track the stock market performance of the most responsible companies. Since its inception in September 1999 to July 2004, the return on the DJSI World slightly underperformed the benchmark Morgan Stanley Capital International (MSCI) World index: -15.16% return on the DJSI World versus -12.49% on the MSCI World.[53] On the other hand (see Figure 4.4), from its inception on January 2000 through June 2004, the JSI achieved an annualized return of 2.67%, while the comparable Standard & Poor's/Toronto Stock Exchange (S&P/TSX) 60 and the S&P/TSX Composite had annualized returns of 0.49% and 1.86% respectively over the same period.[54]

According to a survey carried out in June 2004 by Market and Opinion Research International, these results would surprise retail investors in the UK. More investors expect ethical funds to underperform than outperform the market — 25% compared to 15%. Even with such unnecessarily conservative expectations, two thirds of respondents would still consider investing their money ethically.[55] Imagine what they would do if they learned their expectations could be too pessimistic.

155

Figure 4.5: Business case What-Ifs

Seven Business Case Benefits	Base Case	Less Revenue	Less Productivity	Both Less Revenue and Less Productivity
1. Reduced recruiting costs	-1%	-1%	-1%	-1%
2. Reduced attrition costs	-2%	-2%	-2%	-2%
3. Increased productivity	+10.5%	+10.5%	+4%	+4%
4. Reduced expenses in manufacturing	-5%	-5%	-5%	-5%
5. Reduced water, energy, and consumables expenses at commercial sites	-20%	-20%	-20%	-20%
6. Increased revenue and market share	+5%	+2%	+5%	+2%
7. Reduced risk / Easier financing	-5%	-5%	-5%	-5%
... yielding a profit increase of	38%	35%	23%	20%

Tailored Totals Talk

Few executives are asking for more sustainability case studies. They can too easily dismiss success stories because the examples are from companies in different countries, in different industries, at different stages of growth, or facing different political situations or economies. The companies may be too small or too large, or have different corporate cultures. If executives do not want to be inspired by sustainability case studies, they will find many ways to justify their intransigence.

Executives want to examine assumptions to verify that they are valid for their company and situation. They want to plug in their own assumptions. They should. Using *The Sustainability Advantage Worksheets,* they can substitute their industry's language and their company's assumptions in the Excel spreadsheets to assess the robustness of the sustainability business case for their own company.[56] Service companies would remove the benefit from manufacturing savings. NGOs and public sector organizations would focus on the human resources benefits and commercial site operations benefits. Small and medium-sized enterprises (SMEs) would scale back some factors and emphasize others, as suggested in the appendix. The impact of three changes in assumptions are shown in the "what if" combinations in Figure 4.5.

A benefit is not a benefit to an executive unless it is viewed as relevant to that executive. That is obvious. However, the implications are not always as obvious. Too often, sustainability champions do not understand that executives responsible for different corporate functions are driven by their measurement and reward systems, and these systems are not uniform throughout executive ranks in the same company. Is the executive's pay based on increased revenue or increased profit? Does the executive get rewarded for reducing operating expenses or for attaining a minimum rate of return on capital expenditures? The differences matter, and the business case is more compelling if it accommodates the priorities of different executives within the same company.

At the heart of today's business case for sustainable global success lies a cycle of economic, environmental and social interconnections. Economic viability is the starting point, because all companies are first and foremost economic entities. No company can be sustainable over the long term if it is not economically viable.

And by the same token, no company can be economically viable in the 21st century if it fails to accept its environmental and social responsibilities. These three interrelated components of sustainability provide the foundation for global business success.

As media reports confirm every day, a crack or failure in any one of these components can be enough to weaken the entire structure. — Travis Engen, CEO, Alcan[57]

Triple-bottom-line accounting has to come from the CEO level. It has to start there. If it doesn't, it will be perfunctory, at best. Maybe you have a good HR person who feels very passionate about it and he/she sells the CEO on it. It needs the CEO buy-in at a personal level. (Mitch Gold)

Any project that requires capital investment is competing with other projects that require capital. It has to be not just a good business case, but it has to fit within the strategy. If the company is trying to develop a new product to grow the business, then that project competes with environmental projects requiring capital ....

Sometimes environmental projects will stand alone. You are able to go in and say, "It just makes business sense. I'm paying for this energy today. If I put this energy reduction project in place, I'm going to save this much and it will pay for itself within a year or two." It depends on your company's payback clip level — if there is a good return on investment and a good payback period, then most of the time we will get approval to go ahead and do it.

But if you're coming in and you're saying, "It makes good business sense but it's going to take five years to get the payback," and the company wants to invest its capital somewhere else, forget it. (Richard Mireault)

The Catch

There is a catch to reaping all the potential benefits of sustainability. It requires more than cherry-picking the low-hanging fruit or throwing money at a few high-profile projects. To fully capture potential value, a Stage 4 organization must: energize its internal and external stakeholders with a shared vision of a sustainable company; rethink its governance system and the way it distributes power and authority through its information, decision-making, and resource allocation mechanisms; evolve a patriarchal, command-and-control management system toward a team-based, sustainability-educated, empowered workforce; align measurement and management systems to encourage and reward sustainability initiatives; foster learning and experimentation; integrate sustainability with key business strategies; and encourage leadership throughout the organization.[58] It needs to ensure that investing in sustainability-oriented projects is considered strategic when competing with other projects for limited capital funds.

In short, it requires a culture change. Sustainability must be led with the rigorous discipline of any major organizational change initiative to fully capitalize on the potential benefits in Stage 4. Specifically, a company has to do three things:

1. Senior executives have to visibly sponsor and support integration of sustainability into corporate strategy, purpose, and vision. No tireless, senior-level support, no change. Period.

2. The whole company needs to buy in. The five-year, company-wide education investment described earlier covers four things: why the company cares, what it has already done, what it is planning to do next, and how employees can help. Magic happens when everyone is educated, engaged, and empowered to help a company they believe is doing good things.

3. The company has to set up a "Sustainability Profit Center" or indicate in some other way that its efforts are far beyond philanthropy. It is integrating sustainability into its business strategies as a profit-making, value-creating, knowledge-generating, innovation-stimulating engine.

As with any large-scale organizational change, do these three things and be rewarded. Drop any of them and be disappointed.

I would avoid using terms like ethics, morals, or values. It doesn't sit well with a lot of senior managers .... When you talk about ethics, especially, one plausible, natural response from most managers is, "Are you saying that I'm not being ethical?" (Julian Smit)

I just graded a paper on quantifying social return on investment for a nonprofit social venture fund organization. The student had monetized everything, had quantified qualitative things, and had totally given in to the argument that only economics are important. We need to avoid overdoing it. We need to avoid stepping over the line so we fail to adequately account for the qualitative aspects of a project. It is a two-step process: 1) Monetize what you can; 2) Coach them to grasp deeper qualitative aspects and build a coherent and compelling argument that links the parts you cannot monetize to the health and competitiveness of the firm without simply resorting to ethical/moral pleas. (Mark Milstein)

You have to clearly articulate how every sustainability initiative or effort creates value and fits with your other business strategies. If it doesn't create value for you, go figure out something that does. That idea is liberating. I've seen people who are visibly resistant to corporate sustainability go, "Oh. Okay." Some sustainability proponents would argue that you are just letting companies off the hook that way. I don't think we are at all. I think we are pushing hard and are facing up to the reality that if they are not making money from it, they are not going to keep doing it. You can wish that they would all you want, but they won't do it. (Don Reed)

Although a corporation is often referred to as a "legal entity," I believe it is inappropriate to view it as having a singular personality. It is, after all, an organization of many people, with many backgrounds, many views, many understandings of ethics, and so forth, just like any pluralistic, dynamic group. What the people tend to share are the overarching business objectives. I believe that's part of the reason it is easier to enact change by taking a business case approach — it is easier to get a thousand people to agree to common business objectives than it is convince them to change their personal beliefs. (Mel Wilson)

Ethical Objections to a Business Case Rationale

People with strong ethical convictions, who passionately advocate the values-based approach to sustainability, have concerns about the bottom-line approach to sustainability. Their concern is expressed in this question: "What if the business case is not strong enough for a company to behave ethically/sustainably? Does that mean it is okay for that company not to be ethical or not to use sustainable approaches?"

One reply is: "If the business case does not seem to be compelling enough, it is probably too narrow and undervalues or overlooks valid benefits. It should be revisited to ensure all benefits and co benefits have been fairly included."

A second reason the business case may appear weak is executives don't want it to be strong and are not ready to move up the sustainability continuum anyway. They are deliberately lowballing the potential benefits. If that is the case, it is probably best that company leaders not proceed, since the CSR effort would lack executive support required for a successful and sustainable change initiative. It would just tick off good people and leave another layer of cynical scar tissue for the next worthy organizational change to penetrate.

One value of a business case theme is it legitimizes a rather pointed question posed by Paul Hawken. He was asked to speak to a group of businesspeople in Melbourne, Australia, and to make the business case for sustainable development. Instead, he asked them what the business case was for worldwide endemic poverty, for double-glazing the planet with greenhouse gases, and for business models that destroy people and life.[59] The prospect of dueling business cases is encouraging.

Notwithstanding Hawken's moral argument, in today's business community CSR needs a strong business rationale or it will fail. Although hanging our CSR rationale on the assumption the business case will be sufficiently compelling may appear to be giving companies an excuse to act irresponsibly if it is not compelling, they would behave that way anyway. No license from a weak business case is required to justify irresponsible corporate behavior. Extolling CSR values more passionately and stridently will not be effective.

Many executives are not ready for CSR considerations and have succinct objections to support their unwillingness. Given the three motivators for the first wave of companies and the two emerging drivers, how might a sustainability champion handle their objections?

CHAPTER FIVE

OBJECTION-HANDLING CLINIC ON
INHIBITERS TO THE NEXT WAVE

A standard module in sales schools is an objection-handling clinic. Someone plays the role of an unwilling customer, and an aspiring sales representative is required to skillfully acknowledge and address the customer's concerns about a proposal. The sales representative is trained to listen attentively to customer objections, using "Anything else?" probes to ensure all obstacles to the proposal are aired before responding. A "trial close" might be used to ensure all showstopping objections are on the table: "If I can address all these concerns to your satisfaction, would you be willing to sign the contract?"

The sales representative is encouraged to use an empathetic "3F" response to begin the counterarguments. "I understand how you *feel*. Others have *felt* that way before. But what we have *found* is ..." The sales representative proceeds to address each objection, seeking agreement from the customer that the original concern has been convincingly addressed. The clinic is intended to raise the salesperson's comfort, confidence, and competence in the art of handling objections. It reinforces that until customer's needs and concerns are understood, sales efforts are random stabs in the dark at best, and very annoying to customers at worst. Shotgunning features and benefits at customers is less effective than targeting a critical need or objection. As Stephen Covey recommends, "Seek first to understand, then to be understood" is a good habit of highly effective (sales)people.[1]

If sustainability champions are to sell another wave of companies on the benefits of sustainability, it would be helpful to first understand objections to publicly adopting more aggressive environmental and social agendas. Then sustainability champions can selectively use counterarguments to address each concern, resulting in executive commitment to relevant and helpful CSR approaches.

Experts say the four main inhibiters of corporate commitment to sustainability are:

- Lack of support from senior leaders
- Fear of backlash
- Weak business case
- Mindset

In this country, a change to sustainability practices will only happen top-down, not bottom-up. It needs to come from the board and the CEO, not from EHS [Environment, Health, and Safety] or a director of sustainable development.

I was in a board committee meeting a few months ago and we were talking about making an environmental change in the company. The CEO turned to the board members at one point and said, "George (not his real name) can't do this. I have got to do it." The VP of EHS can't do it, the CEO has to do it. He wrote down notes on what he had to do and did it. (Gib Hedstrom)

An unhappy thought is that perhaps executives are only human and are as apathetic as the next person in their general lack of concern for the environment and people. (Stephen Hill)

Inhibiter #1: Lack of Support from Senior Leaders

Unlike leading sustainability companies who have identifiable founders or CEOs who are championing the efforts, lagging companies do not. That is why experts often cite "lack of support from senior management" as a reason companies are not engaging with sustainability. As noted previously, without senior leader support, especially the blessing and active engagement of the CEO, sustainability initiatives almost never get traction.

What is getting in the way? Why don't CEOs support sustainability? How does sustainability differ from the things they do support? To address this inhibiter, we need to understand the next level of "why nots" behind CEO disinterest, namely:

- "We're too busy."
- "Sustainability is not a strategic area for us."
- "I don't feel pressure from important people on sustainability."
- "It is too hard to change the company."
- "I'm tired of all this environmental and social stuff."
- "People won't believe I'm sincere."
- "This just sounds like good business. Why should we bother reframing it?"

On the following pages, I use an objection-response format to address each concern, representing a hypothetical conversation between a skeptical CEO and a sustainability champion. "A Response" instead of "The Response" acknowledges that alternative counterarguments might be equally appropriate — the one offered is just a suggestion. Although quotation marks are used to suggest what each would say, the compressed conversations are not direct quotes from any specific, real person. They are composites of conversational fragments gleaned from personal experience, experts interviewed, or other acquaintances. For impact, some jargon and exaggeration is used.

With those caveats, we proceed with the first one.

It's one of those things that is very important but not very urgent. Operationally, we run on a quarterly focus, which gets us into a monthly and a weekly focus and inspections to meet our business commitments. (Expert B)

Another inhibiter is initiative overload. A chemical company asked me to do a gap analysis and present it to their board. But they just have so many things on their plate right now, and limited resources, like many companies. With 18-hour days, seven days a week, relegated to investment bankers, the combination produces initiative overload. (Gib Hedstrom)

My second reason for lack of corporate attention to CSR is no time, no space or drivers to propagate long-term strategy and thinking. For example, I am shocked at the number of meetings I have attended in my 27 years in business that have been billed as being strategic and which rapidly descend into minute operational detail. (Steven Cross)

"We're too busy"

The Objection:

"I have no time for this. Our company is too busy surviving hard times. We've got to get out and sell more to make our profit line, or cut more expenses. We can't afford to take our eye off the ball — we have to focus on our core business. We can't go spending money on unnecessary frills when we're laying people off and morale is suffering.

"Stockholders are demanding better results this quarter than last quarter. That's what we need now. When you are up to your butt in alligators, you don't have time to drain the swamp. Maybe we'll have the luxury of thinking about sustainability when things settle down. Right now, we are too busy just trying to survive."

A Response:

"I agree. If considering sustainability agendas is just one more thing on your plate to worry about, you can't afford to even consider it as a new goal. What is surprising, though, is how much low-hanging fruit companies find as they get into sustainability, especially in the area of eco-efficiencies and waste management. For example, 3M's Pollution Prevention Pays (3P) program saved $894 million between 1975 and 2002 by implementing 4,973 employee-suggested 3P projects, like eliminating or reducing a pollutant, saving energy or materials, avoiding pollution control equipment, or increasing sales.[2] Initially, the payback period for suggested projects had to be less than a year, so short-term benefits were reaped as momentum built and employees supported the company's commitment to sustainability.

"So you should use sustainability strategies to accomplish your short- and long-term goals, goals you are already being driven by. They are a means to your already-existing ends. If CSR considerations lead you to take your eye off the ball and stop paying attention to your core business, the problem is not that you're doing it at all — it's that you're doing it badly. Well-managed, smart CSR initiatives support company business objectives, build relationships with key stakeholders, energize employees, reduce business costs, and maximize shareholder returns."

167

Too often, CSR is viewed by a company as a nice thing to do but not connected to its knitting — its key strategic thrust as a company. Smart companies know better. Unfortunately, for many others the truth gets lost in confusing terminology. (William Blackburn)

Figure 5.1: *Dilbert* on Multiple Business Priorities

Dilbert reprinted by permission of United Feature Syndicate, Inc.

"Sustainability is not a strategic area for us"

The Objection:

"We pride ourselves on our strategic focus. Sustainability sounds like it might be a useful strategy for companies in the environmental management business or making green products, but we are not. We offer products and services to meet our customer needs, and we are not hearing a lot of requests from customers for sustainability-related offerings.

"Everything we do is related to our key business strategies, and everyone knows what they are, internally and externally. We don't want to clutter our customers' and employees' minds with irrelevant ideas. Sustainability just doesn't connect with our core strategies."

A Response:

"Good for you on having a disciplined strategic focus. Many companies do not, and they ricochet all over the place chasing the latest fad. If sustainability notions were not relevant to your strategic objectives, you would be wise to reject them.

"However, business strategies are usually designed to make the business more successful, and the prospect of cost savings, increased revenue, and enhanced reputation may warrant giving sustainability strategies another look. They are usually a means to existing ends, as defined in your strategies today. Executives have found that by including environmental and social considerations in decision-making processes throughout their organizations, they make better operational and investment decisions.

"For example, companies find that when they consider building new facilities, they can construct them so that the ongoing operational costs of the building — the water, electrical, oil, and gas utilities costs — are a fraction of what a 'normal' building's would be, and the building is better from every point of view — aesthetically, as an asset, as a productive place to work, and as a proud corporate showcase in the neighborhood. By including environmental and social factors in building design, a much smarter facility results for little or no extra cost.

"The same is true for other strategic decisions. Think of sustainability as a decision-making lens that helps meet today's strategy, not a net additional one to worry about."

Impediment #1 [to companies integrating sustainability into their business strategies] is the boards aren't asking. The people who are charged with responsibility for taking a longer view than quarterly earnings are not asking. There is a whole set of complexities that, based on my experience with about 40 board meetings over the years, boards made up of American or Canadian captains of industry find it hard to see the same way Europeans or Asians would. (Gib Hedstrom)

Often it is the CEO who has not grasped the importance of CSR. The CEO really sets the tone. Unless there are direct pressures from board members or shareholders, they are not going to move on it. (George Khoury)

Maybe those whom you supply start demanding certain attributes in your practices and products .... Some companies are driven by customers. In fact, if you trace back the Ray Anderson [CEO of Interface] story and why he was going to give a speech to his employees that caused him to think about what his environmental policy was, it is because just when the book [Paul Hawken's *Ecology of Commerce*] landed on his desk in the early '90s, his customers had started to ask "What are you doing for the environment?" None of the salespeople knew, and the question got bounced up to him, as chairman and CEO. (Amory Lovins)

If your customers are asking about this stuff, you pay attention. I am working with a US chemical company right now that produces a chemical that is a $500 million business and is listed as a suspected carcinogen. It doesn't mean it is a carcinogen; it is "suspected," so they still make it and have lots of controls about how they handle it. They are hearing about "product de-selection" from customers in Europe. The customers decide they don't want this, even though there is no regulation that prohibits it.

Some auto companies have a list of chemicals and compounds that they just don't want to buy. This precedes regulations. If customers say something, companies pay attention. (Gib Hedstrom)

"I don't feel pressure from important people on sustainability"

The Objection:

"I keep hearing about pressure on companies to adopt CSR pressures. I know NGOs are trying to turn up the heat, but our important stakeholders don't have the same passion. Our shareholders don't seem to be voting with their wallets or their proxies. In fact, they would be really upset if it looked like we were doing anything which interfered with them getting maximum returns on their investment. Staying focused on the real bottom line, versus the triple bottom line, is what our boards and our investors want us to do.

"Our sales are still good, so customers must be okay with what we are doing. We pride ourselves on being market-driven. I suspect that surveys showing customer preference for green products or green brands may not be accounting for the 'halo effect' — how attitudes espoused in surveys are more righteous than actual behavior at cash registers.

"Finally, I don't hear much about big investors or the financial community getting all excited about sustainability dimensions of our operations. Until some of these stakeholders show more interest in sustainability, it is prudent to stay the course."

A Response:

"If you haven't seen customer interest yet, wait for it. Europe is usually five years ahead of North America on the CSR continuum, and companies there are feeling consumer pressure. The debate about how accurately values and attitudes reflect consumers' behavior has kept psychologists, sociologists, and marketing experts fully employed for years.[3] Even if you factor down what surveys say about green consumers, it is still significant.

"The international investment community is waking up too. In 2000, the UK amended pension fund regulations to require disclosure of whether ethical, social, and environmental issues were considered in investment decisions.[4] Germany, Belgium, and Sweden have similar requirements for pension trustees.[5] In February 2002, France announced that all companies listed on the French stock exchange must include social, environmental, and labor information in their annual reports to shareholders.[6] If you are in global markets, you'll recognize these trends. It's not a question of whether interest will be there from important stakeholders, it's when."

An inhibiter is the change of processes. It is the change itself. You are up against change. (Richard Mireault)

There is always the classic resistance to change. (Marlo Raynolds)

One aspect is what I term the "middle layer of clay" — middle management. There may be chairman-level rhetoric in the environmental or sustainability report, and there may be information collectors and ideas bubblers, but often that does not penetrate middle management because their concern is only the double bottom line — finance and finance. (Martin Charter)

When I talk about challenges, I'm talking about challenges integrating different elements of CSR under one umbrella .... Resistance from business units or line managers. They want to do their own thing .... I've seen it when I have worked with companies — how business units are protective of their pet projects, and they are afraid to lose control if it is integrated throughout the organization. It's very shortsighted, but it happens. (George Khoury)

In strategy, what I have learned is there are at least two mega-elements. One is the building of the strategy itself, based on fact-based marketplace insight, business design, innovation, and a clearly articulated strategic intent. Then there is the execution. Are general managers tightly tied to it? Do they understand the root causes that are in the way of actually getting it done? Can you build a set of critical tasks and action plans with a team and satisfy yourself that you have the right people and skills, the right culture, and the right formal organization to execute the strategy? If you can do that, you can execute a strategy. That's what our whole model is based on. (Gerry Pelletier)

A lot of companies are followers. Very few are leaders. "Show me that it is successful and I can be a quick learner/follower, not make those mistakes, and avoid the bleeding edge." (Stephen Hill)

"It's too hard to change the company"

The Objection:

"Okay. I get it. You're not talking about a thin veneer of CSR gloss being laid on top of what we already do. You're talking about a profound change in the way we make decisions about the design of our products and services; about how we engage with all our stakeholders, not just our stockholders; about how we educate and encourage our employees to help us on the sustainability journey; about living our core corporate values and improving our governance; about voluntarily being so far ahead of government regulations that they are irrelevant; about making a positive contribution to the well-being of the world while being a more successful business.

"It's all good stuff, but it's exhausting just to think about it. We've tried implementing significant changes before, and, I must admit, many of them failed. Climbing 'Mount Sustainability'[7] looks a tad harder than selling life jackets on the *Titanic*."

A Response:

"You are right to view becoming a truly sustainable business as being a significant change project. It is. But that is what leadership is all about. It's about (re)grounding the company with a shared vision and core values that resonate with the leadership team, all employees, and important stakeholders. It's about having the wisdom to interpret marketplace and stakeholder signals and steer the company in a direction that transforms risks into competitive advantage opportunities. It is about leadership, and leadership is about change.

"Doing it all at once is daunting. As with any significant change initiative, be smart about how you stage it, tap into expertise to help you approach the journey wisely, ask stakeholders for help, and learn from leading CSR companies. Existing, faltering internal change efforts can be reframed within the more powerful context of sustainability and reenergized. The unifying context helps reprioritize and capitalize on change projects already underway. Deciding to be the most sustainable company in your industry is the kind of 'Big Hairy Audacious Goal'[8] that can galvanize momentum, tear down departmental silos, and build teamwork toward a common, worthwhile goal. It can be an exciting leadership opportunity."

In terms of blockages to CSR, there are a lot of mixed messages from government and government policy. That came out repeatedly in our study of CSR in deprived areas. Some things were encouraged by government and then they weren't encouraged, and so on. Companies are trying to do things with inner cities and are using NGOs as a vital bridge to understanding local markets. NGO funding is largely from government, and the government is constantly changing priorities — funding will be cut or funding will be put in and replicated by different players in the market. There is a real blizzard of initiatives, and sometimes they get in each other's way. (John Swannick)

Absolutely, regulations are a driver. I watched what happened in the textile industry. All the favorable changes that occurred with respect to greening textile processing and inclusion of industrial ecology in new process development came about because of forward-thinking regulators who put some real-world parameters in water quality regulations. Had it not been for these regulations, I'm not sure all the positive changes that occurred in water quality during the 1980s and 1990s could have occurred.

We had a regulator in Raleigh who, together with his staff, decided that the most important criteria for the river basin water quality in North Carolina was decreasing toxicity to fish and their habitat. This started by elimination of acute toxicity and then expanded into elimination of reproductive problems with fish. People understood that. They might not understand the effects of 20 parts per billion of trivalent chromium, but they damn well understand that if you deliver water that fish can't reproduce in, you are breaking the law. This is clarity in vision. (Sam Moore)

"I'm tired of all this environmental and social stuff"

The Objection:

"We've been working on CSR stuff for years. In fact, we are getting battle fatigue. We've seen it all, and every time we think things are settling down, something else crawls out of the woodwork as an issue, and we have to re-justify and explain everything we are doing all over again. Just following the bouncing ball on government funding support for corporate social programs makes me dizzy.

"On the environmental front, we try to work with governments to ensure new regulations and policies make better sense, but they keep coming out with convoluted approaches that are more about doing it their way than really avoiding pollution. It takes a lawyer to understand what they want. I just wish the regulators would make up their minds on what we are supposed to do so we can do it. We just want to beat our competitors at the game, but that's hard to do when the guys on the sidelines keep changing the rules."

A Response:

"I understand your desire for a more stable set of public and regulatory expectations around social and environmental issues. Your shield to fend off criticism has to be continuously re-forged, and your relationships with NGOs keep changing as funding vacillates. It would be nice if all these areas would settle down. It would be even nicer if they were easier to understand and expressed in layperson's terms. Unfortunately, there is no sign that will happen. In fact, you can count on the bar of public expectations being continuously raised, just as it is for other business performance issues like quality, responsiveness, and price/performance.

"The best strategy is to get so far ahead of the regulations and your competitors that your corporate responsibility initiatives become competitive differentiators. Rather than waiting for the next wave of requirements to hit you, position yourself so that regulations and policies are irrelevant. Your leadership position may also enhance your credibility when you ask regulators to adjust the playing field to encourage your continued efforts while putting your competitors in catch-up mode.

"The best defense is a good offense."

I was at a meeting not long ago at a company and was told by some employees that the CEO was adamant that the terms "corporate social responsibility" and "sustainability" not be used in the company's external reports and communications. The CEO preferred the term "corporate risk management" to address what falls under the sustainability umbrella. When I stated that the CEO must have a strong shareholder/investor focus, the employees at the meeting said "Absolutely. That's the whole point. He views these issues as risks, and what he wants to communicate to shareholders is that the company is doing its utmost to manage the risks." (Mel Wilson)

The owners don't have the values, so the probability of others in the organization having those values is reduced. If you said, "I don't really buy into this," but somebody is telling you it is the right thing to do, maybe you decide to go there. If you do, you need to find a champion who will drive it through. You need someone who is quasi-fanatical about it to make it work. (John Szold)

The main obstacle to embracing CSR in organizations is the inability of managers and leaders of most organizations to handle ambiguity. We all know that focus wins. A company with a great strategy and poor focus will be defeated by a company with a lesser strategy and better focus. Focus wins. Period. So senior leaders work hard to provide clarity and focus. When something comes along, like CSR, that is ambiguous or is a highly subjective goal, organizations have little ability to handle it.

I'm convinced that the work of organizational development people is to help people deal with ambiguity .... CSR requires values-based, long-term thinking, not narrow rules. So comfort with ambiguity is at the top of my list for handling CSR initiatives. (Steven Cross)

"People won't believe I'm sincere"

The Objection:

"I'm known as a pretty hard-nosed, some would say ruthless, business leader. That's my reputation, I like it, and I'm proud of it. If all of a sudden I get all mushy about saving the world, people's eyes will roll right out the back of their heads. My like-minded colleagues in the boardroom echo chamber won't believe I suddenly really care about the environment and society. NGOs will say it is just a sneaky trick by a greedy CEO to make more money, rather than a sincere desire to make a positive contribution. So will employees.

"It's a damned-if-I-do, damned-if-I-don't situation. If I can convince people I am sincere, shareholders and investors will think I'm losing it and suspect my stewardship of their capital will be less diligent than before. That's not a healthy seed of suspicion to plant. My public commitment to CSR looks like a lose credibility/lose my job proposition to me."

A Response:

"You keep thinking of CSR and maximizing shareholder returns as opposites, or at least conflicting goals. They're not. CSR is a 'both/and' opportunity, not an 'either/or' dilemma. It is great that you have a reputation as a profit-obsessed CEO. Now you can explain that if you did not recast the company in a CSR mold, you would not be managing risks and would be shirking your fiduciary responsibility to investors. You need to get more comfortable with that ambiguity. Despite how trite the phrase has become, you really can 'do well by doing good.' As a CEO of a publicly traded company, if you can't, you shouldn't.

"If NGOs take issue with your mercenary motives, suggest they look at your actions instead of your motives. If you are earning a reputation as a leading CSR company based on the substance of your environmental and social deeds instead of your moral rhetoric, who cares what people say about your motives? Aren't those co-benefits better than being irresponsible about your impacts on society?

"Initially, you might consider putting an up-and-comer in charge of your 'CSR Profit Center,' someone who is better known within your company as an outspoken advocate for CSR agendas. Have him or her report directly to you, to signal your commitment and the importance of this business strategy. The combination of that person's personal passion and your hard-nosed reputation will reassure people this is a win/win strategy, not lose/lose."

"

There is no single aspect of the business case I disagree with. However, I don't believe that today's organizations' reporting systems are structured so they can easily and directly identify benefits resulting from sustainability improvements. To use a crude analogy, if $500,000 dollars of health care costs are avoided or saved by introducing flexible benefits, it isn't directly labeled as HR savings per se and attributed to HR benefits. Rather, it is more inherently represented as an overall operational efficiency, which ultimately contributes to a company's profitability and/or competitiveness.

So the challenge is to find a way to more directly link any real savings resulting from sustainability and to demonstrate that they were generated because of these sustainability actions. (Neil Cooney)

They may have done these things without ever thinking "We're into sustainable development," as if it were some magic label. They just used good business practices, and one day they wake up and the World Business Council for Sustainable Development says, "What you are doing is sustainable development." They say, "Okay, fine. We're doing it because it is the sensible thing to do." (Alan Willis)

It is an extension of efficiency and cost reduction. It might be new markets or getting to different markets in a different way — the traditional marketing matrix. This may also apply to some who are not consciously adopting sustainability. Whether it is 90% efficiency, cost reduction, doing good business, or being a good community citizen, if they are already doing it, then they may not need or want to put up the sustainability banner. (Steve Rice)

"

"This just sounds like good business. Why should we bother reframing it?"

The Objection:

"The more I hear what you are counting as sustainability initiatives and strategies, the more I think we have been doing it for years. Some of it was accomplished under the quality and reengineering efforts we launched. Some of it was an extension of our customer service thrust. Some of it was driven by our innovative and empowering human resources practices. Some it was through our community liaison work.

"I don't want to sound too presumptuous, but I think our management team has built on our core values and innovatively bridged the relationship between principles and competitiveness. I think we are doing better because we have combined improved competitiveness with a strong positive impact on all our stakeholders and the environment.

"Using your language, I'd say we are at Stage 4 on our sustainability journey already — we just haven't called it that. What is the benefit of rolling out another strategic priority for people to worry about?"

A Response:

"From what I understand about how your company operates and your innovative products and services, I think you are right. You are ahead of the pack already.

"That's why it would be great to learn from your approach. In fact, there was a European project in 2003–04 designed to learn from 'silent business leaders' like you who quietly integrated sustainability principles into their business strategies and operations before the corporate responsibility dialogue began in earnest.[9] Going public about your lessons learned would be a big boost for others who are uneasy about the business benefits of sustainability commitments.

"By coming out of the closet, you also would reap the benefit of improved image and reputation as a role-model company with a credible track record of 'getting it' on sustainability long before it was in vogue. You would be celebrated as a high-performance leader among your peers and would be in a good position to influence regulators to foster incentives and market forces that reward leaders."

Despite all the efforts and time, there are still no significant "Buffalos of Sustainability." For most companies, until they see substantial, reliable, substantive financial or business success by doing this, they keep asking, "Where's the proof?" .... At best, there are no buffalos that are stomping around, changing the landscape significantly, saying, "Pay attention to me. Look at this. You can't fail to notice me." (Steve Rice)

In order to be successful, you can't promote it. It can't be something that you do to give yourself a reputation gain, although it may trickle down from it on a more subtle level. People hear of it through hearsay, or they know different things about the company. But if it becomes your point of distinction, you run the risk of setting yourself up for a certain kind of scrutiny that you may not want. (Julian Smit)

Inhibiter #2: Fear of Backlash

There are several somewhat subtle and often understated reasons that companies keep their heads down on CSR issues. The reasons are especially relevant to companies that are not in sectors such as oil and gas, paper and forest products, mining and metals, chemicals, electrical utilities, and heavy manufacturing. These high-impact companies are already facing strong regulatory, stakeholder, or capital market pressures. Food companies are starting to feel the heat. Companies in "cleaner" industries like telecommunications, technology, banks, insurance, media, and drugs are still mostly in the safety of the shadows, enjoying not being subjected to the spotlight of activist NGO scrutiny that high-impact corporations have experienced ... so far.

The irony is that many of these "silent CSR leader" companies have excellent stories to tell. With a few notable exceptions, companies reaping financial benefits and competitive advantage from their sustainability efforts seem reluctant to go public. Possibly concerned about bad reactions to their good news, they would rather quietly keep doing good things without being celebrated as sustainability leaders.

For sustainability momentum to reach its tipping point, we need a critical mass of vociferous proponents from the ranks of respected business leaders. The best candidates for the next wave of CSR leaders are ones who have quietly been building good track records before going public. Sustainability champions need to help them overcome their fears.

Six backlash fears that inhibit next-wave companies from being more outspoken about their CSR progress are:

- "We don't want to blow our own horn."
- "We don't want to be accused of green-washing."
- "We don't want to open the floodgates."
- "We are concerned about guilt by association."
- "We could lose customers or get sued for skeletons in the closet."
- "We could lose our competitive advantage."

In this section I will explore these fears and possible counterarguments.

We participate in these community outreach things, but we don't exploit them. United Way is a good example. We promote a massive internal campaign that generates a couple of million dollars through employees as a way to give back to the community. I don't see us exploiting it. We feel very good about doing it, but we don't splash it around. (Expert B)

"We don't want to blow our own horn"

The Objection:

"We do good CSR things, but we don't like to brag about them, especially our social programs. We undertake our CSR programs because it is the right thing for us to do as good corporate citizens, not because we want to gain from them. Twisting our donations and community work into a marketing theme would distort our intentions and make it look self-serving instead of genuine. It feels like our deeds would be tainted if the company received any benefit from our giving.

"We are proud of awards we win for being good corporate environmental and social stewards, but we don't like to blow our own horn. We already get more requests for help than we can possibly satisfy. Everyone thinks we have deep pockets and their little request would get lost in the rounding of our business results. Raising our profile would make us even more of a target for donation requests and for criticism we should be doing more. Trumpeting our CSR work would cause misunderstandings about our motives."

A Response:

"To be candid, if you are really uneasy about publicity tainting your philanthropy, you would give corporate donations anonymously.

"Being humble about your good deeds is admirable, but how are all your important stakeholders supposed to know about your good CSR initiatives if you don't tell them?

"CEO surveys show that 60% of the market capitalization of corporations is based on 'hard' financial data, while 40% is dependent on 'reputation,'[10] and 80% of CEOs say that CSR initiatives contribute at least moderately to their companies' reputation, citing the primary business objectives of CSR initiatives as recruiting and retaining employees (71%), favorable media coverage (51%), and promoting transactions and partnerships (40%).[11]

"Those are all good business considerations. If you communicate the good things you are doing in a balanced, transparent, and candid manner, you will help interested stakeholders appreciate how much you are doing. That doesn't taint your good deeds. It contributes positively to your company's reputation as a great company to deal with, work for, and have in your community. Effectively communicating your CSR story builds brand value."

One of the problems is that companies' public policy work is not in alignment with their sustainability marketing initiatives. It may actually step all over their public relations message, or contradict it. We have yet to see any really good examples of companies breaking out on the market side and reinforcing that by breaking out on the public policy side to create synergy. (Don Reed)

A CEO looks at negative press stories about Ben & Jerry's and the Body Shop and says, "I don't need that aggravation. I have enough trouble with the stockholders" .... I think when a company steps up to the plate and says, "We want these values to run through the organization," we somehow expect them to be without fault. I think that is an unfair standard ....As a sweeping generalization, I don't think companies understand how to use the media and PR to their advantage. The perception becomes, "If we say something, somebody is going to find out that we didn't do it perfectly and we're going to get slapped." Even Ben & Jerry's had a fair amount of negative publicity. (John Szold)

"We don't want to be accused of green-washing"

The Objection:

"As soon as we go public about what we are doing, we will be labeled 'green-washers' — overhyping our initiatives and pretending we care about environmental and social causes when our products and operations say otherwise. The validity of our claims will be challenged. If we publicize that we donate a percentage of sales to social causes, civil society activists will scream that we are just 'perfuming the pig.' If it can happen to the Body Shop and Ben & Jerry's, it could happen to us.

"We're not perfect and don't pretend to be. We just are trying hard to have less negative impact on the environment and society. Being criticized for going public about our efforts is too much hassle. We are damned if we do and damned if we don't."

A Response:

"NGOs are experts at smelling a rat. If they sense that a company is duplicitously exaggerating its claims, papering over cracks in its corporate reputation, or showing no real signs of changing its stripes, the company deserves criticism. Planting a few trees and scattering a few thousand dollars to charities is just lip service if your operations and products are part of the problem in the first place. Spending as much or more on your advertising campaign to communicate CSR activities as you are on the CSR activity itself risks green-washing accusations. For example, BP spent $200 million on its two-year 'Beyond Petroleum' advertising campaign, about the same amount as its six-year investment in renewable technologies, drawing the ire of green activists who felt BP was just appeasing critics and trying to achieve a PR advantage over competitors.[12] In 2004, Shell was criticized by Friends of the Earth and Christian Aid for not living up to its promises to communities around its facilities worldwide.[13]

"The secret is not to hide. The secret is to be open and transparent in your communications. Talk about first steps and initial efforts instead of implying you have done it all. Partner with vocal critics — often they are hopeful friends masquerading as cynics — to learn how to improve the credibility of your communications. Be smart about how and when you stage your communications. People will respect you for it, your reputation will be enhanced, and you'll reap the upside advantages instead of the downside risks."

Another inhibiter is management fear of opening up the floodgates. A lot of companies don't know what's coming at them. They fear that if they open the doors, all the responsibility and associated costs are going to come flooding in and there is not going to be any way to control it. They fear that opening up may expose them to ever-increasing obligations that have traditionally fallen in the remit of government responsibility. Some companies may want to keep the doors tight so that government won't offload all of the work onto the private sector. (Devin Crago)

Being a leader carries a cost. In 1997, BP very publicly reinforced our green agenda by breaking away from the rest of the major oil companies to acknowledge that climate change was a serious issue and that we would begin standardizing and greatly stepping up our internal efforts to reduce our emissions. Since then, the biggest surprise to me is the amount of criticism we receive from some environmental groups who say we are not moving fast enough. At the same time, they generally ignore other companies who have yet to step forward and make the commitments that BP has. Perhaps it's because we make clear commitments with quantifiable targets that are specific enough to be challenged and tested. It may also be because we listen and engage our critics in discussions. That makes us more exposed to criticism.

For a large company, particularly one in an extractive industry, the journey toward sustainable development is long. When we look backward, we see real progress that has been accomplished. Looking forward, we can see a bright future for cleaner fuels and alternate energy sources, but our evolution in achieving those goals will be measured in decades rather than months. (Steve Elbert)

"We don't want to open the floodgates"

The Objection:

"There is a corollary to my concern that our CSR claims will be dismissed as overhyped green-washing veneer. It's not so much that what we are doing is not what we say we are doing; it is that we are not doing enough fast enough. We say we are reducing our emissions; they want them eliminated. We say we are cutting back on our use of fossil fuels; they want us to use only green energy. We say we are helping communities in which we operate; they want us to save the world.

"Containing expectations is a never-ending battle. Once NGO wolves taste blood, they go into a feeding frenzy. It is a lot simpler to stay below their radar and not attract their attention. Let someone else be first. Some NGOs are really high-maintenance organizations and just won't quit. Some things they ask us to do are way over the line into government areas of responsibility. We prefer to avoid confrontations and use our executive's energy more constructively than ironically defending our good works."

A Response:

"As in sales, expectation control is critical to CSR communication and credibility. There is no question that some NGOs will never be satisfied, but that's true of some customers, too. The surest way to build trust is to engage in real dialogue. What seems to be working for some leading CSR organizations is building a partnership with vocal NGOs, as encouraged at the World Summit on Sustainable Development in Johannesburg in 2002.[14] It is tricky for both parties to make these relationships work, especially for NGOs so they are not accused of selling out. However, if partners are open and candid with each other, NGOs can be very effective in diffusing unwarranted criticism and demands.

"There is no question that the tide of expectations about how corporations can be powerful contributors to economic, social, and environmental solutions is relentlessly rising. King Canute, standing on his throne on the shore with waves lapping at his feet, could not command the incoming sea to stop. Neither can corporations stem the sea change in stakeholder expectations. That may not seem fair, but it is a fact. Corporations that partner with demanding stakeholders will earn their respect and gain a competitive advantage that opens the floodgates to rising profits."

Figure 5.2: Partial list of Business for Social Responsibility Companies, November 2003

ABB	Kmart
Adidas-Salomon	Levi Strauss
Agilent Technologies	Liz Claiborne
American Express	Marks & Spencer
AT&T	Mattel
Ben & Jerry's	McDonald's
The Body Shop USA	Nestlé
BP	Nike
British Telecommunications	Nordstrom
CH2M Hill	Oracle
Charles Schwab	Patagonia / Lost Arrow
Chevron Texaco	Pfizer
Chiquita Brands	Phillips-Van Heusen
Cisco Systems	Placer Dome
Citigroup	Procter & Gamble
Coca-Cola	Reebok
Colgate-Palmolive	Rio Tinto
Deloitte & Touche	Sears, Roebuck and Co.
Edison International	Shell International
Exxon Mobil	Sony Corporation
Ford Motor Company	Starbucks
Gap	Sunbeam
General Motors	Timberland
GlaxoSmithKline	Tom's of Maine
Hallmark Cards	Toys "R" Us
Hewlett-Packard	Unilever
Home Depot	United Parcel Service
IKEA	VanCity
Inco	Verizon Communications
International Paper	Wal-Mart
Johnson & Johnson	Walt Disney

"We are concerned about guilt by association"

The Objection:

"You know, when you look at the list of companies that are on the speaking circuit about their CSR efforts, it reads like a docket of companies that are case studies of what not to do. The dirtier the industry, the more likely it is that it publicly trumpets its ethical policy and sustainability initiatives. Most have had PR crises about something bad they did, or for something good they didn't do, and are into glorified damage control to recover their reputations.

"I'm not saying they are bad companies. I'm just saying that people are known by the company they keep, and so are corporations. It is like a total abstainer showing up at an Alcoholics Anonymous meeting. People will think they have a problem and are coming out of the closet. That's why we don't join organizations of companies working on sustainable development. It would look like we had problems in that area."

A Response:

"Maybe your description of organizations that are committed to sustainable development was once true, but not anymore. Look at the mix of companies in Business for Social Responsibility (see Figure 5.2).[15] Members represent all industries and are at a range of stages in their CSR journeys. Some had a PR crisis whack them on their corporate heads to trigger their interest, but many are doing it because it makes good business sense and they want to use best practices to accelerate their competitive advantage.

"You can't hide forever. Sooner or later, stakeholders will be asking awkward questions about your CSR performance. That includes big investment houses that realize companies paying attention to environmental and social aspects of their business are better investment prospects. Learn from companies that have been through PR battles. Then skip that first painful wake-up call and go straight to the business benefits derived from smart sustainability initiatives that these same companies describe.

"In fact, your argument is being stood on its head. It is not about guilt by association. It is about guilt by disassociation — if you are *not* a member of leading CSR organizations and on the speaker circuit, people will think you don't care or have something to hide. Being a member of sustainability groups gives you innocence by association."

Suppose you ran a company that had not yet been subjected to adverse publicity. Would you want to be publicly celebrated as a company that had just removed a toxic substance from its product line?

Apparently not. Trudy Heller and Jeanne Mroczko studied why Giftco (a pseudonym), a producer of fine-quality keepsakes, did not publicize the elimination of a toxic ingredient, "T," from its products. They found three reasons for secrecy.

Customers typically kept Giftco's products for a long time. By highlighting that new products were T-free, Giftco would alert loyal customers that previous products had contained T, arouse safety concerns about ongoing exposure to levels of toxicity from T-contaminated keepsakes, erode hard-earned trust, and potentially expose itself to liability suits or recall demands. Heralding the elimination of T could be viewed as an admission of guilt about not disclosing that previous products were dangerous.

Giftco did not want to draw community attention to T-contaminated lagoons of toxic sludge that had been behind its factory. It had successfully cleaned them up, but was reluctant to admit that that the lagoons had been there for years and might have had undesirable local environmental impacts.

Giftco had a reputation for being customer oriented and a producer of high-quality goods for life's happy occasions. Acknowledgment of negative environmental issues, and the image of T-tainted toxic lagoons behind the on-location store, would jeopardize that carefully crafted strategic identity.

The environmental impacts were not being kept secret; the environmentally friendlier products were. Giftco's walk was greener than its talk. Disclosure of good news was viewed as a threat. This irony contrasts with companies that have been publicly taken to task for environmental transgressions and welcome publicity about their clean-up efforts.

— Based on "Information Disclosure in Environmental Policy and the Development of Secretly Environmentally Friendly Products"[16]

"We could lose customers or get sued for skeletons in our closet"

The Objection:

"We could shoot ourselves in the foot by talking about how much more environmentally friendly our products are now, especially if it is just one new product line. What does that say about all the products we are still producing the old way? By definition, they are dirty or environmentally irresponsible. So are our competitors' products, but we could kill our 'cash cow' products if customers just saw the contrast within our product lines and assumed our competitors' products were cleaner.

"If our improvements eliminate toxic materials from a big seller, and a lot of good customers still own or use the old version, we are setting ourselves up for lawsuits. They could sue us for putting them in harm's way or for a whole bunch of ailments they ascribe to toxins in our products. It is better to keep a low profile."

A Response:

"This is a tricky issue. Companies like Toyota and Honda can introduce hybrid cars and still sell gas-guzzling vehicles. Electrolux introduced a Green Range of products, with 3.5% higher gross profit margins, and still sells all its other standard appliances.[17] If the government regulates elimination of a substance, like CFCs, then doing it faster and more completely than competitors is a good thing. However, I agree that an announcement about voluntarily eliminating a toxic component can backfire. Do it carefully, with legal counsel.

"With that caution, let me hasten to add that this concern should not be an excuse to clam up about all the other good things you are doing that are less prone to invoke a litigious response from customers, neighbors, or government agencies. Tell the rest of your story and tell it proudly. It helps build your reputation as a responsible corporate citizen and will serve you well if or when you are taken to task for some CSR oversight.

"Be careful that you don't duck what might be a great opportunity to show your commitment to values and customer service. Johnson & Johnson's handling of the Tylenol scare in 1982 earned it worldwide accolades and customer loyalty. If your customers are truly at risk from your old product line, offer to exchange their old product for a new one. If they are not at risk, inform them anyway and make the same offer if they are still nervous. Think of the goodwill this would generate. You couldn't buy that kind of positive publicity."

BP's businesses are commodity businesses. Many of the products we sell are like products that others sell and, in many customers' eyes, are fungible [interchangeable] products. Customers have a choice regarding where they buy. They make that choice based on several criteria, but one extremely important one is that they see our company's social and environmental values are aligned with their personal values. In this regard I believe, and our survey data show, we are distinct from our competitors. (Steve Elbert)

You have to subdivide customers into four key channels. You have domestic consumers, business-to-business, intermediaries [i.e., retailers and wholesalers], and government. The domestic consumer side is always a very fuzzy issue — high levels of awareness quoted in studies and low levels of purchasing behavior. There's always that action/awareness gap. However, one thing that's not picked up often is the boycotting. It's the negative, saying "We positively won't buy from this company. We'll decide not to purchase from that company." That's going to be a critical issue also in business-to-business and intermediary markets. It's not whether you have a particularly strong environmental performance. If there is a certain thing you haven't done, then that's a de-selection criterion. That may also increasingly come into government procurement. (Martin Charter)

I think sometimes it comes from competitive pressure. This is the one we are most interested in. Our basic model has been to work with high-leverage, bright, early adapters of natural capitalism and help them achieve such conspicuous success at it that their rivals are forced to follow suit or lose share. (Amory Lovins)

"We could lose our competitive advantage"

The Objection:

"Our CSR measures are paying off. We are saving expenses, it is easier to attract and retain top talent, our employees are energized and innovative in their contributions to the success of a company they are proud of, our revenue has improved, and surveys say our reputation has benefited from our actions. As promised, our CSR strategies are yielding us a competitive advantage over others in our industry.

"So why would we want to tell the world how we did it? Companies we compete with would just copy our ideas, catch up fast, and perhaps even pass us. We prefer not to disclose our secrets. Our competitors can figure it out on their own."

A Response:

"Giving away trade secrets would be crazy. It is a question of how detailed your discussions of your CSR efforts are. It's common knowledge that you can save over half your energy bill just by changing lighting fixtures to energy-efficient models, but disclosing blueprints for a re-engineered manufacturing process that improves worker productivity, quality, materials use, energy efficiency, and waste reduction would be a bit much. Saying you did it hints at the possibility and reinforces your commitment to CSR. Not revealing the details protects your competitive lead.

"There is strength in numbers, so there is merit in not being a lonely leader. If more companies acknowledge the benefits they are harvesting from CSR strategies, it helps build a critical mass of companies that can be respected consultants on industry and government policies to encourage CSR activities. Together, they can help identify ways to level the playing field so that sustainable practices are rewarded instead of being penalized, as is all too often the case. This will put competitors that lag you on sustainability initiatives in catch-up mode, which strengthens, not weakens, your competitive advantage.

"Also, remember that it is a lot easier for competitors to copy products than it is for them to clone culture. Once you have diffused sustainability strategies throughout your organization, it is impossible for any other company to duplicate your success. When sustainability is that integrated, it gives you a unique and protected competitive advantage."

The inability to quantify the financial benefits is self-explanatory. It is fundamental to the business case .... When you want to champion the benefits, if you don't have the tangible numbers that you can put in front of people who are used to having those kinds of numbers, it's difficult to spread the commitment. (Devin Crago)

If you are going to run a more sustainable company, the first thing you have to run is a profitable company. Green can be a part of it, but if that is the sole driver for your company, you are probably not going to make it. There is this strange bedfellow that must be considered — the customer. We feel that we must work within a "sustainability space," an acceptable area bounded by the triple bottom line, which certainly includes profitability and cash flows.

Being committed to sustainable development, we are going to scrutinize our products and services within this "sustainability space," and we are going to make the best economical choice we can, balancing sustainability with the bottom line. Sometimes we have to make decisions that are purely economic. If we are not successful economically, we will not exist. Once an enterprise ceases to exist, it no longer participates and influences nothing.

We're running a corporation. This type of enterprise has limitations based on its obligations to its shareholders. However, we are committed to running a business in a manner that emphasizes sustainability as an asset to build value. We believe this inherently, but we cannot go crazy and let the "greenness" of a product drive the customer and his satisfaction out of the equation. There are always discussions of where a new product or service fits within our "sustainability space." We might be critical of ourselves and say, "This product is not 'green' enough. I want something perfectly 'green' before it goes out." Of course, that's what a lot of NGOs would like everyone to do, but technology development just doesn't work that way. Technology development is always improved, however, when it is performed within the limits of a space bounded by the triple bottom line rather than consideration of only profitability.

When I began in this business in the 1970s, there was no discussion of "social responsibility" within our design teams. Now, consideration of a product's impact on people, planet, and profits begins with the initial brainstorming for its development and continues throughout its lifecycle. We have found that this expansion of our definition of success increases the value of products for our customers. (Sam Moore)

Inhibiter # 3: Weak Business Case

Previously, I referred to the reasons companies gave for adopting sustainability practices, as reported by the PricewaterhouseCoopers' "2002 Sustainability Survey Report." The same survey found that the top three reasons 25% of US respondents were *not* engaging in sustainability were:

- No clear business case (82%)
- Lack of key stakeholder interest (62%)
- Lack of senior management commitment (53%)[18]

We have already addressed the second and third objections, but lack of a clear business case is the number one objection to sustainability. Other objections may camouflage it, but lack of a compelling business case was the objection most stressed by the experts — the assumption that costs outweigh benefits. If it made good business sense to adopt sustainability strategies, why would executives not do it? Accordingly, the holy grail of the sustainability movement has been a compelling business case, one that acknowledges costs but also thoroughly accounts for the value of CSR's co-benefits.

How do CEOs express their skepticism about sustainability's business case? Six concerns cause pushback on the business case for sustainability.

- "We're already doing enough. We can't afford to do more."
- "I need short-term results. Sustainability is about long-term results."
- "Perverse subsidies erode our business case."
- "Investments in CSR don't meet our payback criteria."
- "If CSR made such good business sense, we'd already be doing it."
- "It's too good to be true. It's not credible."

We look at these next.

If you are asking why companies have not committed to sustainability, a lot of companies would say that they have. A lot of companies that I would say hadn't, would claim to have done so. There really is a continuum of involvement. (Martin Whittaker)

This is a particularly intriguing objection. These companies are not saying they don't agree with aggressive social and environmental policies and practices. They feel they already have them. "We're doing fine. Why should we do more? What's the problem?" (Susan Burns)

The last one on my list [of why companies ignore sustainability strategies] is assuming "We've done that already. We're already in compliance. We already got this environmental award. We have all these smart engineers and if there were any further way to save our resources cost-effectively, they'd have done it by now." (Amory Lovins)

Another thing is the real lack of understanding what the problem is — the whole notion of not only maintaining but restoring the carrying capacity of the earth. It is extremely difficult to measure, but until you get your mind around that and sit down to figure out how you are going to deal with that, it is too easy to pick the low-hanging fruit or say, "Aren't we wonderful because we do X or Y." Then someone like me comes along and says, "That's not good enough," and they say, "These guys can never be satisfied." (David Powell)

It is still easy to gloss over in the environmental report. A client once described peanut butter as a verb. It is so easy to peanut butter over warts with an environmental report and putting a senior person in charge of sustainability. You know — find the good projects we are doing anyhow and put a sustainability spin on them. That's kind of tongue in cheek, but it is still easy to peanut butter over warts. (Gib Hedstrom)

"We're already doing enough. We can't afford to do more."

The Objection:

"I agree that companies should be socially and environmentally responsible. We are, as our Environment, Health, and Safety (EHS) report shows. We are reducing our pollution, cutting workplace accidents, and saving energy. At considerable cost, we have installed filters and other devices to cut our emissions to water and air. We give to local charities as much as we can. We treat our people well and support diversity.

"Maximizing shareholder returns is paramount. We are doing all the stuff we are supposed to and it is already costing us too much. Give us a break."

A Response:

"What you have described is a great start. However, what you are describing are foundational costs rather than investments. Especially in the US, corporate citizenship is often viewed as synonymous with compliance with regulations and corporate philanthropy.[19] CSR is more than altruistic philanthropy that donates money to high-profile social causes, or good HR practices, or a good EHS track record. Instead, CSR includes strategic philanthropy that leverages the firm's unique core competencies to make contributions that others cannot, and which have a direct relationship to its industry. Reputational capital accounts for an increasing component of corporate market value, and therefore smart donations pay dividends to shareholders. However, CSR goes far beyond philanthropy.

"To reap the full benefits of CSR strategies, the company needs to re-brand itself as a company committed to environmental and social responsibility, integrate sustainability considerations into critical decision processes, and ensure that the business benefits of being proactive are reaped. CSR that is not maximizing profits is risky and costly. Not recognizing the full value of CSR initiatives is usually caused by an overly myopic business case or a misunderstanding that CSR is the responsibility of the HR, donations, or EHS departments. That is just majoring in the minors — they are small pieces of the total sustainability picture. Ensuring that the full spectrum of potential benefits from CSR initiatives is considered helps reframe their costs as strategic business investments that maximize shareholder value."

Another obstacle is what I call the "disconnect from the business trinity." The current business trinity is a high probability of significant financial gain by Friday. Sustainability is the possibility of an unknown financial gain sometime in the future. It is a complete disconnect. (Steve Rice)

When corporations are in a financial pinch, they revert back to their primal instincts and protect the almighty dollar. In tough times, companies need short-term economic benefits. Leaders that don't deliver them aren't around long. (William Blackburn)

The market, just by its own nature, forces companies to think in the short term, quarter to quarter, which means people have their heads down pushing to get the stock price up at any price. As a business, you can't ignore the short-term reality, but if you want to be around for any length of time, and your shareholders are interested in creating value over more than a three-year time frame, companies have an obligation to consider sustainability strategies. (Devin Crago)

CEOs are beholden to short-term investors and day trader mentalities .... I was talking to a CEO about a year ago and asked him what he spent most of his time doing. He said, "I spend most of my time explaining to the analysts why our profits are up 23% and our share price is down 42%." That really had an impact on me. Here you have a talented person who is going around trying to justify or explain why the share price is down. So the thing that is driving CEOs' and executives' decisions is the short-term share price and analyst and investment community pressure to keep the share price up. It's like a dog being twisted by the tail. (Laurent Leduc)

The influence of stock options and share price on corporate behavior is tragic. I'm a big capitalist at heart, but the thing I find most damaging to both business and society is the way we have structured things to drive short-term behavior. (Steven Cross)

"I need short-term results. Sustainability is about long-term results."

The Objection:

"Much as I recognize the benefits of sustainability, shareholders demand short-term results and don't have the patience to await long-term results. Wall Street pressure for quarterly growth is relentless. Without good quarterly results, the stock price will drop. If the stock price drops, shareholders get upset. So does the board. Executives with stock options are affected. The stock price and the short-term quarterly focus prevent us from having the luxury of long-term sustainability initiatives.

"Public companies are ruthless. CEOs who can't deliver the goods on a steady, quarterly basis are toast. I'd be jeopardizing my job and shirking my fiduciary responsibilities to shareholders if I took my eye off short-term numbers."

A Response:

"First, I agree that executives of publicly traded companies are mercilessly driven by shareholders' unrelenting short-term expectations of quarter-to-quarter growth and a rising stock price. However, CEOs are also charged with the long-term health of the organization. Next year's quarterly target is this year's long-term plan. If CEOs intend to be around for a while, it makes sense for them to protect time for attention to future returns as well as today's. It is not a question of paying attention to important long-term opportunities instead of urgent short-term ones. You have to look at both. An integrative corporate vision of sustainability drives everyday decision making and defines short- and long-term success. CSR is a strategic investment in the future, and smart leaders pride themselves on making good investments.

"Secondly, the perception that you have to grow old waiting for sustainability investments to pay off is wrong. As we discussed before when you said, 'We're too busy,' 3M's success with its Pollution Prevention Pays (3P) program reinforces that CSR reaps short-term dividends by eliminating or reducing a pollutant, saving energy or materials, avoiding pollution control equipment, or increasing sales.[20] Smart CSR initiatives maximize shareholder returns in both the short and long term.

"Third, companies that set aside ethical and responsible behavior to temporarily meet expectations of fevered stockholders usually set themselves up for a fall. Enron, anyone?"

Fiscal reform is critical to driving sustainability forward. There are many perverse subsidies and perverse regulations out there. We see some of those around cogeneration, where companies have been impeded by provincial regulations and taxation rules where it has not been to their benefit to do it. The current fiscal system tends to tax or provide a disincentive for things we want, such as employment, but provides no disincentive for things we do not want, such as pollution. From a regulatory perspective, there are not enough carrots out there. And maybe not enough sticks. (Marlo Raynolds)

I think the biggest problem is implicit or explicit subsidies. If alternative energy got half the subsidies that the fossil fuel industry does, it would be attractive. You either level the playing field with subsidies or you eliminate them. Sometimes companies say, "I agree with you, but the subsidy exists, so what am I supposed to do about it?" (David Powell)

We need to plug the tax and depreciation laws. Get rid of perverse subsidies that encourage unsustainable consumption of natural and living capital. Change the way we do discounting. I envision a world of "demurrage" — a charge on hoarding money, or what Bernard Lietaer calls a "sustainability fee," which is mathematically equivalent to negative interest rates — for discounting investments in sustaining natural, human, and social capital. When a sustainability (demurrage) fee is charged, or negative interests are used in discounting, the future becomes more valuable over time, which is exactly the opposite of what happens with our positive interest rate discounting. During the great cathedral-building era of the Middle Ages, they employed demurrage to encourage and justify these century-long building efforts. Using negative interest rates in an NPV formula allows us to justify planting trees that mature in 100 years or building sustainable, living economies. (Mark Anielski)

The second one, and excuse my French on this, but the tax system is [messed up]. There should be a tax on consumption. The current tax system is so complicated and tends to emphasize the wrong things. (Sam Moore)

"Perverse subsidies erode our business case"

The Objection:

"As we come to grips with how we can be better stewards of the environment, it is becoming obvious we have to pay a premium for some sustainable options. That is especially true if we are to reduce our greenhouse gas emissions by cutting back on fossil fuels. Green energy from wind, solar, run-of-the-river hydro, biomass, and geothermal is more expensive than heavily subsidized fossil fuel and nuclear alternatives. That means we have to cover the green energy premium from our energy efficiency savings, instead of being able to flow all those savings to our bottom line, weakening our business case for doing the right CSR thing. We were hoping for big net benefits, not a break-even project. It makes the business rationale for all our effort to green our corporate energy sources less compelling."

A Response:

"There is no question that government subsidies to the fossil fuel and nuclear industries create a very unlevel playing field for green energy. Although not yet approved by the Senate, the US House of Representatives passed an Energy Bill in 2001 that would give away more than $38 billion in spending subsidies and tax breaks to oil, gas, coal, nuclear power, and other polluting industries.[21] Green energy assistance is pitifully small compared to 'perverse subsidies' that foster unsustainable personal and industrial habits. For now, I agree that market signals for environmentally smart material, energy, water, and building alternatives are not helpful, making commitment to green alternatives an unnatural act in some jurisdictions.

"Even so, the good news is that it still pays off. The premium for greener energy can be more than offset by the savings from today's smart eco-efficiency approaches. Rather than waiting for governments to convert perverse subsidies to sustainability subsidies, it is smart to get on with your green initiatives and position your company to quickly reap even greater savings as market signals are better balanced in the future.

"Actually, even with perverse subsidies, the business case for sustainability is so strong that perhaps the counterchallenge should be, 'What is the business case for not integrating sustainability into your business strategies?'"

We need to understand how to address their concerns in their language. That's not always straightforward. In almost every plant we go into, we find that operating engineers have been told to do a one- or one-and-a-half- or two-year simple payback on energy savings, which is on the order of six times their marginal cost of capital. The comptroller never bothered to find the "Rosetta stone" for translating between the discounted cash-flow measures she uses and the simple payback metric. You actually put these two people at the same table, and the comptroller says, "My after-tax return target is 17%," or whatever the number is.

Then you say, "You realize that you could be telling this engineer, then, to go for about five-and-a-half years, say, simple payback."

"Now, where do you get that?"

"Well, here's the formula."

"Oh! So he's way under-investing in energy efficiency."

"Yes, because you told him to do an 18-month simple payback. You have to tell him what you want in his language."

Lack of internal communication is very common .... The counterarguments have to be specific, they have to be in the right language for the specialists you are dealing with — law, accountancy, public affairs, HR, IT. (Amory Lovins)

I sit on the environmental advisory committee of the university. We are always frustrated because the payback on green design of buildings is too long even though it will cost them more to operate them in the long run. The operations people are tearing their hair and saying, "We get handed this damn building and I have to maintain it. To save money upfront, it is costing me more in the long run and has negative environmental consequences, as well" ....

That is another major impediment. How can you afford to spend X amount of capital now to save 2 X later on operating expenses? I don't have X right now. That is a huge problem. Either they don't have the money now or the payback period is too long. (David Powell)

"Investments in CSR don't meet our payback criteria."

The Objection:

"You say we should treat some costs associated with our sustainability programs as investments of capital, not expenses. Okay, suppose we did. Our capital budgeting process has required hurdle rates [the minimum rate of return required on capital invested in a project] and payback periods [the time it takes to recover the initial investment in the project]. From our experience and what we have heard from others, some capital projects that are required for us to get maximum CSR benefits, like major building retrofits and production line redesign and retooling, do not meet our investment criteria.

"Even if they do, they are competing with other capital projects that often have better rates of return on investment [ROIs] or payback periods, so sustainability investments don't make the cut as candidates for limited available capital. They are good ideas, but are not good enough to make it through our CFO's capital budgeting process. It is not personal, it's business."

A Response:

"Sure, some CSR capital projects will be approved and others will be challenged, postponed, or rejected. That's life in the corporate world and it is true for any capital project. Sometimes sustainability champions' paranoia makes them lose sight of that reality.

"There are a couple of thoughts that might support a more favorable decision, though. First, make sure you are talking the CFO's language. ROI and payback period calculations can lead to very different go/no-go decisions — ROI is preferable. Secondly, make sure a full set of present and future stakeholder costs and benefits are included in the ROI calculation, not just traditional ones. For example, employee productivity gains in day-lit retrofitted facilities can far surpass energy bill savings and should be included in retrofit ROI calculations.[22] The ROI of other projects competing for capital funds may suddenly look iffy by comparison. Thirdly, propose that some financial returns from CSR initiatives be squirreled away in a special rotating pot of capital to fund some CSR-related capital projects, using different hurdle rate and ROI criteria.[23]

"This is one case where clarifying language is crucial. It pays to clarify what terms the CFO is most focused on."

There is an underlying skepticism that sustainability pays off. Many business leaders have been brainwashed, and they think a compelling business case is too good to be true. It is the environment or the economy, not both. This belief has been indoctrinated in society, and abetted — if only by default — by many business schools. (Rodney White)

One of my favorite quotes from Matthew Kiernan, the founder of Innovest, is the old adage about two economists walking along the sidewalk together and there's a hundred dollar bill lying on the ground. Neither of them picks it up because it is just impossible in the free market that there could be a real hundred dollar bill just sitting there. (Devin Crago)

At the top of my list is not seeing what's right under your nose. Not noticing that you are wading ankle-deep in low-hanging fruit that's already fallen down and mushing up around the ankles and meanwhile the tree is putting out a whole new crop. Not having *muda* [the Japanese word for waste, purposelessness, or futility] spectacles — you know, the special glasses that let you see waste that's designed in. A lot of my role in plant visits is just to walk around asking dumb questions. There are lots of stories there. (Amory Lovins)

Executives don't understand sustainability, partly because the ideology of capitalism, which is hedonistic and financial wealth maximizing without limits, cannot be reconciled with an economy of ethics that includes subsistence, frugality, self-sufficiency, and "enough," or in another word: sustainability. They went to school, got their MBAs and learned the art of making money, are making a million dollars a year, and you want to tell them they are not doing it right? "Get serious. I'm doing fine, thank you very much." (Mark Anielski)

"If CSR made such good business sense, we'd already be doing it"

The Objection:

"I find it rather amazing that you say the business case for sustainability is so compelling — that we could increase our profit by 38% if we commit the company to CSR strategies, and that an estimate that big could possibly be the low end of the range of possibilities. We'd kill for a 10% improvement and pride ourselves on running a lean and mean operation. How could we have missed these benefits?

"Frankly, suggesting that we have somehow left that much money on the table is verging on being insulting. We are smart, aggressive, highly paid executives. Surely we would have discovered these benefits and captured them by now if they were real."

A Response:

"My apologies. My intent wasn't to be insulting — just to get your attention. In fact, I factored down the assumptions derived from hundreds of real documented cases several times to get the increased profit down to just 38%. The reason the profit increase is still so high is that the quantification methodology is more holistic and complete than previous attempts. It includes human resources co-benefits, risk-management aspects, and potential revenue opportunities that could result if a company re-branded itself as being serious about sustainability strategies. You may be pleasantly surprised that your potential returns are actually higher than those for the composite company used in my model.

"One reason smart leaders like you miss the potential from CSR is they are locked in a limiting mindset. I remember being locked in a limiting paradigm as an IBM sales manager in the early 1980s when IBM first introduced personal computers. I was firmly convinced my quota for PC sales was impossible. When someone jokingly suggested I change my selling paradigm from door-to-door salesman to department-store operator, it triggered breakthrough thinking that enabled me to make ten times my 'impossible' quota that year. Same person, same product, same territory, different thinking, very different results. At the time it was a breakthrough. Now the idea is ho-hum, just as using CSR as an enabling lens on business strategies will be soon. If you think of CSR as a strategic, integrative business paradigm instead of a compliance paradigm, the business possibilities will blow you away."

The business case needs to be quite specific to their business, their situation, and not generic. People go, "Yeah, yeah, but what's the situation in my industry or my company?" when they see the generic business case. To get to that level of specificity requires company-specific effort that includes things that only they themselves will know. (Don Reed)

The lack of a business model is still there. What does business sustainability actually mean? Let's see the financials on it. That's a key issue. (Martin Charter)

One of the biggest obstacles is the assumption that the costs are too great and that the benefits are too fuzzy. You clearly discuss that in your book. That is really important. (David Powell)

"It's too good to be true. It's not credible."

The Objection:

"I see how you work through each line item in your financial business case model, and I understand how you derived your assumptions from benefits that companies have actually achieved from their best practices in sustainability. Each detailed benefit looks okay. It is the size of the total that I have trouble with, especially for us. It is just not credible.

"Maybe the companies you studied were in other countries, in other industries, different sizes, or at a different stage in their growth than we are. Although you say you don't start counting the benefit until its cost has been repaid by its savings, something must be missing. It is too good to be true."

A Response:

"I understand your amazement. At first I, too, was surprised at the size of the potential profit improvement. There is no guarantee that you will capture the full range of benefits that others have or that you can replicate their best practices in your environment. You may already have a head start and have captured some of the benefits. On the other hand, you may have missed some co-benefits that deserve to be included.

"You are the experts and you know your company best. What you might want to do is insert your company's financial parameters into the spreadsheet used to quantify the financial benefits,[24] tailor the assumptions to reflect your experience and best judgment about what is possible for you, and see how compelling the CSR business case is for your company. Some benefits may be lower than what others have achieved. Some may be higher. The model assumes it takes five years to realize the full value of CSR benefits. You may be able to accelerate some, and others may take longer.

"Only when you see the benefits calculated using your company's own data will the credibility gap be closed. Try it."

"
Your commitment to sustainable development is shaped by how you see the world evolving. A lot of people miss information. We have tried to put something together called "Tomorrow's Markets," a collection of 19 trends that the WBCSD [World Business Council on Sustainable Development] members selected as the key environmental, social, and economic trends that are going to shape markets and companies.[25] Companies don't have all that information in one place. There are silent or weak signals. They are not something you will read about on the first or second page of the *Financial Times* or the *Wall Street Journal*. The signals that we could be moving towards a social or environmental crisis are weak, gradual and they are complex. You don't get crisp and clear information about risks and opportunities, and you may find out too late. (Claude Fussler)

A skeptical executive pushes back on the business case. Insisting the numbers work is always the gatekeeping, fail-safe argument against something. That is, if you don't want to support something, keep saying you are not satisfied with how the numbers work ... forever. (Mark Milstein)

A manager in Europe sees things very differently from his American counterpart. In Europe, there is no extra land for dumps. The Netherlands is the third-most-densely populated country in the world. One's perspective is driven by where you live .... Germany passed a law in 1991 on designing automobiles for disassembly. The US and Canada would not need a law on that for decades with our low population growth. In Germany, there is no more space for dumps. (Gib Hedstrom)
"

Inhibiter #4: Mindset

Changing someone's mindset is a fun challenge. However, when someone else tries to change ours, it is aggravating. Of course our worldview is correct. If it were not, we would have changed it by now. Besides, it has worked well for us as a foundation for our beliefs, values, and behaviors. Why would we change?

Our mindsets include assumptions about how the world works. There are remarkably impervious master programs stored in our brains that tell us how best to behave in the world. They are independent of intelligence and motivation. In fact, smart people are especially defensive about their worldviews to avoid the potential embarrassment of having to admit that perhaps their reasoning, premises, and inferences are incorrect.[26]

Our whole belief system is based on its ability to persist in the face of contradictory evidence. Once a belief is entrenched, it is a given. We don't need supporting evidence, and we defend against even small suggestions that might be the thin edge of a big wedge penetrating the fortress of our beliefs, which are essential to our survival in a complex world. Our brains need to maintain a sense of wholeness, consistency, and control in life.[27] They unconsciously filter and dismiss ideas that jeopardize our intertwined fundamental philosophies. Worldviews are brittle. Pick at one peripheral belief and the whole structure might start to crumble.

Thinking of CSR as costly, regulation-driven, philanthropic gestures on the periphery of real business is consistent with a mental model that the sole purpose of business is to maximize shareholder value. If sustainability is presented as a worthy end for business to pursue in partnership with all stakeholders, it is perceived as an attack on a sacred economic model. Instead, smart sustainability champions meet executives where they are — where their mindsets say their priorities should be. Is it the role of CEOs to maximize shareholder value and improve profits? Terrific. Show how corporate responsibility is a means to accomplish that real business goal.

The evolution of executives' mindsets on the sustainability journey will occur at a pace and manner of the executives' choosing, as they gradually "get it" at a more profound level. But it is their choice, not yours. Acknowledging their initial mindset is critical to our credibility as sustainability champions.

Figure 5.3: The *Wizard of Id* on Global Warming

Reprinted by permission of John L. Hart FLP and Creators Syndicate, Inc.

"What environmental and social problems?"

The Objection:

"From what I hear, all the concern about environmental degradation and social problems is a lot of hooey. For every scientist who says the climate is changing, there is one who says there's no problem. In fact, didn't a Swedish professor who used to belong to Greenpeace write a book that debunks all the 'sky is falling' rhetoric of environmentalists?

"Until the debate about the environmental stuff is settled, I think the best approach is to get on with doing what we've always done."

A Response:

"I understand how you might feel the scientific community is evenly divided on some of the big questions like climate change. When you look behind the news stories, however, you'll see the number of scientists raising alarms is far higher than the number saying we have nothing to worry about. For example, the book you are referring to, *The Skeptical Environmentalist*, is by Bjorn Lomborg, a Danish statistician working at Aarhus University in Denmark.[28] It was published in 2001 and contended that the state of human welfare, ecosystems, and progress was much better than the litany of ills described by the world's scientists. You should know that after an extensive review, the Danish Committee on Scientific Dishonesty concluded in 2003 that Lomborg was guilty of systematically biased representation of the facts, selective use of statistics, and scientific dishonesty.[29] Rest assured that the majority of scientists are warning us we can't continue exploiting natural resources as we are. As early as 1992, 1,700 of the world's leading scientists, including the majority of Nobel laureates in the sciences, issued the 'World Scientists' Warning to Humanity' about the state of the planet's air, water, soil, forests, oceans, and living species.[30] Things have not improved since then.

"Some say the last refuge of scoundrels is uncertainty. There will always be scientists who point out that we can't be sure about ecological problems — that they are just theories. The 'Precautionary Principle' says we should be careful if we are not sure, because by the time we are sure, it may be too late. So don't wait for certainty any more than you would when managing any risk. Whether you believe the science is less important than if other stakeholders believe it and are acting on it. Manage that risk."

"I don't really have a name for this impediment. It occurs when companies believe that it's a power play. Essentially, they believe if they give in to this "socialist agenda," they will tip the balance of power to favor the non-capitalist groups. I'm talking in colorful terms here to make the point. There are groups that believe that all this talk about corporate sustainability and corporate social responsibility is some type of socialist conspiracy, so to speak. They believe it's all about giving additional power to the NGOs of the world that have no vested interests in these companies, so it is an unraveling of the capitalist system, and an undermining the responsibility of CEOs and executives to the shareholders. (Mel Wilson)

Companies don't "get it." People do. Most companies have been based upon the Milton Friedman model of economic thinking. There is no corporate social conscience, as shown in the film *The Corporation*. The people in the company have it. (Mitch Gold)

1514: Copernicus produces the first feasible model of a sun-centered system.
1597: Galileo says the Copernican model of the universe makes sense.
1632: Distribution of Galileo's *Dialogue Concerning the Two Chief World Systems* is stopped by Pope Urban VIII. The Pope refers Galileo's case to the Inquisition.
1633: Galileo is interrogated before the Inquisition and sentenced to house arrest for an indefinite term.
1641: Galileo dies, blind and under house arrest.
1820: The Inquisition is abolished.
1835: Galileo's *Dialogue* is taken off the Vatican's list of banned books.
1992: The Catholic Church formally admits that Galileo's views on the solar system are correct.
— "Chronology of the Trial of Galileo" from the Famous Trials website[31]

"All this environmental and social stuff is anti-capitalist propaganda"

The Objection

"I get a little suspicious that all this rush to ill-defined corporate social responsibility is a thinly disguised plot by labor unions to promote their socialist agenda. Capitalism is what made this country great. It makes sense that the risk-takers and innovators be rewarded for their courage and accomplishments in a market economy. We don't need more misguided regulations slowing up progress, and we don't need higher taxes getting in the way of shareholders' returns on their hard-earned investments. Suggesting that businesspeople are supposed to feed, clothe, shelter, and educate the poor as well as save the world is ridiculous. No reasonable, informed person would suggest that is the purpose of business.[32]

"Social responsibility is just code for socialism, and socialism is just one step away from communism. I see corporate social responsibility as the thin edge of a big wedge bent on destroying our hard-fought capitalism, free market, competition, and democracy."

A Response

"You are reinforcing how sustainability language is not helpful. It is easy to see how corporate *social* responsibility sounds like a communist plot. The good news is that it is just the opposite. Smart sustainability is embedded into the management system to help set priorities, shape strategies, and choose alternatives that produce competitive advantage. It is about strategic investments, not misguided costs. Sustainability-oriented strategies enable a corporation to protect its license to operate, practice enlightened self-interest, generate higher shareholder returns, and reinforce the positive power of responsible capitalism. They are more a plot to promote capitalism than destroy it.

"It took a while for the Catholic Church to agree that the earth not being the center of the universe was compatible with its dogma. Such views were considered heresy in Galileo's time, just as a broader role for business in society is viewed as a dangerous idea by some businesspeople today. Be sure that you leave face-saving space to capitalize on a beneficial idea that originally looked like a threat."

If every company chases only those sustainable development projects with a business case, do we end up with significant gaps in the range of social and environmental issues that get attention? What about issues such as homelessness — how many companies do we know that are chasing this issue because they find it sexy or of strategic business value?

This is where considerations regarding the role of governments in promoting corporate sustainable development practices become important. How can governments make sure they are leveraging what companies are doing and helping channel it into areas that may otherwise be overlooked? This is an important area for consideration in the future. (Ron Yachnin)

CSR goes beyond looking at a company's philanthropic efforts. CSR is not about how companies spend a proportion of their profits. It is about the more fundamental question of how they produce their goods and provide their services. It is about how they make their profits. While philanthropy can be a worthy element of a company's external affairs strategy, it is not an indicator of responsible behavior. — Dr. Gary Dirks, president of BP China[33]

"CSR is the government's domain, not ours"

The Objection:

"Saving the world is not my responsibility. It is unfair to pile a whole lot of feel-good environmental and social responsibilities on our already overloaded shoulders. In fact, as Milton Friedman would say, 'The business of business is business.' It is irresponsible — effectively, theft — to undertake CSR initiatives using funds that rightfully should be shareholder returns.[34] The sole purpose of a corporation is to enhance shareholder returns. Do-gooder shareholders can decide what causes to support with their dividends, not us.

"Besides, who are we to decide what cause to cherry-pick among all the worthy ones out there? We're not trained to do that and would probably mess it up. We know how to make profit. We pay taxes so that governments can look after the stuff they are trained to do. If we started to meddle in the government's cultural, political, and educational 'public interest' jurisdiction, we'd be setting ourselves up for more regulations on how they want us to do their job, which would be stupid.[35] Our taxes enable governments to fulfill their role and we applaud their good work. We leave social programs to the experts."

A Response:

"Sustainability does not contradict Friedman's idea that the fundamental purpose of a corporation is to enhance shareholder returns, it simply broadens how executives go about doing this. CSR is not simply about obeying the law and paying taxes. It is about managing the demands and expectations of opinion leaders, customers, local communities, governments, and environmental NGOs. It is about managing risk and reputation, and investing in community resources on which companies depend.[36] The business of business is staying in business. Ironically, smart sustainability initiatives contribute to shareholder value and support Friedman's contention."

"CSR is not philanthropic 'giving away' of shareholder returns. CSR is a process by which the firm manages its relationships with a variety of influential stakeholders who can have a real influence on its license to operate and reputation.[37] It is a strategic investment in the company's future, just as much as R&D is. It ensures the reputation component of a corporation's market valuation is an asset, not a liability. It's good business."

Another impediment is viewing sustainability drivers as environmental, and therefore sticking responsibility in the corporate environmental, health, and safety (EHS) function. If you stick it in EHS, it is almost guaranteed to fail. (Gib Hedstrom)

My view is that most executives do not have an integrated view of sustainability — that "We are not doing it because ...." I do not give the business credit for that sophisticated thinking. The organizational matrix, the size, the complexity often gets in the way of an integrated view, and I think it is a missed opportunity. How do you get into someone's mind space so they recognize that? That is an enormous challenge. (Neil Cooney)

The main reason there isn't more action on sustainability is that people don't see that it adds shareholder value. They don't see it as a business issue or they don't see the paths that would enable them to add value. (Don Reed)

A very small group have not committed because they do not think their industry is relevant to the environment. For example, MCI WorldCom would say, "Sure, we look at sustainability. We have an engineer who goes out and makes sure we don't break any rules when we're laying the cables." To them, that's sustainability. There is absolutely no awareness of the role of telecommunications in creating a more sustainable society in terms of dematerialization, avoiding unnecessary travel, and things like that, and calculating reduced emissions the way Deutsche Telecom are doing. (Martin Whittaker)

A more charitable reason is that the executives have simply never thought about the potential business benefits. Their lack of action is not deliberate. It is just a lack of understanding and lack of awareness of options. (Stephen Hill)

"I never thought of it that way"

The Objection:

"You keep talking about how committing to CSR is a strategic business decision, but I must admit it never crossed my mind that it might be. Environmental issues are the responsibility of our EHS department. They ensure we don't pollute and that we keep our noses clean on regulations and legal liabilities. Social and philanthropic concerns are dealt with by the experts in our corporate relations department — they interface with the community, government, and organizations that we donate to.

"Meanwhile, the rest of us get on with running the business and making the money that funds their activities. It works fine for us."

A Response:

"What you describe is quite typical in large organizations. The Work Foundation's 2003 survey of 277 human resources specialists in the UK found that, despite the advantages CSR offers for generating public trust in the post-Enron era, 58% of organizations surveyed have no strategy for social responsibility or corporate citizenship.[38] Of these, 32% say they have never thought of a CSR strategy, 27% say it is not a business priority, and 13% have never even heard of CSR. Experts in EHS and corporate affairs are respected but marginalized when it comes to strategic business decisions. At the corporate, business unit, and operational decision-making levels, sustainability factors are an afterthought, at best.

"As we have discussed before, a whole new world of possibilities opens up when corporate responsibility is considered as an enabling agent for innovation, productivity, leadership, teamwork, revenue, savings, and profit. Done properly, it can ensure better business decisions are made and build the company's reputation. Start thinking of it that way, and everything else falls into place."

In many cases the environment just generates a negative reaction. "Well, you know, the environment stuff, right?" Kyoto is a prime example of that. It always evokes a defensive reaction. Because the door to sustainability is usually opened through the environment, it ends up being managed to a level like "What do we have to do here to keep ourselves out of trouble?" They don't come at it from a broad management, decision-making point of view around "How do we manage overall?" (Louise Comeau)

Beyond environmental compliance, at least in Canada, many citizens and companies think environmental responsibility is about costs, penalties, and fines — bad news. It is at least a risk, it could be expensive, it means filing things, keeping our nose clean, having auditors. It is a bad-news cost of doing business. Some businesspeople's eyes would pop wide open if they heard a Rick George [Suncor] or Travis Engen [Alcan] describe what it is all about to them. There is a lot of ignorance and myth out there about what this is all about. (Alan Willis)

We don't use the "S" word [sustainability]. [Chuckle] Our terminology depends on what we are talking about. If we mean "natural capitalism," we say that. If we mean "ecologically restorative practices," we say that. If we mean "resource productivity," we say that. We try to be more explicit. If we mean "socially responsible behavior," we say that .... We do see some adoption of what you're calling "sustainability" — a word we don't use because it means so much to so many people. (Amory Lovins)

"Environment has negative connotations in business"

The Objection:

"As you admitted before, there is a lot of baggage around the term 'environment.' In the US, it is hard for big business to disassociate the hated, expensive Superfund regulations on pollution liability from the word 'environment.' Since the UN Intergovernmental Panel on Climate Change led the charge in alerting the world to the dangers of climate change, even 'climate change' may evoke negative perceptions because many US businesspeople are not enamored with the United Nations.[39] Of course, left-wing, permanently-panicked tree-huggers don't help the environment's image in business circles, either.

"Fundamentally, two unpopular notions are imprinted on corporate perceptions of environmental issues: regulations (and all the bureaucratic red tape associated with them) and costs (to install expensive filters or retrofits to reduce pollution). Regulations and costs are unpopular in business circles. Therefore, so is the environment. Corporate responsibility includes environmental dimensions, so it gets tarred with the same negative brush."

A Response:

"This is one of the most challenging aspects of sustainability discussions — the baggage around the language we use. As we discussed previously, even the 'social' in 'corporate social responsibility' has caused some to dismiss it as a subversive socialist plot. Word associations are insidious.

"There is no easy answer to this except to acknowledge historical perceptions and move on. When dealing with outside stakeholders, it is especially wise to understand that they may have the same aversion to your language as you have to theirs. Profit may equate with greed in their lexicon. It helps to listen closely to the language the other person uses and echo terms they are comfortable with. You can encourage each other to get behind the labels to the meanings of what you are trying to achieve and to how CSR-grounded approaches can help, rather than debating labels."

All the efforts by government and intergovernmental agencies to try to spread best practices are practically pointless .... We published information about 3M's 3P program all around the world in several languages in 1984, on the tenth anniversary of 3P. We documented and used 3M's examples about how much money you can save doing eco-efficiency, and there was no take-up. It was a waste of time. Everyone documenting the economic value of eco-efficiency and pushing case-study data banks since then has had the same result. (Antony Marcil)

Many companies are not aligned well with, or in touch with, societal, community, or customer values and what their key stakeholders expect of them. (Alan Willis)

It's "They're going to attack me, therefore the hell with the environment." That's really important, especially if the company has a lot of influence in their sector. It is a mindset that "We have a right to do whatever we want." You have people who claim that environmental problems are greatly exaggerated by environmentalists, for example, Lomborg in his book *The Skeptical Environmentalist.* (David Powell)

"How come I don't hear more about this?"

The Objection:

"I am pretty well-read. I make it a point to stay on top of issues that are relevant to my business. I don't see much about sustainability in them. If I do see an article on it, it is about how a company is being sued, or it debunks climate change predictions. I can't remember seeing articles about sustainability agendas leading to higher profits, or hearing topics like that at industry conferences I attend. Am I missing something?"

A Response:

"At birth, no one slips a copy of *Sustainability for Dummies* into our cribs as a lifelong manual on how things work. It is not a prescribed text in schools or universities. There is no daily 'How are We Doing?' column on the front pages of our newspapers, reporting back on the world's ecological, social, and corporate progress. But the messages are there.

"I don't know about you, but I see what I look for. Emerging themes are sometimes hard to spot. I wonder how much attention Kodak paid to cell phones when they first came out, before they became phone/cameras.

"When I become aware of an issue, suddenly I see articles about it everywhere. Is it just synchronicity, or were they always there and I didn't notice them before or filtered them out? When I started thinking about and researching sustainability issues 15 years ago, I was amazed how much material I found that had been around for years, in sources I had monitored before for leadership, organizational development, innovation, teamwork, and productivity themes. Once I used a sustainability lens, I discovered how many of these same books, journals, and articles were about sustainability as well. I just hadn't noticed that theme before.

"Cross-industry conferences on CSR are usually attended by the converted, although recently CSR topics have been popping up in mainline industry gatherings. The same is true for magazines, journals, and books you read. Now that you are aware of sustainability and its relevance to business, you may be surprised what you (re)discover. Some commentary will be from sustainability skeptics. Some of it will be from CSR champions. Now you are in a more informed position to critically evaluate them and form you own judgments."

They don't understand it. They went to school, got their MBA, are making a million dollars a year, and you want to tell them they are not doing it right? "Get serious. I'm doing fine, thank you very much." Mandating of reporting functions may be a more effective process than moral suasion. (Mitch Gold)

Back in the '80s, there was a huge assumption that the younger the corporate leader, the more environmentally and socially progressive he would be. We had great optimism that by now, many of these people would be in executive positions and the world would be a different place. It didn't turn out that way. There has to be something within the corporate educational and learning system that does not adequately draw the link between environment and economy. The people are very bright, but, too often, they just don't seem to connect the dots to the different elements of sustainability. (Paul Muldoon)

Despite all the good efforts of the corporate and business champions of the sustainability movement, I feel that their efforts to pursue a genuine sustainable economy are impossible without serious understanding and restructuring of the nature of our debt-based money system, which compels all agents in an economy to keep growing and producing more stuff to service a mountain of unrepayable debt, even if these economies have reached a level of satiety, "enough" or "genuine sustainability." (Mark Anielski)

"They didn't talk about CSR in my MBA courses"

The Objection:

"Business leaders are good people, but in my MBA school we were educated to think of the economic well-being of companies as being at odds with, or irrelevant to, the environmental and social well-being of the planet. Business schools encourage students to be compliant with environmental, labor, and human rights regulations, but seldom suggest that there are any significant benefits to be gained from going further.

"Maybe MBA schools have changed since I graduated, but a colleague just finished her executive MBA, and I don't recall her saying anything about sustainability being covered in her courses. If it were a legitimate concern for business, surely they would include it."

A Response:

"Your observation is substantiated by "Beyond Grey Pinstripes 2003," a report by the World Resources Institute and the Aspen Institute.[40] They surveyed 100 MBA schools in 20 countries and determined which business schools ranked the best at integrating social and environmental responsibility into their curricula. Compared to their previous survey in 2001, they found a marginal rise in the infusion of environmental and social-impact management in required core courses such as accounting, economics, finance, marketing, operations, and strategy. However, they found a 70% rise in elective courses with CSR content, which bodes well for future core courses including more soon.

"The 'Beyond Grey Pinstripes' findings show that business schools are still mostly overlooking one of the most compelling win/win business opportunities available to companies. They can support the profit orientation of companies, and at the same time show how a well-executed sustainable development strategy can be one of the largest contributors to savings, revenue, productivity, competitiveness, lower risk, and new markets. Convincingly quantifying the bottom-line benefits of corporate social responsibility is doable. It should be included in required business school courses, and it would be extremely useful in convincing current and future corporate leaders to embrace sustainable development to reap business benefits. Business schools are just catching on to this."

Engaging senior management in sustainability is tough. We have developed an idea bank for our clients' sustainability change agents on how to engage executive decision makers in various parts of the organization in the management discipline of sustainability. They need to create tangible projects that demonstrate the business benefits of sustainability and set up the context for embedding it into the corporate culture. They need to make the business case and show compelling reasons why the company should change. As Scott Noesen, SD manager at Dow Chemical told me one time, "We have to build support for sustainability slowly, one conversation at a time." (Kevin Brady)

Figure 5.4: Two Mental Models of Sustainability Concepts

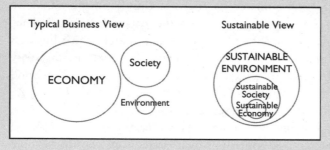

Changing Worldviews Is Tough

We should not be surprised if responses suggested to each objection do not result in gushing gratitude from skeptical executives, thanking us for helping them see the light. We are messing with people's worldviews.

As discussed earlier, your worldview helps you understand how things work and relate to each other. By definition, it is correct. Otherwise you would change it. That is exactly how the skeptical executives feel about their paradigm, an extreme view of which is depicted on the left-hand side of Figure 5.4. If your paradigm matches the model on the right-hand side, trying to ram it down the throats of others is cathartic, but futile.

A U-shaped personal change curve is sometimes used to describe stages we go through when suffering a major loss or traumatic change in our lives. The sequence starts down one side of the U when the prospect of change triggers shock and denial. Then we get into anger and blaming before entering grief and nostalgia. We bottom out when we accept the change and start climbing up the recovery slope, reassessing our values, then committing and adapting to the change, and finally growing and prospering as we integrate the new framework into our lives. If we ask people to change their worldviews, we should expect their initial reaction to be shock, denial, anger, and blaming — just as anyone subjected to a significant change would react.

At the organizational level, there is a 4D-defense that is analogous to early reactions to personal change: Deny that there is a problem or that the organization is contributing to it. Delay by asking for more studies or evidence of a problem. Divide and isolate the heretic(s) who suggest there is a problem or wrongdoing. Discredit the credentials and motives of the proponents of change.

Variations of these personal and organizational reactions are found in the sample skeptical executives' objections. The intent of the responses is to nudge them through their change curves.

When you are gone, all that is left is your reputation. Your legacy. We do care about these things .... I think it takes leadership, foresight, and vision. It has to be incorporated into our core values, and I know we will get there. (Expert B)

My experience is that people have two agendas when buying:
1. The reasons they give you for buying
2. The hidden, real reasons
Most people pretend they are buying out of a logic base — for good, sound, logical reasons. But the more I sell, the more I'm convinced that emotional reasons influence buyer decisions much more than logic ....

In using logic, you show the good sense of investing in your product or service.

In using emotion, you get the prospects visualizing themselves enjoying having it or enjoying how it will make them look to others; or you help create mental pictures in their minds of suffering from suddenly needing it and not having it.

Here are some suggestions for appealing to people's emotions as you demonstrate: get them feeling; get them tasting; get them looking; get them doing; and get them experiencing.

Get them emotionally experiencing the rewards of having your product or service. Get them experiencing the shock or loss of not having it ....

Use vivid word pictures that help them visualize themselves enjoying the benefits of your product or service.

The more you adapt these ideas to what you're selling, the more successful you'll become in influencing buyer behavior.
— Ron Willingham, *The Best Seller!*[41]

What Color Would You Like?

Pssst! Want to know a secret? From my experience, over half of business decisions are made by gut instinct and then retroactively rationalized with hard-nosed data. It is the same way we buy cars. First we decide what car we really want, and then we selectively create the objective criteria that led us to that judgment. Business decisions in the end are made with good judgment, not just calculators.[42]

When I was selling mainframe computers, a "trial close" I sometimes used on a sales call was to casually ask the data-processing director whether red, blue, or ivory computer panels would best fit the décor of the computer room that would proudly showcase the latest-and-greatest leading-edge technology. Chatting about floor plans and color schemes created an emotional desire to have the new computer. Then we would work together to justify it.

So when you are deep into the "carrots and sticks" of the business case with executives, you might consider surfacing for air and ask them whether they would prefer wearing their dark blue or grey pinstripe suit at the annual awards ceremony for being the most respected company in their industry. Criteria for being the most respected company include tough financial attributes as well as other societal dimensions of brand image. Standing a typical argument on its head, you could suggest that they would be shirking their fiduciary responsibilities and leaving money on the table if they did *not* take advantage of sustainability strategies to mitigate risks, improve their corporation's bottom line ... and look like heroes. Then show them how.

Perhaps they could wear the dark blue suit to the "most respected company" ceremony and the grey pinstripe to the "most macho, hard-nosed champion of shareholder returns" ceremony the same year. Just a thought ...

CHAPTER SIX

CONCLUSION

I have looked at three drivers of the first wave of companies already on the sustainability continuum. Some were inspired by a passionate founder whose values-based convictions shaped the environmental and social purpose of the company. Some were shocked by a public relations crisis into revisiting the way they operate or the products they produce. Once they rectified the cause of the criticism, many were pleasantly surprised to discover that a more sustainability-friendly way to conduct business was enhancing business results. A third group of companies in the first wave was concerned about existing or impending legislation and took steps to avoid fines, penalties, or the need for more stringent regulations.

I then examined two emerging drivers of the next wave of companies. Some companies will be attracted by a compelling set of financial benefits that can be realized when sustainability considerations are integrated into corporate strategies. Some will take action to avoid the risk of market forces raising the bar of expectations above their level of corporate responsibility. Many will be motivated by a combination of both emerging drivers. Without a compelling business case, trying to maintain momentum on sustainability would be like pushing a rope.

Anticipating pushback from harried executives, I explored comebacks to 26 likely objections to the relevance of sustainability in current business paradigms.

Stepping back, I will now position the drivers against the five stages on the sustainability continuum, revisit climate change as a seminal mega-issue driving change, review trends in sustainability reporting, and consider five encouraging signs that corporate sustainability's tipping point is close.

Figure 6.1: Stage-to-Stage Drivers

Positioning the Drivers

I have identified three drivers that triggered early corporate responsibility adopters and two emerging drivers. How and when are they effective motivators for the next wave of CSR leaders? What are the most convincing rationales for companies moving to the next stage on the sustainability continuum that I discussed in Chapter 1? It depends where they are on the continuum, as shown in Figure 6.1.

For companies in get-away-with-whatever-you-can Stage 1, enforced regulations or a PR crisis will work. These companies are the sustainability laggards. They may never "get it," insisting to the end that they are just trying to be as efficient as possible and avoiding costly environmental or social measures not strictly required by law.

Compliant companies in Stage 2 will be driven by the pleasant prospect of savings from eco-efficiencies and move beyond compliance to Stage 3. These are often the companies that had a PR crisis, cleaned up their act, and then discovered that the new approach was actually a better way to run a business — increased savings and revenue resulted from their corporate responsibility actions. A high-performance corporate culture helps at this stage. Companies that pride themselves on doing whatever they do very well, once awoken, commit to ensuring they go beyond compliance and never are subject to public embarrassment again.

Transformation from Stage 3 to Stage 4 is not trivial. Risk management expands to ensure the company is better positioned to weather a wider "perfect storm" of potential market force risks on the horizon. These companies capture the benefits of re-branding themselves as responsible corporate citizens and quantify them as business value. Day-to-day corporate decision-making processes ensure sustainability's financial rewards are reaped and accounted for. The momentum feeds on itself as these companies get smarter about how to do well for their stockholders while "doing good" for a wide network of stakholders.

The transition from Stage 4 to Stage 5 is rare. In Stage 5, sustainability becomes a legitimate end in itself, not a means to business ends. Instead of being a co-benefit, making a worthy contribution to society becomes the purpose of the firm. Few public corporations will be able to make this transformation, which does not concern me. A critical mass of companies in Stage 4 would make a world of difference.

There is no bigger problem than climate change. The threat is quite simple; it's a threat to our civilization.
— Professor Sir David King, chief scientific adviser to the UK government[1]

It would be too great a risk to stand by [and] do nothing. Fighting climate change later, when it becomes a serious problem, instead of now, while there's still some chance it can be controlled, could be so disruptive as to cause serious damage to the world's economy.
— Sir John Browne, Group Chief Executive, BP[2]

The Climate Change Lightning Rod

Earlier, I looked at climate change as an ecological mega-issue in the "perfect storm" discussion. As a comprehensive, front-page sustainability issue and a lightning rod for demanding stakeholders, it is the next "ozone hole."[3] Climate change injects a huge amount of uncertainty into our daily affairs. Only recently has the enormity of the implications of this risk factor truly penetrated the minds of the business community.[4] It is a unifying, galvanizing issue that is an energy source for all demanding stakeholders.

The relevance of mega-issues like climate change to corporations is not so much their direct impact, as it is the fallout from unmet expectations that companies should have used their power, influence, and ingenuity to help us avoid the disaster in the first place. Citizens' anger and blame will be stoked by memories of corporate dismissals of environmentalists' earlier dire predictions and by accusations that corporate complicity or willful ignorance allowed climate change to happen — that companies should have taken earlier, stronger steps to eliminate their greenhouse gas emissions and foster green energy alternatives.

Climate change is a national security issue. In 2004, Sir David King, the chief scientific advisor to the British government, urged the United States to take climate change more seriously, saying, "Climate change is the most severe problem we are facing today, more serious even than the threat of terrorism."[5] A leaked Pentagon report in early 2004 echoed the concern that climate change is a threat to national security and global stability. In surprisingly alarmist language, the Pentagon report predicted global chaos, anarchy, and nuclear threats in the next 20 years as nations scramble to secure food, water, and energy supplies, dwindling due to climate change catastrophes.[6] In July 2004, British prime minister Tony Blair declared that climate change is the biggest problem facing the world today.[7]

With luck, these are all just possibilities, and we will not have to face the abyss. Scenario planning exercises are used in corporations to assess possibilities. By including climate change possibilities in strategic planning scenarios, companies can position themselves to weather stakeholder storms and capitalize on stakeholder energy channeled to their support when they proactively work on this critical mega-issue.

The detailed science is still provisional. There are many things we don't know. But science is always provisional and in business we are used to working in circumstances where we don't know all the facts for certain.

You have to make judgments in conditions of uncertainty and in my view the right judgment on the basis of the available evidence is that there is a powerful case for precautionary action. ... I believe the aim of that action should be to limit any increase in the world's temperature to around two degrees Celsius.
— Sir John Browne, Group Chief Executive, BP[8]

Climate Change Predictions

Global temperatures have risen by about 0.6 degrees Celsius since the 19th century, and the average concentration of carbon dioxide in the world's atmosphere has risen from some 280 parts per million to around 370 ppm. The trend is undoubtedly due in large part to substantial increases in carbon dioxide emissions from human activity.[9]

Climate models predict that the Earth's average temperature might increase by between about 1.4°C and 5.8°C over the next 100 years. A warming of this magnitude could significantly alter the Earth's climate. A summer 2003 heat wave killed 15,000 people in France and 1,300 in India.[10] That same year, scientists at the World Health Organization and the London School of Tropical Medicine said that 160,000 people, mostly children, die each year from side effects of global warming — like the spread of malaria, diarrhea, and malnutrition in the wake of warmer temperatures, floods, and droughts — and that number could almost double by 2020, especially in developing nations.[11]

If summer temperatures increase slightly, carbon dioxide levels could double, resulting in a 17% to 28% increase in the number of wildfires and a 143% increase in really severe wildfires.[12] Storm patterns and severity might increase, a rise in sea level would displace millions of coastal residents, and regional droughts and flooding could occur. The agriculture, forestry, and energy sectors could all be significantly affected, with most other sectors being indirectly affected.[13]

Insurance and re-insurance companies are already being hammered by climate change. Over the past 15 years there have been over $1 trillion in economic losses due to "natural" disasters, three quarters of which were directly related to climate and weather. Losses in 2001 totaled $100 billion and appear to be doubling every decade.[14] Insurance companies are reinforcing the message by factoring the cost of global warming into their premiums. Severe weather events are making it harder for companies to get insurance. Worldwide insurance claims for extreme weather events and disasters like drought and forest fires have jumped tenfold in the last 40 years, hitting $55 billion in 2002. The world's second-largest re-insurer, Swiss Re, is telling its corporate clients to come up with strategies for handling global warming or risk losing their liability coverage.[15]

Sharp, non-linear change of the global climate could pose the greatest environmental challenge to our species in the past 10,000 years. We may be far closer to such a threshold than we dare admit. Scientists are particularly concerned about the possibility of a sudden shift in the Atlantic Ocean's currents — a shift that could, paradoxically, make many of us much colder.

Ocean scientists have discovered that the North Atlantic is one of only two places on Earth where large quantities of water descend from the ocean's surface to its depths (the other is near Antarctica). They've also learned that the process is a key element of a planet-wide flow of water — often called the Great Ocean Conveyor — that snakes from the Atlantic through the Indian Ocean and into the Pacific Ocean. The Conveyor plays a vital role in moving the sun's heat energy around Earth.

But the whole phenomenon depends upon vast quantities of water sinking in the North Atlantic, and whether this happens depends in part on the water's salinity. So it seems that the relatively balmy climates of eastern North America and Northern Europe — and more generally the movement of the sun's heat around Earth — are highly sensitive to the balance of fresh and salty water in the North Atlantic.

Global warming could upset this balance. A warmer atmosphere boosts precipitation of rain or snow over the North Atlantic and adjacent lands and oceans, like the Arctic Basin. Global warming is also rapidly melting the region's glaciers and ice sheets, including those covering Greenland. As all this fresh water flows into the North Atlantic, it makes the water arriving in the Gulf Stream from the south less salty and less likely to sink....

So here's the paradox: While Earth is, on the whole, getting hotter — very quickly so by historical standards — some large regions could become much colder, because of radical shifts in the way heat circulates around the planet.

— Thomas Homer-Dixon, "Cold Truths about Global Warming"[16]

Potential for Sudden, Irreversible Disasters

Climate change scientists are particularly concerned we may be on the brink of disrupting the Gulf Stream flow. Why might that happen? As the excerpt on the opposite page from Thomas Homer-Dixon's article says, the Gulf Stream acts as a great oceanic conveyor belt because its warm, salty water sinks when it reaches the North Sea (since it becomes cooler and its salinity makes it relatively dense) and then returns to the South Atlantic tropics via deep ocean currents. If increasingly warm rains and melting Arctic glaciers dilute the water at the North Atlantic end of the Gulf Stream so it is relatively warmer and less salty, the whole conveyor belt could slow down ... or stop. In the same article, Homer-Dixon goes on to describe how researchers have recently found a 20% decline in the amount of deep water flowing southward through a crucial, kilometre-deep channel between the Faroe and Shetland Islands near Scotland.

Why does this matter? A slower or extinct Gulf Stream would produce much more extreme winters in eastern North America. Shipping lanes, rivers, and harbors would freeze far earlier; crops would fail; and our energy use would soar. Northern Europe would be as frigid as Siberia and probably unable to feed itself.[17] The leaked Pentagon report, mentioned above, argues that even a mid-range disruption of the Gulf Stream could generate mass migrations and interstate and civil war across Europe, Asia, and Latin America.[18]

The 2004 movie *The Day After Tomorrow* was a dramatic — and unscientific — depiction of what could happen if the Gulf Stream conveyor belt suddenly stopped. It exaggerated the suddenness of the impact, and the special effects were more sensational than plausible. However, it helped raise awareness and discussion about climate change in a way that scientific debates could not.

I think there is growing pressure from the investment community. Regardless of the pressure for short-term gains, any investment banker will tell you that if a company can demonstrate that it has potential for long-term growth and long-term sustainability, that they're going to be around for a long time, that they are going to continue to grow over a long period, he will reflect those considerations in his investment decisions.

The issue again comes up of transparency. That's what the investment community is pushing for, transparency. Not necessarily more corporate social responsibility, but transparency. As you become more transparent, these issues surface and they need to deal with them. I think it is a growing trend internationally. The UK is very much ahead of the game. The United States is very much ahead of the game in this one.
(Julian Smit)

Shareholders Are Getting Restless

Internationally, pension funds, with assets of over $1 trillion, have begun to use their collective financial muscle to promote greater climate change disclosure and accountability from the world's largest corporations.[19] The United States Public Interest Group says resolutions concerning global warming won about 18% support from shareholders at a dozen or so companies in 2002 and over 25% support at more than twice that number of companies in 2003. Putting this in perspective, an Investor Responsibility Research Center spokesperson said in the 32-year history of shareholder activism on shareholder issues, only board diversity proposals have had shareholder support levels topping an average of 20%.[20] In 2003, shareholder activists filed a record 31 global warming resolutions, up from 19 in the 2002 proxy season, and 6 in 2001[21] — it is the fastest-growing area of shareholder activism.

For the 2004 proxy season, activists filed 28 climate change resolutions at 27 companies. The five largest carbon dioxide emitters among US power companies — American Electric Power, Cinergy Corp., Southern Company, TXU Corp., and Xcel Energy — simultaneously faced global warming and related shareholder resolutions at their 2003 annual meetings.[22] The level of support for the resolutions was 32% at Exxon Mobil, 27% at American Electric Power, 24% at TXU, 23% at Southern, and 21% at Chevron Texaco.[23] Additional resolutions at other big utility companies were withdrawn when the companies agreed to write reports on climate change risks.[24]

Even if they are defeated, resolutions get the attention of companies. Two of America's largest coal-fired generators, American Electric Power and Cinergy, made significant commitments to manage climate change risk, including promises to assess impacts of several legislative proposals that would limit GHG emissions. Chevron Texaco and ConocoPhillips committed to set GHG targets, while Exxon Mobil provided more detailed emissions reports for operations in 2003.[25]

The 13 members of the Investor Network on Climate Risk include state pension funds in California, Connecticut, Maine, New York City, New York State, and Vermont, and other major US pension funds controlling nearly $800 billion in assets.[26] In early 2004, the network called on the US Securities and Exchange Commission to clarify that climate change is indeed a material risk and to require that companies disclose, in corporate security filings, their potential financial exposure from global warming and their plans to respond.[27]

One reason that important elements of the private sector, including some energy producers, have become supporters of policies to reduce emissions is that the trading of reduction credits could become a huge and lucrative business .... It would still require an international agreement to cap emissions at successively lower levels in order to reduce the speed at which climate changes. But the driving dynamic would be provided by the profit motive, not simply regulation and enforcement. Likewise, a market approach would still need agreement on measuring and continually verifying compliance ....

Under the market approach some people — the successful emissions reduction experts, the carbon traders, and the providers of their trading infrastructures, such as lawyers and consultants — will begin to benefit immediately.

Even while the Kyoto process is still struggling for definition and ratification, carbon trading has already begun .... Companies like BP, Shell, and TransAlta set their own reduction targets and established in-house trading systems between different business units. The United Kingdom, Denmark, Norway, and Switzerland have established — or are in the process of establishing — the rules for national trading schemes. In the United States a regional scheme is under development at the Chicago Climate Exchange .... The European Union scheme is scheduled to begin in 2005.

Although these are very early days, it is not impossible to imagine that carbon trading might evolve like other commodity markets. At first trading may be local, perhaps even confined to national boundaries, but these regional schemes will link up to become a global system with international standards for payment and quality.
— Sonia Labatt and Rodney White, *Environmental Finance*[28]

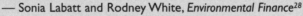

The Carbon Trading Lure

An awakening financial sector has become a powerful catalyst, causing companies to pay more attention to environmental liabilities and risks. When big investors start showing an interest in CSR attributes, sustainability agnostics suddenly get religion.

Enter carbon trading. If/when governments impose limits or caps on the annual amount of CO_2 emissions permitted by a company, the organization has two ways to achieve the reduction. It can either actually reduce its greenhouse gas emissions or purchase a credit from some other company that has exceeded its own required reduction and therefore has a carbon reduction credit to sell. Suddenly a carbon credit becomes a commodity. Commodities are tradable. Mercantile and commodity exchanges all over the world know how to handle futures and options for all sorts of commodities, including pork bellies, crude oil, aluminum, cocoa, wheat, cotton, and soybeans. Carbon credits are just another commodity. Presto: carbon credit exchanges are being formed.

The Chicago Climate Exchange (CCX), the world's first multinational and multisector exchange for reducing and trading greenhouse gas emissions, traded over one million metric tonnes of carbon dioxide in its first six months of operation, January to June 2004.[29] CCX members like Ford, Dow Corning, DuPont, IBM, Motorola, Bayer, and Baxter lend credibility to the viability of carbon trading. Europe anticipates $7 to $10 billion worth of carbon emissions trading per year by 2010 under schemes such as the 2004 European Emissions Trading Directive, which covers the power sector, oil refining, cement production, iron and steel manufacture, glass and ceramics, and paper and pulp production.[30] CO2e.com estimates the potential market for greenhouse gas trading is $10 billion to $3 trillion by 2010.[31]

There are still many wrinkles to be ironed out — the allocation of caps, verification and certification procedures, baseline years and amounts, eligible traders, and so on. However, the success of a similar scheme for sulfur dioxide emissions trading, sparked in 1993 by the US Clean Air Act in the war against acid rain, is encouraging.

The business case outlined earlier did not assume revenue from carbon emissions trading. Soon, that revenue stream may be a real possibility for companies aggressively cutting back their greenhouse gas emissions.

- Be clear about motives for reporting.
- Use a tone and style that is consistent with other communications.
- Engage the entire organization in the process.
- Ask stakeholders to review drafts or even contribute to the review.
- Listen and respond to feedback.
- Be prepared for the process to take longer than expected.
  — Experts' Advice on Sustainability Reporting

Getting the Word Out

Public companies are required by law to publish annual financial reports, plus mandatory environmental reporting is done for hazardous pollutant releases. However, broader nonfinancial reporting is growing in significance internationally as corporations and their shareowners and stakeholders recognize that nonfinancial issues impact financial performance. Both regulatory and voluntary pressures are in play.

What is the point of excelling in the sustainability arena if no one knows about it? The degree to which company efforts are useful in mitigating threats from demanding stakeholders is directly related to communications credibility, openness, transparency, and consistency. Beyond ongoing dialogue and press releases, the primary stakeholder communications technique is the annual corporate sustainability report, published either in hard copy or on the company website. It is usually separate from the annual financial report and includes information about company social and environmental policies, efforts, and results. Sustainability reporting can add real value to a company's reputation capital.

For many companies, CSR reporting is unfamiliar territory. Experts in the area offer the advice on the opposite page to those preparing their first CSR review.

Mandatory reporting of a company's environmental and community impacts is an essential starting point for any regulatory framework. By prompting recognition of a need for improvement, regulated reporting could actually diminish the need for further environmental regulation. As the trend toward mandatory CSR reporting continues, companies that have voluntarily been communicating with stakeholders on these issues will find they have a very useful head start.

Two reporting issues are intended audience and verification.

The third inhibiter is the slippery slope argument. Adherents of this argument state that once you give in on one demand, there will soon be another demand. Once you give in on that one, there will be another, and so on. Many companies and CEOs feel they have already been pushed down the slippery slope too far as it is, so they are digging in their heels. When asking companies to provide an objective, balanced measurement of their performance, some will say, "When's it going to stop? We're being asked to open our cupboard doors and show the world what we are like as a company. What's the next thing that's going to happen?" (Mel Wilson)

Sustainability Reporting — For Whom?

Everyone who has produced a CSR review stresses the need to be clear about the intended audience. While annual financial reports are almost exclusively directed at investors, annual sustainability reports can be directed at operations managers, employees, suppliers, neighbors, skeptical customers, nervous investors, suspicious regulators, and troublesome nongovernmental organizations.

How well a company communicates its sustainable development accomplishments can affect its reputation and sales. The findings of a 2004 Ipsos-Reid poll underlined this. More than half of the respondents (55%) said they have consciously decided to buy a product or service from a company because they felt it was a good corporate citizen. Similarly, half of the respondents (52%) have consciously refused to do business with a company that has not conducted itself in a socially responsible way. Ipsos-Reid concluded it is no longer acceptable to provide stakeholders with financial information only. They want to know how the company achieved that financial performance; they want to know the extent of its corporate social responsibility.[32]

Governments are another interested constituent, especially for reporting of environmental liabilities, which makes reporting less optional. A 2004 report by the US Government Accountability Office (GAO) called for a standard of reporting material liabilities from environmental risks ranging from hazardous waste contamination to greenhouse gas emissions. As a result of the report, the Securities and Exchange Commission has agreed to work more closely with the Environmental Protection Agency (EPA) to systematically track problems involving corporate environmental disclosure.[33]

Lack of clarity about who will read the report can water down the message and complicate decisions about content, format, and stakeholder contributors. To accommodate the wide diversity of stakeholder audiences, CSR reports, like financial reports, are moving online, allowing stakeholders to quickly and easily access the information they need. Internet publishing may fuel a trend to report every two years and complement this biennial report with shorter, more targeted, online communications.

And what is it that clients hope to get for their money? In essence, two things: an independent review of the robustness of their process and, as a result, stakeholder trust ....

As trust falls, we move from a world where key actors in business and government insist that the public "trust us," through the later stages where the public increasingly wants to be told what is going on — and then insists on being shown real world evidence of commitment and progress. The best way to turn the corner and move towards high levels of trust, the logic goes, is to actively involve stakeholders in key decisions ....

Is the current state of assurance, say, or sustainability management systems really what stakeholders have been asking for? Is it verification they want or is it truth? Are they the same thing? Is it standards they want or is it a whole new way of doing business? — SustainAbility and UNEP[34]

Sustainability Reporting — Says Who?

How good are the reports? Are companies "just pretending?" The SustainAbility and United Nations Environment Programme (UNEP) "Trust Us" study of 235 sustainability reports in 2002 revealed reports had grown in size by 45%, but had no associated increase in overall quality.[35] Some reports seemed to be "carpet bombing" readers with data and facts, but providing little or no context of their significance, materiality, or relevance to company financials. According to NGOs surveyed by Burson-Marsteller in late 2003, the most important approach a company can take to improve the credibility of its sustainability report is to acknowledge noncompliance, poor performance, or significant problems. Standardized reporting and third-party certification came next.[36]

Independent verification of CSR reports by third-party auditors or NGO organizations is gaining momentum in Europe and the US. European auditors certified to use AA1000 (launched in 1999 by UK-based AccountAbility[37]) and American auditors using the S8000 verification system (launched in 1998 by the US-based Social Accountability International [SAI] as a standard for workplaces based on International Labour Organization [ILO] and other human rights conventions[38]) provide credibility for CSR reporting. The proportion of sustainability reports externally verified grew from 4% of reports in 1994 to 28% in 1997, 50% in 2000, and 68% in 2002.[39] Even so, verification tends to focus on management processes rather than facts, and many companies still prefer not to use third-party verification.

Companies that adhere to the Global Reporting Initiative (GRI) guidelines gain credibility for their reports. GRI is gaining support because its standardized set of indicators allow stakeholders to compare various companies' environmental and social reports. The "Trust Us" analysis found that 60% of the top 50 reports in 2002 used GRI guidelines.[40] As of June 2004, GRI reported 450 organizations worldwide were using the GRI reporting guidelines,[41] and it planned to have at least 600 companies on board by 2005.[42] On balance, this is a positive prediction.

Sustainability reporting, or corporate disclosure on social, environmental, and economic issues that make up the triple bottom line, is relatively young — only about a decade old, according to Julie Gorte, director of social research at the Calvert Group. An expert on the subject, Dr. Gorte sits on the judges' panel for the North American Sustainability Reporting Awards, sponsored by the Association of Chartered Certified Accountants (ACCA) and the Coalition for Environmentally Responsible Economies (CERES). Auditing of sustainability reporting is even younger, but as such reporting becomes more commonplace, independent, third-party verification stands to grow concomitantly in importance.

"The current state of auditing of sustainability reports produced by corporations is best described by analogy: it's probably graduated from kindergarten, but it hasn't yet got an official diploma," Dr. Gorte told SocialFunds.com. "But it isn't an infant, either."

Andrew Savitz, a partner in the sustainability services group at PricewaterhouseCoopers (PwC), calls the auditing of sustainability reporting a "leadership activity," opted for only by companies that are corporate social responsibility (CSR) leaders. PwC audits the sustainability reports of such CSR leaders as Sony and Shell as well as auditing the process by which Sustainable Asset Management (SAM) rates companies on the Dow Jones Sustainability Index (DJSI).

PwC audits sustainability reporting in two different but related ways, according to Mr. Savitz. First, it audits the processes by which companies report their information, and sometimes it takes the second step of auditing the data itself through site visits, interviews, and document reviews.

"There is no generally accepted reporting standard for corporate social responsibility — there's no equivalent to the financial side's GAAP," said Mr. Savitz, referring to the generally accepted accounting principles that guide financial accounting and auditing.

Dr. Gorte concurs, but clarifies that there is no dearth of sustainability reporting guidelines: "there are many, and the pinnacle is the GRI," said Dr. Gorte, referring to the Global Reporting Initiative. GRI and other standards organizations, such as the International Organization for Standards (ISO), are working on developing suitable GAAP-like standards for sustainability reporting auditing, she added.
— William Baue, "Auditing Sustainability Reporting"[43]

Reporting Fatigue

As companies are inundated with requests from NGOs and ethical investment analysts about social and environmental aspects of their business, "questionnaire fatigue" sets in.[44] In an effort to address this, SRI World Group announced "OneReport" in 2004, an electronic reporting network that would enable companies to more efficiently report their sustainability and corporate governance information to investors, the financial community, and other stakeholders. It consolidates data requests from research firms with the Global Reporting Initiative (GRI) framework, provides companies with data management tools, distributes sustainability data to the marketplace, and provides Web reporting tools.[45] Similarly, the London Stock Exchange launched its Corporate Responsibility Exchange in September 2004, to help companies respond to the duplicate questions making up 80% of questionnaires about corporate governance and social responsibility policies.[46]

To support benchmarking, Future 500 released the Corporate Accountability Practices (CAP) Gap Audit in 2004. It allows a consolidated assessment that ranks corporate sustainability performance according to the criteria of 17 leading systems of standards in a single, easy-to-use tool. Via a 195-point survey, indicators of risk are flagged, performance is documented, and results are delivered in a concise, high-impact, executive report, an on-site presentation, and other customized formats.[47]

Sustainability reporting is undergoing the same growing pains financial reporting did before its contents were standardized. Efforts to accelerate sustainability reporting standards are welcome.

I think it is more likely to happen in Europe than in North America. The position of business in society is rather different here. The strength of the shareholder value issue is less in Europe. There is an acceptance of institutional mechanisms. (Nigel Roome)

UK Reporting Sets the Trend

The UK seems to be a bellwether jurisdiction for the evolution of both mandatory and voluntary catalysts for regulation. As of December 2000, publicly traded companies in the UK had to conform to the Combined Code of the Committee on Corporate Governance, also known as the Turnbull Report. It requires boards of all companies listed on the London Stock Exchange to consider long-term financial, environmental, and social risks from business activity that might adversely affect share price, company reputation, or longer term commercial prospects.[48]

Further, in July 2002 the UK Pensions Act was amended to require pension fund trustees to produce a statement of investment principles (SIP), setting out the extent to which social, ethical, and environmental (SEE) considerations were taken into account in the investment process.[49] This creates a domino effect: to take SEE factors into account, pension fund administrators require appropriate information from corporations; if corporations are to provide it, they have to gather it; gathering it for pension fund administrators leads to more open reporting, since corporations now have the basic data required.

What's next? In early 2004, the Corporate Responsibility (CORE) Bill would have made CSR reporting mandatory in the UK, but it was defeated. However, the Company Law Bill, which includes a requirement for companies to produce a more inclusive operating and financial review (OFR), is destined to become mandatory for the 2006 reporting season.[50] OFR guidelines require the top 1,000 companies to disclose in their annual report any nonfinancial risks, including social, environmental, and other issues that are likely to materially affect future performance. The guidelines could mark a sea change in attention to CSR among the investment community.[51] Clearly, social and environmental risks are now considered material information — information that is sufficiently important to have a financial impact on a company's short- or long-term performance, or that would be important to a prudent investor making an investment decision.[52]

In 2003, 132 of the top 250 UK companies produced some form of CSR report.[53] Already, members of the Association of British Insurers (ABI), which represents 96% of UK insurance companies, require companies to disclose how social and environmental risks are being handled.[54] It would be hard to categorize that reporting as "voluntary."

The financial sector — insurers, reinsurers, lenders, investors, analysts — is beginning to wake up to a range of non-financial issues. Even the best current non-financial reporting by companies may not yet meet their needs, but the convergence of the financial and non-financial worlds is now underway ....The good news is that this latest survey finds that some companies have made massive progress in responding to demands for improved transparency on key issues of corporate responsibility .... But the bad news is that most companies still fail to identify material strategic and financial risks and opportunities associated with the economic, social, and environmental impacts captured by the "triple bottom line" agenda.
— SustainAbility, *Risk & Opportunity*[55]

Sustainability Reporting in Other Countries

Sustainability reporting is being institutionalized. Globally, more companies are publishing reports on their environmental, social, and sustainability performance. The 2002 KPMG "International Survey of Corporate Sustainability Reporting" revealed that, of the top 250 Global 500 companies, 45% published a separate corporate report on their environmental, social, or sustainability performance, up from 35% in 1999.[56] An Accountability Rating study found 48% of the world's 100 companies with the highest gross revenues issued sustainability reports by 2003, jumping to 72% by 2004.[57]

A 2002 PricewaterhouseCoopers study of triple-bottom-line reporting by multinational companies found that 68% with headquarters in Western Europe did such reports, compared to 41% headquartered in the US.[58] France is the latest jurisdiction to require companies listed on the stock exchange to publish information on the environmental and social impacts of their activities. Europe is leading the way, but others are catching up. The Australian Financial Services Reform Act 2001, like the UK Pensions Act, requires sellers of investment products to disclose how labor standards or environmental, social, or ethical considerations are taken into account in the selection of the investment.[59]

Beyond the quantity of reports, the quality of reports still needs work. Companies need to better explain how their social and environmental nonfinancial performance impacts the financial bottom line, as indicated by SustainAbility's assessment of the top 50 sustainability reports in 2004 on the opposite page.

High-impact Canadian companies with heavy environmental or social footprints — i.e., mining, forestry, chemical, and energy companies — or those operating in heavily regulated sectors, such as banks, have responded to pressures from external stakeholders for responsible conduct and disclosure practices. The number of companies listed on the Toronto Stock Exchange (TSE) publishing sustainability or integrated annual reports has continued to grow: 57 in 2001, 79 in 2002, and 100 in 2003.[60] As a 2004 Conference Board of Canada report pointed out, however, two thirds of the top 300 Canadian companies do not yet report. And the ones that do report focus on their processes instead of measurable outcomes.[61]

Figure 6.2: *Dilbert* on Corporate Social Responsibility

Dilbert reprinted by permission of United Feature Syndicate, Inc.

Five Signs that Sustainability's Tipping Point Is Close

Something is going on out there. As shown in Figure 6.2, even Dilbert is talking about the three-legged stool of CSR.

First, we are getting past the "shock and denial" and "anger and blaming" phases of the sustainability change curve. Originally, some economists and corporate executives viewed CSR as ominously anti-corporation, anti-capitalism, and anti-business. On the other side, skeptical activists dismissed early CSR efforts as a placebo for the enemies of globalization, a PR smokescreen, and capitalism's last-ditch attempt to save itself by co-opting its opposition.[62] Companies were viewed as greedy institutions throwing a few philanthropic crumbs to the masses and expecting to be loved for it. And so on.

Fortunately, few are still stuck in those early rancorous phases of change, and we can get on with more productive NGO-corporate partnerships as both sides move past the "acceptance of change" phase. CSR is morphing from optional, marginalized philanthropy to mainstream strategic corporate practice; from a feel-good factor into a fundamental risk-management factor; from charity to enlightened self-interest; and from being fashionable to being a strategic business imperative. "Sustainability" is becoming synonymous with "high performance."

Many of us are encouraged by sustainability momentum. Perhaps it is the cumulative effect of a number of related levers, a confluence of forces rather than a single cataclysmic event. A couple of experts feel we have already passed the "tipping point," the point at which the sustainability idea becomes contagious and spreads like an epidemic through the business community.[63] I do not believe we are there yet, but we are close — within two to five years? There are encouraging signals that the tectonic plates of corporate mindsets and practices are starting to shift.

I am often asked why I am optimistic that sustainability is gaining currency as a strategic business lens. Sometimes I jokingly say things have to get bad before they get better, and they are getting really bad now. More optimistically, I refer to five signs of hope that are especially encouraging because they indicate corporate mindsets are changing and starting to think of sustainability as a legitimate business issue.

The Carbon Disclosure Project cites a range of developments as responsible for the greater attention to climate change, including:

- Companies are facing pressure from financial market authorities and fiduciaries to deal with climate risk. The introduction of "Generally Accepted Carbon Accounting Principles" appears likely, and litigation against major emitters is possible. Companies in the OECD face rules favoring a shift to a low carbon economy;
- More FT500 firms took strategic positions in climate change solutions and opportunities. Investing in the "clean tech" sector has quadrupled to $2.5 billion over the past two years;
- Climate change awareness and action is not just coming from energy intensive sectors, as companies recognize that impacts on product use and disposal, and on the supply chain, will affect every industry from tobacco to ice cream;
- Greater volatility now exists in certain industrial and commodity markets due to more extreme weather. Weather-related disasters cost US$70 billion in 2003 (an increase of six times from 1960s);
- Rising wholesale electricity prices are expected to impact profitability and encourage energy risk management and efficiency.
  — *GreenBiz.com* news item about the Carbon Disclosure Project[64]

1. Financial Markets Are Poking with Sharper Sticks

An awakened investor community is a powerful driver of corporate CSR attention. The financial sector gets involved in sustainability as investors of capital, as developers of financial products that encourage sustainable development, and as stakeholders who are leery of businesses exposure to environmental risk. Fed by a steady diet of corporate scandal, the world's major institutional investors are starting to ask questions about governance, ethics, and broader corporate citizenship issues. Dots that matter are being connected.

The Carbon Disclosure Project ties market valuation to climate change.[65] When 95 investment institutions representing $10 trillion of assets ask the 500 largest companies in the world how they see climate change affecting their market value and what they are doing about it, all companies sit up and take notice. Throw carbon trading possibilities into the mix, and suddenly corporate environmental sustainability becomes a mainstream business issue.

A 2001 Conference Board of Canada report, which analyzed the performance of seven prominent funds and indices, and also looked at 18 research studies, found compelling evidence that investment portfolios consisting of companies committed to sustainable development have matched or outperformed their benchmarks.[66] Given this positive correlation, investment analysts are starting to request company environmental and social reports as information sources about holistic company health and competitiveness. At a minimum, sustainability scores are a good proxy for superior management of intangible assets and critical organizational capabilities such as business efficiency, management competency, human capital, strategy execution, stakeholder relations, and reputation management.[67]

A 2004 study showed 86% of institutional investors across Europe believe that social and environmental risk management will have a significant long-term impact on companies' market value.[68] A 2003 poll conducted by GlobeScan showed 51% of Canadian shareholders had punished a socially irresponsible company in the previous year.[69] And a survey reported in *The Wirthlin Report* in April 2004 indicated that 74% of adult Americans say their view of a company's ethical behavior and practices has a direct influence on their willingness to purchase the firm's stocks.[70]

Retail and institutional investors are waking up. Stand back!

Regulations work sometimes. The Toxic Release Inventory (TRI) is probably one of the most successful examples in history. It was very clever. The numbers didn't have to be accurate. They could just be your best guesstimate. "We're not going to do anything with the numbers. Just make sure the CEO signs off on them and gives them to us." It is probably the single most effective action the US government has taken since 1969 when the EPA was formed ....

I would implement a TRI analogy in the private sector and government ministries .... They both need to sit down and keep an off-the-books tally of the value of all the unwanted outcomes from their operations: sick days, accidents with company vehicles, amount of raw materials not processed into useful product (i.e., waste), etc. You put it on the CEO's desk once a quarter and it will have a wake-up effect on the amount of leakage that occurs .... I would force them to do an on-the-books accounting of all the total leakage or the losses of value.

They are not stupid. The number would be so big, they couldn't stand the heat from their shareholders if they didn't do something about it, especially from institutional investors. Waste doesn't show up in normal accounting, so it doesn't seem to have any value. Waste of all kinds is numbers that are not there. I would make waste numbers that are there. (Antony Marcil)

It was an incredibly crafty move in the UK a few years ago when pension fund legislation was introduced to require disclosure of environmental and social criteria when investing. It was incredibly simple and innocuous, but it has had a powerful trickle-down effect. We need something like that in Canada, too. (Alan Willis)

2. *Sustainability Reporting Is Becoming Business as Usual*

Following the 1992 Earth Summit in Rio de Janeiro, the concept of sustainable development gained common currency. Existing environment, health, and safety reports began to include wider community issues, and "sustainability reports" started appearing. According to CorporateRegister.com statistics, the percentage of reports focusing exclusively on the environment fell from 63% of nonfinancial reports in 2000 to 42% in 2002, while sustainability reports rose from 5% to 15% over the same period, suggesting some environmental reports morphed into sustainability reports.[71] Sustainability reporting has moved from the fringe to mainstream accounting practice, and "sustainability" is increasingly the term used to label all nonfinancial reports.

There was concern that the Kasky case would inhibit CR reporting. In 1998, California activist Marc Kasky sued Nike for violating California's truth in advertising law. After losing business in the mid-1990s to charges of funding sweatshop conditions overseas, Nike issued press releases denying there were major problems and claimed it enforced a code of conduct that prohibited overseas factories from abusing workers. Kasky's lawsuit claimed Nike knowingly lied about working conditions to improve sales, which amounted to advertising, and therefore the denials were commercial communications, subject to the truth-in-advertising law, rather than free speech protected under the First Amendment. The case was settled out of court, but the signal that public statements may be considered information for investors could make companies leery of describing their CR intent in official reports.[72]

One of the most enduring business clichés is "what gets measured gets managed." Reporting and disclosure leads to awareness and tracking, tracking leads to improvement strategies, and improvement strategies lead to new actions that enhance corporate performance and image. Almost by osmosis, it becomes evident that paying attention to CR metrics is good for business, and as a result, sustainability considerations are integrated into key decision-making processes throughout the firm.

As sustainability reporting becomes as commonplace as financial reporting, stand back!

> The different departments in business schools are in bunkers — policy, strategy, economics, technology management, etc. Sustainability is more holistic. We have a lot of depth and not much breadth. Sustainability affects every dimension of the business, from finance through to human resources. There are very few people with the competence to do that. (Nigel Roome)
>
> If the next generation of business leaders is to excel at managing enterprises for greater competitiveness, it will need the knowledge and skills to tackle not only the financial but also the social and environmental challenges faced by today's corporations. Business schools provide the foundation for the analytical reasoning, strategic thinking, and decision-making frameworks used by future business leaders the world over. In the United States alone, over 100,000 master's degrees in business are awarded each year.
>
> In October 2002, the "Beyond Grey Pinstripes" survey was mailed to 426 schools accredited by either the Association to Advance Collegiate Schools of Business (AACSB) or the European Foundation for Management Development (EFMD) and to more than 100 other leading MBA programs around the globe. Schools from 20 countries — 68 from the United States and 32 from Africa, the Americas, Asia, Australia, and Europe — completed the survey.
> Findings from this survey show that business schools have broadened their coverage of social and environmental stewardship ....
>
> "Beyond Grey Pinstripes 2003" identifies the leading schools and faculty that are devoting the deepest attention to social impact and environmental management as well as those that are beginning to weave together this triple bottom line. Ultimately, graduates from such programs will be better equipped to lead competitive businesses that are outstanding performers in terms of financial success, social value, and environmental quality.
> — "Beyond Grey Pinstripes 2003" [73]

3. Business Schools Are Legitimizing Sustainability Strategies

Business schools shape the thinking of current and future business leaders. In the US, more than 100,000 master's degrees in business are conferred each year.[74] "Beyond Grey Pinstripes", mentioned earlier and further described on the opposite page, highlights the MBA programs and faculty at the forefront of incorporating issues of social and environmental stewardship into their curriculum. The worldwide report is prepared every two years by the Aspen Institute and the World Resources Institute.[75]

According to the 2003 report, sustainability issues are becoming part of the business vernacular and are addressed in many MBA programs through elective courses and extracurricular activity. The six top schools in the 2003 survey were, in alphabetical order: George Washington, Michigan, North Carolina (Kenan-Flagler), Stanford, Yale, and York (Schulich).[76] Integration of sustainability into core courses — including accounting, finance, marketing, operations, and organizational behavior — that most powerfully shape the MBA experience is still a work in progress. Three MBA programs have deliberately been designed from the ground up to integrate sustainability seamlessly into all courses: Bainbridge Island Graduate Institute off the coast of Seattle, Presidio World College in San Francisco, and the Green MBA at New College in Santa Rosa, California.[77]

"Beyond Grey Pinstripes" is to MBA schools what the Carbon Disclosure Project is to large companies. Just asking what schools are doing to integrate sustainability into the core MBA curriculum — and publicly ranking them — gets their attention.

What is even more encouraging is the Net Impact MBA student group. Its 90-chapter, 10,000-strong membership is working with MBA schools and future employers to legitimize sustainability interests.[78] Net Impact's professional membership option allows alumni and other business professionals to stay connected with a network of like-minded peers after graduation. Net Impact members are a beneficial virus of sustainability champions infecting mainstream business communities. A 2004 survey of MBA students found that 97% said they were willing to forgo 14% of their expected income to work for an organization with a better reputation for corporate social responsibility and ethics.[79]

MBA schools shape the mindsets of corporate leaders. Stand back!

In the States, if it is promoted as a standard, it is a commitment. It is a forward-looking statement that has to be reported under SEC reporting requirements, and people might invest because of your commitment to this performance standard. "I will achieve XYZ." If you don't achieve XYZ, it might be considered securities fraud. There is a very strong legal implication of committing to something, people investing based on that commitment, and then not achieving it ....

That is a very subtle deepness that may be a substantial issue. A couple of financial lawyers that I have talked to agree that is a real consideration. That may be why the standards become process based, not performance based ....They don't want performance-based standards that commit them to doing things they may not want to do tomorrow. It has investment fraud or securities fraud implications, at least in the US. (Steve Rice)

4. ISO Is Developing a New Standard for Social Responsibility

ISO 9000 standards gave a big boost to quality. ISO 14000 standards gave a big boost to environmental management systems. In June 2004, after 18 months of rigorous study of CSR trends and initiatives by various stakeholders, the International Organization for Standardization (ISO) decided to develop a new international standard for social responsibility.[80] Perhaps it will give a big boost to sustainability.

ISO openly acknowledges that the sustainability topic involves issues that are qualitatively different from issues it has traditionally dealt with. The standard is intended to add value to, not replace, existing agreements such as the UN Universal Declaration of Human Rights and Global Compact.

Wisely, the ISO task force plans to make its efforts open to anyone interested and to make it as easy as possible for experts from stakeholders in developing countries, NGOs, international and broadly based regional organizations, business, government, labor organizations, and consumer associations to participate. The challenge will be to develop practical guidelines that provide easy-to-use guidance to this wide range of stakeholders.

This will be a different kind of standard. It is not intended for certification, so it will be interesting to see if, without that rigor, it draws attention to CSR. Given the comments on the opposite page, perhaps the focus on process rather than results will make the new standard more attractive to companies. The idea of extending existing corporate strategies to embrace sustainability could be a clever move. Some companies that achieved ISO 9000 certification for their quality management system viewed ISO 14000 certification for their environmental management system as a natural extension. When an ISO standard for corporate social responsibility is established, companies with ISO 14000 certification may view applying for the new standard as an extension of their environmental management system base.

If an ISO CSR standard awakens the supply chain anything close to the way ISO 9000 did, stand back!

The Natural Marketing Institute's second annual survey of the Lifestyles of Health and Sustainability, or "LOHAS," marketplace reveals consumers have strong and growing interest in various environmental, social, personal development, and values-based issues.

According to the survey, nearly one-third of U.S. consumers, or 68 million adults, are concerned about various environmental and social issues and are conscientious of those issues when making purchase decisions — a 7% rise from a year earlier.

Overall, consumers indicate high interest levels in protecting the environment (91%), socially responsible business practices (83%), and preference for purchasing products made in a sustainable manner (59%).

Perhaps of greatest interest for manufacturers and marketers is that many consumers incorporate those related attitudes into their purchase decisions across many different products. As proof of the growing LOHAS marketplace, consumers show strong interest in a variety of specific products including energy efficient appliances (96%), renewable power (74%), organic food (53%), hybrid vehicles (56%), and many additional products and services that were included in this NMI research study.

— *GreenBiz.com* news item[81]

It's About Innovation, Productivity, and Competitive Advantage ...

I started the book with a discussion of sustainability terminology. I urged less focus on the language of sustainability and more focus on the language of its results. When attempting to move sustainability strategies from the fringes to the mainstream of the business world, sustainability champions might get a warmer reception from CEOs if they suggest executives adopt "smart business strategy X" instead of "sustainability strategies."

When my publisher and I were working on the title for *The Sustainability Advantage*, we considered *Show Me the Money!* made famous by the movie *Jerry Maguire*. We decided against it because the phrase was overused at the time, but the idea of highlighting the end result of sustainability strategies was good. In retrospect, a better title might have been *Innovation, Productivity, and Competitive Advantage: The Sustainability Trinity*.

Sustainability provides a vitamin supplement for corporate health. When executives are scratching their heads wondering how they can unleash the innovation of their workforce to give them a competitive advantage, they too often overlook the Big Hairy Audacious Goal (BHAG)[88] of being the most sustainable company in their industry. BHAGs get employees going. People find them stimulating, exciting, adventurous. They are willing to throw their creative talent and energies into them. A sustainability-related BHAG would be a powerful statement about the company's ideology and unleash incredible, productive commitment in the workforce.

Sustainability is an innovation and productivity engine waiting to be turned on. Wise executives have the key.

If left to its own the capitalist system is efficient but ruthless. It creates enormous wealth but can leave poverty and inequality in its wake. It increases productivity but discards employees. Capitalism powers the stock market but closes factories and abandons whole communities. It reduces consumer prices but lowers the wages of workers. It balances budgets but deprives governments of resources needed for investment. It offers access to the wonders of the World Wide Web but leaves millions behind in a new digital divide. It generates marvelous inventions but leaves environmental pollution in its wake. It democratizes information but marginalizes people. It speeds up the flow of goods, services, and money but creates increased volatility, vulnerability, and insecurity. Globalization creates unprecedented riches but widens the gap between those who have and get ahead and those who don't and are left farther and farther behind.

As with the corporate governance challenge, the onus is on the private sector to demonstrate that it can be part of the solution, rather than part of the problem. Far and away the vast majority of business leaders have operated with high standards of integrity, but this is not how much of the public sees it. The private sector must demonstrate that it is worthy of public trust and confidence. Companies need to show that they can work in partnership with governments and others to help make the process of globalization not only profitable, but also more equitable and more beneficial for more people, without destroying the world's environmental capacity to nurture future generations.

For many businesspeople these leadership challenges represent uncharted and choppy waters, but they cannot be ignored. Together, they represent a powerful and unprecedented collision of forces — what many corporate leaders are describing as the economic and political equivalent of a "perfect storm."

Business leaders need to face this "perfect storm" and navigate with a new compass. Despite the ongoing pressures of relentless competition, and the need to deliver short-term financial performance, no major company can ignore and fail to respond to the following threats to long-term corporate success and viability: The crisis of trust, the crisis of inequality, and the crisis of sustainability.

— Ira A. Jackson and Jane Nelson, *Profits with Principles* [89]

Leaders, Followers, and Laggards

Sustainability leaders are in Stage 4 or Stage 5 on the sustainability continuum. They integrate social and environmental considerations into investment, research and development, and procurement decisions. They clearly understand the power of human ingenuity and let the spirit of the company's corporate culture shine through. They measure, manage, and transparently report their ecological impacts, their waste and emissions, and their social impacts. They work with stakeholders to minimize the ecological and social footprints of their supply-chain members. They educate customers and encourage them to demand more sustainable choices. They influence capital markets and analysts to recognize lower long-term risks compared to competitors less engaged in sustainable practices. They influence regulators to implement progressive, smart regulations that reward leaders and punish laggards, strip away perverse subsidies, unleash market forces, and introduce market-based regulatory approaches like emissions trading. To them, CSR is no longer about buffing up one's corporate reputation. It is about a comprehensive way of doing business to yield intelligent profit maximization, which is as pro-business as it gets.

Sustainability followers are at Stage 3 on the sustainability continuum. They are starting to see benefits and are paying attention to further possibilities. They are proactively learning from the leaders, intelligently experimenting, and courageously pushing the edges of their envelopes of status-quo comfort. They are starting to see that CSR marries profit and purpose, results and inspiration. Once a critical mass of followers is on board, the tipping point is reached and we can all enjoy the momentum as it kicks into overdrive.

Sustainability laggards are in Stage 1 or Stage 2. They may never "get it" or they may experience a rude awakening from their reactive rut by a PR crisis in time to get on board.

Corporate responsibility is no longer a luxury for companies. In today's global economy, it is critical for companies to embrace social and environmental responsibility in order to meet the demands of their investors, consumers, employees, and communities they serve. Smart sustainability champions can help executives and directors of forward-looking companies recognize that sustainability strategies serve these goals.

SME-RELEVANT BUSINESS CASE

Why bother with small and medium-sized enterprises (SMEs)? Their aggregate environmental and societal impact is immense. What they lack in size they make up for in numbers. Of the 73 million legally constituted firms in the world, at least 65 million (89%) are SMEs.[1]

In 1998 in the European Union, 99.8% of enterprises were SMEs and they employed 66.4% of employees. A medium-sized enterprise is defined as one that has 50 to 250 employees, while a small enterprise has 10 to 50 employees and a micro-sized enterprise has fewer than 10 employees. Interestingly, micro-enterprises represent a massive 92.5% of EU enterprises and 32.4% of employment, compared to small enterprises (6.3% of enterprises and 18.9% of employment) and medium-sized enterprises (0.9% of enterprises and 15.1% of employment).[2] Clearly, the small-enterprise sector enjoys a big piece of economic action. Small is beautiful ... and important.

Industry Canada defines an SME as a company with annual revenues of less than $25 million and up to 300 employees in the services sector or up to 500 employees in the manufacturing sector.[3] The Canadian Federation of Independent Businesses uses slightly different definitions. Medium enterprises have 50 to 500 employees, small enterprises have 5 to 50, and micro-enterprises have fewer than 5.[4] Based on 1999 statistics, 75.3% of Canadian businesses are micro-enterprises, 22.1% are small, and 2.4% are medium.[5] That is, 99.8% of Canadian businesses are SMEs, the same as in the European Union, even though they are categorized differently.

In the United States, SMEs are companies with fewer than 500 employees. They represent 99.7% of enterprises and employ 50% of private sector employees in the US, slightly lower than the 55% of the Canadian workforce and 66% of the European workforce working in SMEs.[6]

SMEs deserve special attention. As we shall see, SMEs' level of interest in environmental issues is generally high and is often linked to the values of the owner. However, the concepts and tools used for larger organizations are not easily transferred to SMEs. These organizations need simple tools with step-by-step procedures. Ideally, these tools should link directly to customers and have clear and immediate benefits.[7]

Obstacles to CSR for individual SMEs:

1. Perceived and/or actual costs (e.g., for verification for big business customers' codes of conduct)
2. Lack of awareness of business benefits
3. Conflicting time and other resource pressures
4. More immediate pressures from the daily struggle to survive commercially (some SMEs live below the poverty line)
5. Lack of know-how and know-who (e.g., to relate CSR as a mainstream issue; to make the business case; and where to find technical support)
6. Being reluctant and too slow to seek external help
7. Tools, business case, measurements, and verification procedures so far are primarily aimed at large businesses
8. The language of CSR is off-putting
9. Lack of awareness of the environmental and social impacts
10. Lack of good record keeping to prove CSR track record
11. Limited rewards for responsible business practice
    — European Multi Stakeholder Forum on Corporate Social Responsibility, "Report of the Round Table on Fostering CSR Among SMEs"[8]

How SMEs Are Different

What distinguishes SMEs from larger firms? First, they have a less-well-defined formal management structure and specialized positions, so environmental and social responsibilities lie with busy staff who have several other responsibilities. They do not have the time, or the skilled staff with technical expertise, to sort through confusing communications from regulators or sustainability experts. The growing number of sustainability-related codes, standards, and regulations are so complicated that SMEs without specialist resources have difficulty complying because of ignorance, not because of a lack of intent. Second, they seldom have dominant market positions, so are driven more by cash flow than by year-end profits. Third, they do not have the money, resources, or time to focus on environmental and social issues, and they cannot fall back on funding and expertise support from parent companies.[9] In some situations, if the SME is lucky, a larger company to which an SME is a supplier may lend its experts to assist with sustainability audits and initiatives in the SME, to help the large company's own green procurement objectives.

As the list of inhibiters on the opposite page shows, SMEs also lack the time, money, and resources to tell the world about the good environmental and social things they are doing. Driven by brand image and reputational considerations, large companies have whole departments to publicize their CSR initiatives, produce annual sustainability reports, apply for awards, respond to surveys, and generally get the word out. Although 91% of UK SMEs feel they have socially and environmentally responsible business practices,[10] they are not able to invest time and expertise in publicity, so they suffer from a "no news is bad news" image: if they are not known as sustainability leaders, they are suspected to be poor stewards of the environmental and social aspects of their operations and products.

Too often that is an unfair conclusion, since they are practicing "silent" CSR. SME employees and management are more likely to have local roots, and SMEs may be less mobile than large organizations. As local residents, they care more about stewardship of the local environment and community because it is where they and their children, relatives, and friends live. They may be less inclined to soil their own nest than impersonal multinational corporate nomads seeking jurisdictions with the best tax breaks.

Commitment to corporate stewardship is more personal in SMEs.

Drivers of CSR for individual SMEs:

1. Personal beliefs of the founders/owners-managers and employees
2. Attracting, retaining, and developing motivated and committed employees — especially because the speed of market and technology change requires flexible and engaged staff
3. Winning and retaining consumers and business customers (supply-chain pressures and opportunities), especially because economic stagnation means SMEs need to find new markets/revenue streams
4. Being a good neighbor — maintaining a license to operate from the local community
5. Responding to pressure from banks and insurers
6. Reputation — with internal and external stakeholders
7. Changing perceptions of the role of business in society (not only as a source of profit) through the media, education, and actions by stakeholders
8. Cost and efficiencies savings (e.g., reduced insurance and landfill costs)
9. Networking opportunities
10. Product/market innovation, differentiation, and competitive edge, and the need for more sources of creativity and innovation in business
11. Anticipating future legislation/getting practical experience of compliance in ways that help business
    — European Multi Stakeholder Forum on Corporate Social Responsibility, "Report of the Round Table on Fostering CSR Among SMEs"[11]

Sustainability Drivers for SMEs

In 2002, the European Commission launched the European Multi Stakeholder Forum on Corporate Social Responsibility, a pan-European initiative composed of representative organizations of employers, business organizations, investors, consumers, trade unions, and civil society.[12] Its goal was to create a common understanding of corporate social responsibility and to promote it as a credible and effective aid to achieving EU economic, social, and environmental aims. One of the forum's four themes was fostering the concept of CSR among SMEs. It held a series of roundtables in 2003 and 2004, during which it received presentations from SMEs in Belgium, France, Germany, Greece, Italy, Spain, and the UK and assembled 100 SME case studies. It delivered its "Report of the Round Table on Fostering CSR Among SMEs" in May 2004.[13]

The report provides excellent insights into the drivers, obstacles, and critical success factors for implementing sustainability initiatives in SMEs. It acknowledges that the findings will be more valid for some than others, depending on the size, age, ownership of the company; the reasons for its start-up; its growth ambitions; and its attitude toward risk and innovation.

Just like large enterprises, SMEs are driven by a combination of minimizing risks and maximizing opportunities. The list of 11 factors that drive SME attention to the sustainability aspects of their operations is shown opposite. They look familiar. About 90% of the rationale discussed in this book for large enterprises paying attention to sustainability applies to SMEs. However, there are some differences in degree and some unique inhibitors, as we shall see in the next sections.

Some companies had the benefit of founders whose personal convictions led them to create companies that overtly appealed to customers whose values resonated with theirs. They have identified a really good marketing opportunity and found a niche. The classic examples are the Body Shop and Ben & Jerry's. (Marlo Raynolds)

Current environmental regulations have far more impact in triggering change in behavior of a 100-employee firm than in a 5-employee firm. For a five-person firm, personal views of the employer count the most. And not to be forgotten is the fact that 78.4% of Canada's business population are firms employing fewer than five people. Hence, the data suggests that a regulation, no matter how well defined, would not change behavior as much as enhancing the business owners' understanding on environmental issues. Information and education are the key strategies toward better environmental protection that governments should use when dealing with SMEs.

Regulations are not the root of improvements in environmental behavior. In fact, among all the firms that have "made progress," 47.3% are not regulated by any level of government. About one third, 34.7%, of the firms that have "made a great deal of progress" are not regulated either. Almost 50% of the firms that have stated "some progress" are not regulated as well, and two-thirds of the ones that have "made little progress" have improved without being under any kind of environmental regulation. Hence, being regulated does not constitute a necessary condition for improvement.
— Canadian Federation of Independent Business[14]

Relevance of First-Wave Drivers to SMEs

How do the three drivers triggering the first wave of sustainability companies apply to SMEs?

- *Founder's Personal Passion:* In a survey done in 2001 by the Canadian Federation of Independent Business (CFIB), the personal environmental conscience of the business owner was found to be the leading motivator for 86.8% of SMEs' environmental stewardship.[15] In a 2003 NetRegs survey in the UK, 54% of SMEs said they were motivated by a general concern for the environment, echoing similar owner conviction.[16] If the business owner is a values-driven, voluntary sustainability champion, the firm's commitment may be informal and implicit. It is at Stage 5, by definition. The founder's personal passion and ethical core philosophy are more significant drivers for SMEs, because of their size, than for large, publicly traded corporations. CSR is the enterprise version of personal integrity.[17]

- *Public Relations Crisis:* Reputational risk is a big factor for large firms, but most SMEs exist below the radar screens of activists in search of high-profile companies to publicly chastise. Also, an SME's license to operate may be more determined by its relationship with its local community than with global stakeholders, even if it is an exporter. A 2002 study by the European Commission reported that half of SMEs — 48% of micro-enterprises, 65% of small, and 70% of medium — in the 18 countries surveyed were involved in some aspect of local social causes, mostly sporting or cultural activities.[18]

- *Regulatory Pressure:* In a 2003 NetRegs survey in the UK, 39% of SMEs said they felt pressured by environmental regulations to limit their impact on the environment. In Canada, where about 80% of firms in primary industry and agricultural sectors are regulated,[19] 33.6% of SMEs said they felt pressured to limit their environmental impact.[20] Ironically, the only mention of regulations in a Canadian Business for Social Responsibility study was by SMEs in the primary resources and manufacturing sectors who say cost and time burdens from regulations intended for large companies prevent them from implementing more sustainable practices.[21] The CFIB case against regulations being an effective motivator of SME environmental stewardship is on the opposite page.

There is a lot of evidence that a lot of small companies do community work, either because the owner/manager has a particular predilection for that or because in some cases they have discovered their own business case reasons — getting marks for local community engagement, license to operate, all those sorts of things. We did quite a bit of research on this, particularly in relation to inner-city, deprived areas and why companies got engaged there. There were lots of reasons why they did it — making staff feel better about the company; retention and recruitment; profile amongst the local communities; better relationships with, and more loyalty from, customers — all very much on an anecdotal basis. Nobody could really put their finger on bottom-line benefits, but there were very much the standard anecdotal reasons why people do these things. (John Swannick)

Large companies are pushing sustainable development down to small and medium-sized companies through requirements related to supply-chain management. This is one of today's most important trends. (Ron Yachnin)

With supply chains and competitors, if your customers expect you to do things a certain way, if you're half-smart you're going to start doing them that way. So there are different reasons, sector by sector. In the automotive industry supply chain, you may not be a natural philanthropic, altruistic, visionary, sustainable development person but if Ford Motor Company says, "You have got to do this and this and this," that is very motivating. (Alan Willis)

Relevance of Emerging Drivers to SMEs

How do the two emerging sustainability drivers apply to SMEs?

- *Perfect Storm of Threats:* As described earlier, mega-issues are arousing the expectations of demanding stakeholders of large corporations. These pressures have a trickle-down effect on SMEs that supply large companies. Outsourcing does not absolve accountability. No longer simply accountable for their own operations, large corporations are now taken to task if operations of SMEs in their supply chain are violating acceptable labor, social, or environmental standards, whether at home or abroad. Client-driven requirements were cited by 24.8% of Canadian medium-sized businesses and 18.2% of small businesses as drivers of their environmental efforts.[22] When large firms' procurement departments demand an acceptable standard of environmental management and social responsibility from suppliers, it drives SMEs to be more explicit about their sustainability initiatives and to report on them in a transparent manner.[23]

- *Compelling Business Case:* Sustainability is about being productive, producing a better product using as few resources as possible, and distinguishing one's products, processes, and services to become more competitive.[24] In the Canadian Business for Social Responsibility study of SMEs interested in sustainability, referenced earlier, the second big driver, after the founder's personal passion, was perceived business benefits.[25] SMEs with positive environmental and social reputations can differentiate themselves as suppliers. However, in the NetRegs survey in the UK, only 8% of SMEs were motivated by potential business benefits.[26]

The small-capital Winslow Green Growth Fund finished 2003 with a return of +91.74%, compared to +44.77% for all small-cap growth funds, the Russell 2000 Growth Index at +45.51%, the S&P Index at +28.68%, and the Nasdaq Composite Index at +50.01%. The Winslow Green Growth Fund invests in environmentally responsible SMEs. It is reassuring that it ranked second out of 483 small-cap growth funds in 2003.[27] The stock value for SMEs paying attention to their environmental impacts does not seem to be suffering.

However, more work needs to be done to help SMEs recognize and reap business benefits from their good sustainability efforts.

Figure A.1: SME Ltd.

Assumptions for Hypothetical "SME Ltd."		
Revenue	$4,000,000	
Profit	$200,000	5% of Revenue
Employee Population	50	
Employees	43	
Managers	7	
Average Employee Salary	$25,000	
Average Manager Salary	$55,000	

Sample Company — SME Ltd.

To make the business case for large companies in *The Sustainability Advantage,* I used a composite company based on five large, global, high-tech companies to estimate the potential bottom-line benefits. I called it Sustainable Development Incorporated ("SD Inc."). Choosing the size and industry of a typical "SME Ltd." in our business case is tricky, since it would be nice if it were relevant to most SMEs. I have created a generic 50-person firm, with the characteristics shown in Figure A.1. That puts it on the cusp between small and medium-sized companies, regardless of what country's classification scheme is used, so it should be useful to a majority of SMEs.

Assumptions from the literature about real-life case studies are used throughout the business case. Amazingly, the benefits add up to a **46%** potential improvement in bottom-line profit. Would that be possible for a particular SME? People wishing to use their own assumptions and the financials for a specific SME are welcome to download *The Sustainability Advantage SME Worksheets* from New Society Publishers' website <www.newsociety.com> so they can tune the parameters to their own situation. The Excel spreadsheets double as a working checklist of savings areas to explore.

As with SD Inc., I have assumed that SME Ltd. invests in sustainability education for all its employees: the equivalent of two days the first year and one day in each of the next four years. The design, development, and delivery cost of $350 per student per day assumed for SME Ltd.'s five-year education plan are the same as for SD Inc., to acknowledge that assistance from outside consultants may be needed. The first-year education investment for all 50 people in SME Ltd. is $43,000, and an additional $21,000 is allocated for the day of education in each of the following four years. Although that may seem a steep price to pay, the projected annual benefits more than offset the education investment, even though I do not count the benefit until its upfront investment has been repaid. That is, to allow for different payback periods on sustainability initiatives, I assume that 30%, 50%, 70%, 90%, and 100% of the potential benefits are realized in each of the five years.

The business case is still compelling, as we will see.

Typical percentage cost savings for material, utilities, and wastes:

- 1% to 5% on most-often-used materials
- 5% to 20% on ancillary materials
- 10% to 30% of consumable materials
- 10% to 90% of packaging materials
- 5% to 20% of electrical costs
- 10% to 30% of gas and fuel oil costs
- 10% to 60% of water costs
- 10% to 50% of solid and liquid wastes

— Envirowise, *Increase your Profit with Environmental Management Systems* [28]

Then, after risk management, some companies began to find opportunities for cost reductions, savings, and efficiencies by doing more with less. That is an easily sold argument. In about 1993, the WRI [World Resources Institute] came out with a very good book called *Green Ledgers*.[29] When cost accountants began to help management to reassign costs using ABC [activity-based cost accounting] or whatever, they found they were spending a lot of money on waste and wanted to engineer that out of their business to save some money. (Alan Willis)

An SME-Relevant Business Case

I have often been asked if the business case outlined for a sample composite, global, high-tech company in *The Sustainability Advantage* would apply to an SME. When the revenue and profit used in the example are in billions of dollars, there is an understandable question about its scalability and relevance to SMEs.

Cash flow trumps profit in SMEs. The smaller the SME, the more critical cash flow becomes, rather than year-end profit or growth.[30] A positive cash flow requires that a company be ruthless with ongoing expenses and minimize upfront costs required to reap benefits, so the business case needs to focus on benefits from early eco-efficiencies that have quick paybacks and short-term productivity improvements. Starting with eco-efficiencies is also less daunting than undertaking the full spectrum of CSR initiatives.

The good news is there are many descriptions of quick business benefits that can be reaped by environmentally and socially responsible SMEs. See the list on the opposite page for typical percentage savings on specific items estimated by Envirowise. Over 60% of cost-saving environmental projects undertaken by the 500 companies studied by Envirowise cost little or nothing.[31]

The bad news is that utility, waste, and energy costs are often lumped into "overhead" rather than tracked in separate accounts that enable them to be attributed to specific processes, products, services, or activities in an activity-based costing (ABC) approach. Environmental management accounting is a fledgling practice, encouraged by life-cycle analysis. Companies identifying and tracking environmental costs for the first time have often discovered that actual costs are four to five times their estimates.[32] They may be tracked using physical quantities rather than financial costs, so a conversion may be required.

Adequate metering of electricity, water, and fuel usage is critical to understanding where the high-payoff opportunities are. You can't manage what you can't measure, and you can't measure what you don't meter. Ideally, the usage data should be a by-product of good business management rather than just one more thing to worry about.

Figure A.2: SME Business Case for Sustainability

Business Case Benefits	% Improvement for SME Ltd.	% Improvement for Large Companies like SD Inc.
1. Reduced electricity, fuel, and waste costs	-10%	Not applicable
2. Reduced recruiting costs	-1%	Same
3. Reduced attrition costs	-2%	Same
4. Increased productivity	+6%	+10.5%
5. Increased revenue	+5%	Same
6. Reduced risk / Easier financing	-5%	Same
... yielding a profit increase of	46%	38%

Similar and Different Benefits

Earlier, I outlined seven areas of potential benefits for large companies engaging in CSR. Rather than repeat the assumptions and the logic behind each again, I will simply indicate differences. For SMEs, five of the seven benefits for large companies apply.

- Reduced hiring costs
- Reduced attrition costs
- Increased employee productivity
- Increased revenue
- Reduced risk and easier access to capital

The other two areas, "Reduced expenses for manufacturing" and "Reduced expenses at commercial sites," will be lumped together for SMEs under a new "Reduced electricity, fuel, and waste costs" category. This acknowledges that office and plant space may co-exist in the same facility for some SMEs, and areas for potential savings are similar in both parts of the site. Because eco-efficiencies are so important to SMEs anxious to benefit quickly from their efforts, that new category is listed first in Figure A.2.

A 2002 Envirowise report from the UK, "Increase Your Profit with Environmental Management Systems", suggests that potential savings equivalent to 1% to 3% of revenue, or higher, can be achieved from reduced utility, materials, and waste costs, depending on how large a percentage of business costs they are.[33] I will assume 1%, to be conservative. The "Reduced electricity, fuel, and waste costs" category includes savings in the following areas:

- Savings on electricity used for lighting
- Savings on electricity used for appliances and equipment
- Savings on fuel used for heating and cooling
- Savings on fuel used for transportation
- Savings from water efficiencies
- Savings from better waste management

I will consider ideas for potential savings in each subcategory shortly, but first I'll explore why Figure A.2 shows different assumptions being used for productivity gains in SME Ltd. and SD Inc.

Figure A.3: Increased Employee Productivity

Increased Employee Productivity		
Increased Productivity of Individual Employees		Average
Total number of employees	50	
x Percent who will be energized by the company's sustainability initiatives	20%	
x Percent increased productivity from their increased commitment	10%	2.0%
x Average employee's annual salary	$25,000	
--		
Benefit of increased productivity from individuals	$25,000	
Increased Productivity from Improved Teamwork		
Total number of employees	50	
x Percent increased productivity from interdepartmental teamwork	2%	2.0%
x Average employee's annual salary	$25,000	
--		
Benefit of increased productivity from improved teamwork	$25,000	
Increased Productivity from Improved Working Environment		
Total number of employees	50	
x Percent of employees whose working conditions are improved	20%	
x Percent increased productivity from improved working conditions	10%	2.0%
x Average employee's annual salary	$25,000	
--		
Benefit of increased productivity from improved working environment	$25,000	
Total Benefit of Increased Productivity		
Benefit of increased productivity from individuals	$25,000	
Benefit of increased productivity from improved teamwork	$25,000	
Benefit of increased productivity from improved working environment	$25,000	
--		
Annual benefit of increased productivity	$75,000	6.0%
Number of full-time equivalent (FTE) employees	3.0	

Increased Employee Productivity

As with SD Inc., I use three subcategories of productivity benefit for SME Ltd. employees: increased individual productivity, increased teamwork across the company, and increased productivity as a co-benefit of workplace environmental improvements.

In the discussion of individual productivity improvements in Chapter 4 of this book, I assumed the personal values and ethics of 20% of the employees aligned with a sustainability vision for a large firm. I will use the same conservative estimate for SME Ltd. employees. The number, derived from several worldwide surveys, is a lowball estimate, especially after the five years of sustainability education built into the business case.

I then assume these individual employees would be 10% more productive, primarily through more energised and innovative approaches to their responsibilities. This is even more conservative than the 25% increase in productivity assumed for individual SD Inc. employees, yielding an average 2% (10% x 20%) increase in individual productivity.

A worthwhile common cause is a wonderfully unifying factor. As for SD Inc., I assume an additional 2% in productivity from improved company-wide teaming around common sustainability issues that transcend departmental boundaries.

The third productivity area is improved workplace environments, especially daylighting, as a surprise by-product of eco-efficiency retrofits. For SD Inc., I assumed 50% of the employee population would receive these retrofits, and their productivity would increase by 7%, the low end of the 7% to 15% range documented in the literature at the time, yielding an average productivity gain of 3.5% (7% x 50%). For SME Ltd., I assume fewer employees, 20%, have their workplace environments retrofitted, and their productivity increases by 10%, based on more recent estimates of 6% to 26% potential productivity gains, yielding an additional productivity gain of 2% (10% x 20%) for SME Ltd.

Adding individual, teamwork, and workplace productivity contributions together, the overall productivity gain for SME employees is 6%, versus 10.5% for SD Inc. Even so, the contribution of this productivity improvement to the overall business case is substantial.

Figure A.4a: Savings on Electricity

Savings on Electricity	Annual Qty Today	Annual Cost Today	Potential Savings (%)	Potential Savings ($)
Savings on Electricity Used for Lighting				
Install occupant sensors			30%	
Use photo sensors or timers for outdoor lighting				
Use compact fluorescent lightbulbs (CFLs)			75%	
Convert from T12 to T8 fluorescent light fixtures			25%	
Use aluminum reflectors in fluorescent fixtures				
Use task lighting				
Reduce lighting in overlit rooms				
Turn off indoor lights at night				
Use LEDs for exit lights and decorative lights			95%	
Increase use of daylighting				
Other ...?				

Savings on Electricity Used for Lighting

There are numerous ways to save on electricity used for lighting. Here are some of them:

- Save up to 30% of energy used for lighting by installing occupancy sensors in seldom-used areas like storage rooms, washrooms, loading areas, and basements.[34]

- Use photo sensors or timers for internal or external lights left on overnight for security or safety reasons.[35]

- Convert to compact florescent lightbulbs (CFLs), which use 75% less energy and last ten times longer than incandescent lightbulbs.[36]

- Save 25% of energy used by fluorescent lights by converting from T12 technology to T8 technology with electronic ballasts that provide better lighting and do not buzz.[37]

- Use aluminum reflectors with CFLs or T8 fluorescents to increase lighting output with lower wattage bulbs.[38]

- Use task lighting.

- Reduce lighting in overlit areas.[39]

- Increase the use of daylighting with more windows, skylights, or solar tubes.

- Turn off indoor lights at night.

- Use light-emitting diodes (LEDs) for exit signs and other decorative lighting. They only use one watt of energy instead of the usual two 15-watt or 25-watt bulbs normally in exit lights. Since they are on all the time, you can save $20 a year for each exit sign converted to LED technology with a do-it-yourself kit.[40]

Rules of thumb are provided to indicate potential savings for some line items. The absence of a rule of thumb in this and other worksheets should not be interpreted as an absence of savings. The sample percentage savings are there simply to prime the pump for other opportunities.

Figure A.4b: Savings on Electricity

Savings on Electricity	Annual Qty Today	Annual Cost Today	Potential Savings (%)	Potential Savings ($)
Savings on Electricity Used for Appliances and Equipment				
Turn off computers, copiers, appliances after work				
Convert to Energy Star® appliances				
Locate refrigerators and freezers in cool areas				
Consider deferring use to off-peak hours				
Generate power onsite (cogeneration, solar, wind)				
Sell excess electricity back to the grid				
Install energy-efficient pumping motors				
Consider more efficient distribution transformers				
Use thicker electrical wires				
Other ...?				

Savings on Electricity Used for Appliances and Equipment

There are numerous ways to save electricity used for appliances, as shown in Figure A.4b.

- Turn off electrical appliances, computers, photocopiers, printers, etc., after work.[41]

- Use Energy Star® appliances, taking advantage of government incentives to do so.[42]

- Locate freezers and refrigerators in cool locations rather than near ovens, heaters, or in sunlight.[43]

- Plot 24-hour electricity use and consider deferring electrical appliance use to off-peak-rate hours, if possible.[44]

In addition, consider using electricity as a power source instead of compressed air, which costs about 10% more than electricity.[45]

You can also save on electricity used for industrial equipment. Motors use 75% of all industry electricity, and they are most often used for pumping. You can cut electricity costs by installing energy-efficient pumping motors, straightening piping systems, using more energy-efficient distribution transformers, and using thicker electrical wires to lower their resistance and associated heat/energy loss.

Explore ways to generate electrical power onsite, such as cogeneration, solar photovoltaic panels, or wind turbines in locations with a suitable wind regime. If your energy efficiency "negawatt" efforts are really effective, the company may be able to produce more electricity than it needs and sell the surplus back to the utility's grid, converting an expense to a revenue opportunity.

If you are uncertain about which appliances are most inefficient and need to be replaced, or how much electricity they consume even when turned "off," use a Kill-a-Watt meter.[46] Plug the meter into a three-prong grounded wall outlet and then plug the appliance into the meter. The LCD display on the meter shows energy consumption by Kilowatt-hour, enabling you to calculate electrical expenses by the hour, day, week, month, or year. The knowledge gained can conserve energy and reduce your power bill.

Figure A.5a: Savings on Fuel

Savings on Fuel	Annual Qty Today	Annual Cost Today	Potential Savings (%)	Potential Savings ($)
Savings on Fuel Used for Heating and Cooling				
Close entrance doors and windows when heating			30%	
Clean radiators and baseboard heaters				
Change furnace filters regularly				
Use eco-efficient, right-sized fan and HVAC systems				
Ensure HVAC system use is monitored and controlled				
Maximize ventilation with a heat exchanger				
Install reversible ceiling fans to heat and cool				
Use programmable thermostats				
Install plastic insulating sheets on windows				
Use shades and awnings				
Plant trees to shade buildings			40%	
Plug drafty openings and electrical outlets				
Increase ceiling insulation and weather stripping				
Install double-paned or "super" windows				
Insulate hot water tanks and pipes; lower thermostat				
Tap into district heating, if available			10%	
Install a passive solar hot water heater			35%	
Install a solar wall			33%	
Other ...?				

Savings on Fuel Used for Heating and Cooling

Energy used for heating or cooling can be saved by doing the following:

- Close entrance doors when heating.

- Clean radiators or baseboard heaters.

- Change furnace filters regularly.

- Use energy-efficient natural gas furnaces and air conditioners and maintain them regularly. Heating costs can increase by 30% or more if boilers are poorly maintained or operated.[47]

- Ensure the building's heating, ventilation, and air-conditioning (HVAC) management system is monitoring air-conditioning, chiller use, and other cooling and heating components so they operate only when needed.[48]

- Maximize ventilation with a heat exchanger.[49]

- Install reversible ceiling fans that push hot air down in the winter and pull hot air up in the summer.

- Use a programmable thermostat to avoid overheating — each 1° Celsius of overheating raises the heating costs by 6% to 10%.[50]

- Install insulating plastic sheets on the interior of windows.

- Use shades or awnings, and plant trees, to shade buildings. Properly sited trees can reduce air-conditioning needs by 40% and heating needs by 10%.

- Fill draft gaps with expandable foam, and install foam pads to fill drafty electrical outlets.

- Increase insulation in ceilings, and improve weather stripping.

- Retrofit double-paned or "super" windows to reduce air-conditioning needs by 38% and heating needs by 34% in cold climes.[51] You can avoid unnecessary air-conditioning by installing windows that can be opened on hot days.[52]

- Insulate hot water pipes and the hot water tank, and lower the thermostat on the hot water tank. Reducing the temperature by 11° Celsius can cut water heating costs by 10%.[53]

- Use district heating if it is available.

- Install a passive solar hot water heater or solar wall.

Figure A.5b: Savings on Fuel

Savings on Fuel	Annual Qty Today	Annual Cost Today	Potential Savings (%)	Potential Savings ($)
Savings on Fuel Used for Transportation				
Use fuel-efficient vehicles				
Consider using compressed natural gas (CNG)				
Keep the vehicles tuned and tires at correct pressure				
Keep a log of fuel consumption for each vehicle				
Discourage idling on deliveries				
Improve route planning				
Use rail instead of trucks or air freight whenever possible				
Enable employee use of public transit and carpooling				
Consider planting trees to offset carbon-dioxide emissions				
Other ...?				

Savings on Fuel Used in Transportation

You can save additional fuel costs in transportation of raw materials, delivering finished goods, and employee commuting. The following is a partial list of ways to economize fuel used in transportation, echoed in Figure A.5b.

- Use fuel-efficient vehicles.
- Consider using alternative fuels like compressed natural gas (CNG).
- Keep vehicle engines tuned and tires at correct pressure.
- Keep a log of fuel consumption and other costs for each vehicle to provide insights into savings opportunities and fuel-efficient driving habits of employees. Poor driving techniques can increase fuel consumption by 20%.[54]
- Discourage idling when drivers are making deliveries.
- Improve route planning.
- Use rail instead of trucks or air freight whenever possible.
- Enable employee use of public transit and carpooling.
- Consider planting trees to offset carbon-dioxide emissions.[55]
- Use teleconferencing or videoconferencing instead of business travel.

Figure A.6: Savings from Water Efficiencies

Savings from Water Efficiencies	Annual Qty Today	Annual Cost Today	Potential Savings (%)	Potential Savings ($)
Install aerators on taps				
Install spring-loaded turn-off valves				
Fix dripping taps				
Install low-flow shower heads				
Install low-flow toilets or toilet dams			50%	
Use rainwater in industrial processes				
Landscape using native plants that require less water				
Redesign inefficient rinse systems				
Use low-pressure water instead of high-pressure				
Consider closed-loop water treatment				
Consider "living machine" water treatment				
Other ...?				

Savings from Water Efficiencies

Some SMEs pay for water four times: when they are metered for the water in the first place, when they treat the water to production standards, when they treat the water prior to discharge, and when they are charged sewage fees. Water and effluent bills can cost a company as much as 1% to 2% of its revenue.[56] The following measures can help reduce water bills.

- Install aerators on taps.

- Install spring-loaded turn-off valves.

- Fix dripping taps.

- Install low-flow shower heads.

- Install dams in toilets or low-flow toilets. Dams can reduce the cost per flush by 25%, and a low-flow, six-litre toilet can cut water bills by 50% while improving performance.[57]

- Use rainwater instead of drinking water in industrial processes.

- Landscape using native plants that require less water.[58]

- Redesign inefficient rinse systems.

- Use low-pressure water instead of high-pressure water where possible.[59]

- Consider closed-loop water treatment, replacing some or all incoming water with the treated effluent.

- Consider using a "living machine" to treat waste water. Such a system uses tanks, marshes, and reed beds where bacteria, zooplankton, plants, snails, and fish process the organic waste into water that is reusable for industrial purposes.[60]

Cost savings. A lot of people get into CSR from the waste management side. This is how many resource companies got into it in the first place. It is the classic environmental sustainability dimension — managing costs, reducing waste, and making waste useful or, at least, not a problem. (Steven Cross)

Figure A.7: Savings from Better Waste Management

Savings from Better Waste Management	Annual Qty Today	Annual Cost Today	Potential Savings (%)	Potential Savings ($)
Redesign processes to be more efficient				
Substitute benign materials for hazardous ones				
Reduce monitoring and reporting costs if you do the above substitution				
Reduce amount of material used per product				
Reuse materials, solvents, chemicals, and packaging				
Recycle materials at end of product life				
Sort and sell paper, glass, metal, and organics				
Reduce cost of hazardous waste disposal				
Reduce cost of non-hazardous waste disposal				
Use double-sided photocopying				
Require suppliers to take back their packaging				
Use reusable kitchen cutlery, plates, cups, etc.				
Use reusable manila envelopes and file folders				
Return printer cartridges				
Use rechargeable batteries				
Centralize paper filing				
Donate old equipment and furniture to charities				
Remove the company from unwanted mailing lists				
Buy products with high recycled content				
Take back your own products after their end of life				
Other …?				

Savings from Better Waste Management

There are two kinds of waste: non-hazardous and hazardous. The true cost of wasted materials and chemicals is about ten times the cost of disposal when hidden costs like labor, energy, and other added-value costs are included.[61] To reduce waste:

- *Eliminate:* Avoid producing waste in the first place by redesigning processes and procedures to be more efficient and effective. Substitute benign solvents for hazardous chemicals, and reformulate products to use alternatives to hazardous or non-recyclable materials.

- *Reduce:* Minimize the amount of material used and waste generated in current processes, saving money on the purchase of raw materials.

- *Reuse:* Use materials, solvents, chemicals, and packaging as many times as possible to reduce net operating costs.

- *Recycle:* Recycle materials and products when they cannot be reused further; sort them into segregated waste streams for specialist recycling companies, to maximize this source of income.[62]

Reducing hazardous waste correspondingly reduces costs for permits, fines, penalties, inspections, documentation for shipments, labeling, safety training, employee health insurance premiums, and protective equipment associated with their use. Cost of treatment of air and water emissions is reduced, as is the cost of solid waste disposal and treatment of storm water runoff. Further, you can lower costs of record keeping, site monitoring, environmental studies, decommissioning, audits, and legal fees.[63]

You can eliminate non-hazardous waste by: making double-sided copies and reusing single-sided copies as notepaper; requiring suppliers to take back their packaging; replacing disposable coffee mugs, cutlery, and crockery with reusable products; using reusable manila envelopes for internal mail and reusing file folders; using rechargeable batteries; returning printer toner cartridges; centralizing paper filing and using technology to move to a "paperless" office; donating old equipment and furniture to charitable organizations; removing yourself from unwanted mailing lists; and placing recycling containers in handy locations.[64]

To close the loop, buy recycled products or products with high recycled content and take back your own products after their useful life has ended.

Small and medium-sized enterprises have a much more limited capacity to undertake sustainable development than do large corporations. If governments and large companies devote some of their resources to helping these smaller organizations move forward, then everybody benefits. (Ron Yachnin)

The idea of the CEO network is important — learning from your peers and mentors. A sort of buddy network. The moment one person at the golf carts starts wearing a dark green hat, pretty soon they all are, especially if they happen to see the guy with a very prestigious head with the hat on. (Nigel Roome)

Critical Success Factors for Engaging SMEs in CSR Activities:
- Commitment of owner/management to running their business on these principles
- Enthusiastic engagement of employees and other stakeholders
- Core business vision and values based on CSR principles
- Integration into existing mainstream management/operational practice
- Staged approach to build confidence among SMEs hungry for results, incorporating shorter-term results into vision of long-term sustainability
- Networking opportunities for SMEs to learn from their peers
- Availability of good practice examples for other SMEs to learn from
- Understandable benchmark standards to aspire to, and corresponding management tools to help attain them
- Supply chain advice, training, and reward/sanctions from clients
— European Multi Stakeholder Forum on Corporate Social Responsibility, "Report of the Round Table on Fostering CSR Among SMEs"[65]

Food for Thought on Engaging SMEs in Sustainability

It is not the fancy acronyms or big corporate language that will attract SMEs to sustainability. CSR will sell if it represents better business. Small companies can reduce their costs by managing environmental impacts. They can retain their best staff by making employees feel proud to work for them, and by being active corporate citizens in the local community. They can sell more if they nurture strong relationships with customers, their own people, and the community overall.[66] Many SMEs seem to know all this already — a 2002 UK study of SMEs found that 81% believe that CSR activities contribute to a successful business.[67]

However, there is a real danger that sustainability may be oversold as a panacea for poorly run companies. No amount of environmental and community focus will prolong the life of a company that is economically unsustainable and mismanaged.[68] It is a catalyst, not a straw to be grasped by companies drowning in red ink. Further, it is one thing to have a business case in an Excel spreadsheet. It is another to ensure that the balance sheet, profit and loss statement, and income statements track, integrate, and report sustainability potential benefit areas so that their value is actually captured.

Encouragement, support, case studies, and communication tools need to be tailored for SMEs. The Small Business Consortium was set up in the UK in 2002 specifically to produce materials that support SME improvements in social responsibility. The consortium is a collaborative effort of AccountAbility, Arts & Business, British Chambers of Commerce, Business in the Community, CSR Europe, Federation of Small Businesses, The Forum of Private Business, Institute of Directors, Lloyds TSB, and Scottish Business in the Community.[69] As of July 2004, the SME Key database had 57 case studies of SME companies' experiences with CSR initiatives in a variety of industries.[70] More SME-targeted resources are being developed in other jurisdictions, such as the SME Program of Canadian Business for Social Responsibility.[71]

The objective of these initiatives is to provide practical, relevant tools and information to help SMEs learn from each other on their sustainability journeys. The business case outlined here is one more small contribution to that effort.

ENDNOTES

Chapter 1: Introduction

1 Deloitte & Touche, "SD Energy Leaders: Analytical Framework," from a slide deck received by e-mail from Dale Littlejohn, April 2004.

2 World Commission on the Environment and Development (WCED), *Our Common Future*, Oxford University Press, 1987, p. 43.

3 "Understanding Sustainability" [online], [cited July 8, 2004], The Natural Step website. <www.naturalstep.org/learn/understand_sust.php>

4 Lynn Johannson, "ISO 14001: One For All, Or Just For Some?" *ISO Management Systems,* September-October 2002, p. 51.

5 Malcolm Gladwell, *The Tipping Point: How Little Things Can Make a Big Difference*, Little Brown and Company, 2000, pp. 166, 172, and 173.

6 Ibid., pp. 30–88.

7 Jane Nelson, Peter Zollinger, and Alok Singh, *The Power to Change: Mobilizing Board Leadership to Deliver Sustainable Value to Markets and Society,* SustainAbility Ltd., 2001, pp. 4–8.

8 Ibid., p. 14.

9 The SIGMA Project Management Team, *The SIGMA Project: Sustainability in Practice,* The SIGMA Project, 2001, p. 6.2.10.

10 WCED, *Our Common Future,* p. 43.

11 Conference Board of Canada,"Governance and Corporate Social Responsibility" [online], [cited July 8, 2004]. <www.conferenceboard.ca/GCSR/default.htm>

12 "Corporate Social Responsibility" [online], [cited July 8, 2004], World Business Council for Sustainable Development (WBCSD) website.

13 "European Union Multi Stakeholder Forum on Social Responsibility: Final Forum Report" [online], [cited July 11, 2004], Europa website, June 2004. <europa.eu.int/comm/enterprise/csr/documents/final_draft_forum_report_290604.pdf>

14 "Understanding Sustainability" [online], <www.naturalstep.org/learn/understand_sust.php>

15 Lisa Princic, "Sustainability Primer" (draft), Canadian Business for Social Responsibility, April 2004.

16 David Kemker, "Earthkeeper Hero: William McDonough" [online], [cited July 8, 2004], My Hero website, April 20, 2004. <www.myhero.com/myhero/hero.asp?hero=McDonough_Update_04>

17 John Ehrenfeld, "Tomorrow's Challenges," presentation given at York University's Sustainable Enterprise Academy, May 5–8, 2003, Kimberley, Ontario.

18 William McDonough, "Creative Pathways to Sustainability," from personal notes during his remarks made during this panel discussion at Globe 2004, March 31, 2004, Vancouver, BC.

19 Brian Pearce, *Sustainability and Business Competitiveness: Measuring the Benefit for Business and Competitive Advantage from Social Responsibility and Sustainability*, Forum for the Future and Department of Trade and Industry, 2003, p. 7.

20 Mel Wilson, "Corporate Sustainability: What Is It and Where Does It Come From?" *Ivey Business Journal*, March/April 2003, Reprint # 9B03TB06, p. 2.

21 Conference Board of Canada, "The National Corporate Social Responsibility Report: Managing Risks, Leveraging Opportunities," Conference Board of Canada, 2004, p. 2.

22 "Making Corporate Responsibility Work: Lessons from Real Business" [online], [cited August 4, 2004], *Ethical Corporation*, August 24, 2004. <www.wbcsd.org/plugins/DocSearch/details.asp?type=DocDet&DocId=7103>

23 "About Project" [online], [cited August 4, 2004], Conversations With Disbelievers website. <www.conversations-with-disbelievers.net/site/about/>

24 Ibid.

25 Mark Schacter, with Elder C. Marques, "Altruism, Opportunism and Points in Between: Trends and Practices in Corporate Social Responsibility" [online], [cited July 8, 2004], Institute on Governance, 2000, p. ii. <www.iog.ca/publications/csr.pdf>

26 Forum for the Future, *Just Values: Beyond the Business Case for Sustainable Development*, British Telecommunications plc, 2003, p. 16.

27 Coro Strandberg, *The Future of Corporate Social Responsibility*, VanCity Credit Union, 2002, p. 5.

28 Carl Frankel, *In Earth's Company: Business, Environment and the Challenge of Sustainability*, New Society Publishers, pp. 35–94.

29 Marcel van Marrewijk, "European Corporate Sustainability Framework", paper delivered at the 47th Annual Congress, European Organization for Quality, 2003, p. 2.

30 Mark Goyder, *Refining CSR: From the Rhetoric of Accountability to the Reality of Earning Trust*, Tomorrow's Company, 2003, p. 2.

31 The Sustainability Helix was developed by Natural Capitalism Inc. in partnership with The Natural Edge Project (Aus) and The Global Academy. For more information, see www.natcapinc.com. The Chicago Manufacturing Center uses the Helix in its GreenPlants Initiative, see <www.cmcusa.org/initiatives/index.cfm>

32 "2002 Sustainability Survey Report" [online], [cited July 8, 2004], PricewaterhouseCoopers website, unnumbered "Key Statistics" page. <www.pwcglobal.com/fas/pdfs/sustainability%20survey%20report.pdf>

33 Laurent Leduc, "Corporation as Servant: A Contribution to Conversations in Corporate Social Responsibility," unpublished paper, 2003, p. 4.

34 Ibid., p. 14.

35 George Carpenter and Peter White, "Sustainable Development: Finding the Real Business Case," *International Journal for Sustainable Development* 11:2, February 2004, Reprint R110202051, p. 2–56.

36 Bob Doppelt, *Leading Change Toward Sustainability*, Greenleaf Publishing, 2002, p. 36.

37 John Elkington, *The Chrysalis Economy: How Citizen ÇEOs and Corporations Can Fuse Values and Value Creation*, Capstone Publishing, 2001, pp. 71–99.

38 Natural Resources Canada, Interdepartmental Working Group on Corporate Social Responsibility, "Corporate Social Responsibility: Lessons Learned" [online], [cited July 8, 2004], Natural Resources Canada, 2003, p. 4. <www.nrcan.gc.ca/sd-dd/pubs/csr-rse/pdf/csr.pdf>

39 Ibid, p. 6.

40 GlobeScan, "The GlobeScan Survey of Sustainability Experts: 2003–2 Highlights Report" GlobeScan, 2003, p. 6.

Chapter 2: Three Drivers of the First Wave

1 "2002 Sustainability Survey Report" [online], [cited July 8, 2004], PricewaterhouseCoopers website, unnumbered Key Statistics page. <www.pwcglobal.com/fas/pdfs/sustainability%20survey%20report.pdf>

2 William Baue, "CEOs Worldwide Prioritize Corporate Social Responsibility" [online]. [cited July 8, 2004]. *SocialFunds.com*, February 01, 2002. <www.socialfunds.com/news/article.cgi/article769.html>.

3 "CSR shining lights are being hidden" [online], [cited July 8, 2004], Edie.net, July 19, 2002. <www.edie.net/gf.cfm?L=left_frame.html&R= http://www.edie.net/news/Archive/5766.cfm>

4 Memuna Forna, "Could do better! Must try harder! Survey shows that CEOs have been slow to learn the lessons of Enron and Tyco" [online], [cited July 8, 2004], The Work Foundation website, February 20, 2003. <www.theworkfoundation.com/newsroom/pressreleases.jsp?ref=84>.

5 "SustainableBusiness.com Announces This Year's SB20: The World's Top Sustainable Stocks" [online], [cited July 28, 2004], press release from SustainableBusiness.com, July 22, 2004. <www.csrwire.com/article.cgi/ 2901.html> The SB20 list is produced by *Progressive Investor*, published by SustainableBusiness.com.

6 "2003 World's Most Respected Companies Survey" [online], [cited July 8, 2004], PricewaterhouseCoopers website. <www.pwc.com/Extweb/ ncsurvres.nsf/docid/D2345E01A80AC14885256CB00033DC8F>

7   "World's most respected companies — 2001: Tables Index" [online], [cited July 8, 2004], *Financial Times* website. <specials.ft.com/wmr2001/ FT3NGL5G6VC.html>

8   "Business Ethics Corporate Social Responsibility Report, 2004" [online], [cited July 8, 2004], *Business Ethics* website. <www.businessethics.com/ chart_100_best_corporate_citizens_for_2004.htm>. Reprinted with permission from *Business Ethics*, P.O. Box 8439, Minneapolis, MN 55408, 612-879-0695, <www.businessethics.com>

9   Mark Schacter, with Elder C. Marques, *Altruism, Opportunism and Points in Between: Trends and Practices in Corporate Social Responsibility* [online], [cited July 8, 2004], Institute on Governance, 2000, p. ii. <www.iog.ca/publications/csr.pdf>

10 Jeffrey Hollander, *What Matters Most: How a Small Group of Pioneers Is Teaching Social Responsibility to Big Business, and Why Big Business Is Listening*, Basic Books, 2004, pp. 231 and 232.

11 "Companies believe in ethics, poll says," *Deseret News*, July 15, 2003.

12 Stan Maklan and Simon Knox, *CSR at a Crossroads*, Cranfield University School of Management, 2003, p. 13.

13 At IBM, for example, employees are required to annually confirm that they have read, understood, and will follow IBM's Business Conduct Guidelines, which spell out appropriate ethical behavior in various situations.

14 "United Nations Global Compact Announces Milestone: 1,000 Businesses Now Participating" [online], [cited July 8, 2004], *CSRwire*, July 2, 2003. <www.csrwire.com/article.cgi/1949.html>

15 Earth Charter Initiative, "Endorsement Statement" [online], [cited July 8, 2004], Earth Charter website, July 2003. <www.earthcharter.org/endorse/> A pop-up window with the number of worldwide individuals, groups, and organizations that have endorsed the Earth Charter is available by clicking the "View the list of endorsers" button.

16 Jim Kouzes and Barry Posner, *The Leadership Challenge: How to Keep Getting Extraordinary Things Done in Organizations*, Jossey-Bass Publishers, 1995.

17 Marjorie Kelly, *The Divine Right of Capital: Dethroning the Corporate Aristocracy*, Berrett-Koehler Publishers, 2001, p. 62.

18 Simon Webley and Elise More, *Does Business Ethics Pay? Ethics and Financial Performance*, Institute of Business Ethics, 2003, p. 9.

19 Mervyn Pedelty, "A Year in Focus" [online], [cited July 8, 2004], "The Co-operative Bank Partnership Report 2001". <www.co-operativebank.co.uk/ ethics/partnership2001/pr/chief_exec.html>

20 "Henry Mintzberg in the News: Henry Mintzberg on the Bad Side of Big Business" [online], [cited July 8, 2004], *McGill News*, "Alumni Quarterly,"

Fall 2002. <www.mcgill.ca/news/archives/fall2002/mintzberg/>

21 Robert Hinkley, "How Corporate Law Inhibits Social Responsibility" [online], [cited July 8, 2004], "Business Ethics: Corporate Social Responsibility Report", January/February 2002. <www.divinerightof capital.com/change.htm>

22 Kelly, *Divine Right of Capital,* p. 2.

23 Ibid., p. 3.

24 Ibid., pp. 5–7.

25 Penny S. Bonda, "Follow the Leader" [online], [cited July 8, 2004], *green@work,* July/August 2002. <www.greenbiz.com/news/printer.cfm?newsID=22058>

26 Mel Wilson and Rosie Lombardi, "Globalization and Its Discontents: The Arrival of Triple-Bottom-Line Reporting" [online], [cited July 8, 2004], *Ivey Business Journal,* September/October 2001. <www.iveybusinessjournal.com/view_article.asp?intArticle_ID=334>

27 World Economic Forum, *Values and Value: Communicating the Strategic Importance of Corporate Citizenship to Investors,* World Economic Forum, 2004, p. 24.

28 "Voice of the Leaders Survey: 2004 Annual Meeting Survey," [online], [cited October 29, 2004], World Economic Forum website, p. 1. <www.weforum.org/pdf/am04_survey2.pdf>

29 Arthur D. Little, *The Business Case for Corporate Citizenship,* Arthur D. Little, 2002, p. 1.

30 Hill & Knowlton and Korn/Ferry International, "2003 Corporate Reputation Watch Survey" [online], [cited July 8, 2004], Hill & Knowlton website, 2003.

31 Little, *The Business Case for Corporate Citizenship,* p. 1.

32 Joel Makower, "The Seven Attributes of Highly Reputational Companies," *The Green Business Letter,* Tilden Press, June 2003, p. 4.

33 "Reputation Management" [online], [cited July 8, 2004], Harris Interactive website. <www.harrisinteractive.com/expertise/reputation.asp>

34 World Economic Forum, "Values and Value", p. 24.

35 Ibid.

36 Stephan Bevan, Nick Isles, Peter Emery, and Tony Hoskins, *Achieving High Performance: CSR at the Heart of Business,* The Work Foundation, 2004, p. 17.

37 "Boards of Directors Getting More Involved in Companies' Ethics Programs" [online], [cited July 8, 2004], *CSRwire,* March 4, 2004. <www.csrwire.com/article.cgi/2538.html>.

38 "97% of Business Leaders Believe Damaged Corporate Reputations Can Be Restored — Though It Can Take up to Four Years" [online], [cited July 19, 2004], Burson-Marsteller press release, September 16, 2003. <www.bm.com/pages/news/releases/2003/press-09-16-2003>

39 Alison Maitland, "Barclays Banks on a Good Name: A Growing Number of Companies Now Recognise the Importance of Managing Risk to Corporate Reputation" [online], [cited July 8, 2004], *Financial Times,* February 19, 2004. <www.business-humanrights.org/Categories/Sectors/Finance/ Financebanking>

40 David Brinkerhoff, "Dow Investors Seek More Details on Bhopal Disaster" [online], [cited July 8, 2004], *Planet Ark,* May 17, 2004. <www.planetark.com/avantgo/dailynewsstory.cfm?newsid=25123>.

41 Ethical Corporation, "Press Coverage of CSR Increases by Over 400% in Last Three Years" [online], [cited July 8, 2004], *GreenBiz.com.* <www.greenbiz.com/news/news_third.cfm?NewsID=26316>

42 David R. Boyd, *Unnatural Law: Rethinking Canadian Environmental Law and Policy,* UBC Press, 2003, pp. 72–79.

43 Paul Tarr, "Analysis: Is Trying to Kill the Alien Tort Claims Act Digging for Fool's Gold?" [online], [cited July 8, 2004], *Ethical Corporation Online,* May 13, 2004. <www.ethicalcorp.com/content_print.asp?ContentID=2036>

44 Sarah Murray, "Environmental Risk: Investors Demand Action on Climate Change," *Financial Times,* January 16, 2004.

45 Hinkley, "How Corporate Law Inhibits Social Responsibility."

46 "Shellshocked" [online], [cited July 8, 2004], *Economist.com,* March 10, 2004. <www.economist.com/agenda/displayStory.cfm?story_id=2494807>

47 Kathryn Harrison, "Talking with the Donkey: Cooperative Approaches to Environmental Protection," *Journal of Industrial Ecology* 2:3, 1998, p. 67.

48 Environment Canada, *Guide to the Canadian Environmental Protection Act,* Environment Canada, 2000, p. 18.

49 Dianne Saxe, "The Impact of Prosecution of Corporations and Their Officers and Directors upon Regulatory Compliance by Corporations." *Journal of Environmental Law and Practice 1,* September 1990, pp. 104 and 109.

50 Kenneth W. Johnson, "Law, Ethics, and the Federal Sentencing Guidelines for Organizations" [online], [cited July 8, 2004], *Ethical Edge,* May 2, 2003. <www.ethicaledge.com/quest_2.html>

51 Bruce A. Hamm, "Elements of the US Federal Sentencing Guidelines" [online], [cited July 8, 2004], Ethics and Policy Information Centre website, 2003. <www.refresher.com/!bahsentencing.html>

52 Boyd, *Unnatural Law,* p. 219.

53 John Moffat and Francois Bregha, "The Role of Law Reform in the Promotion of Sustainable Development," *Journal of Environmental Law and Practice 6,* December 1995, p. 19.

54 Carl J. Schramm, "The High Price of Low Ethics: How Corruption Imperils American Entrepreneurship and Democracy" [online], [cited July 8, 2004],

paper delivered at the University of Rochester, Meliora Weekend, October 12, 2002, pp. 8, 9, and 12. <www.emkf.org/pdf/schramm_ethics_10_12_02.pdf>

55 Boyd, *Unnatural Law,* p. 334.

56 Canadian Chemical Producers' Association (CCPA), "Reducing Emissions: 2002 Emissions Inventory and Five Year Reductions," CCPA, 2003, pp. 2–4.

57 Jennifer Lynes and Robert B. Gibson, "Appendix: The Alternatives Pocket Guide to Voluntary Corporate Initiatives for Environmental Improvement" in *Voluntary Initiatives,* edited by Robert B. Gibson, Broadview Press Ltd., 1999, p. 260.

58 Colin Isaacs, "An Environmental Lexicon," *The Gallon Environment Letter,* Canadian Institute for Business and the Environment, 9:7, April 7, 2004.

59 Thomas P. Lyon and John W. Maxwell, "Corporate environmental strategies as tools to influence regulation," *Business Strategy and the Environment* 8, 1999, p. 189.

60 Lynes and Gibson, "Appendix" in *Voluntary Initiatives,* p. 262.

61 Harrison, "Talking with the Donkey," p. 67.

62 Richard Teather, "Corporate Citizenship: A Tax in Disguise" [online], [cited July 8, 2004], Mises.org, August 5, 2003. <www.mises.org/fullstory.asp?control =1280>.

63 Boyd, *Unnatural Law,* pp. 87–89.

64 Harrison, "Talking with the Donkey," p. 53.

65 "The Ten Principles" [online], [cited July 8, 2004], UN Global Compact website. <www.unglobalcompact.org/Portal/Default.asp>

66 McKinsey & Company, *Assessing the Global Compact's Impact* [online], [cited July 8, 2004], World Business Council for Sustainable Development website, May 11, 2004. <www.wbcsd.ch/plugins/DocSearch/details.asp?type= DocDet&DocId=NTc2MQ>

67 Ibid, p. 59.

68 Joanna Sabatini, "Banks Begin to Evaluate Impact of Project Financing: Lowering the Risk May Aid Shareholders" [online], [cited July 8, 2004], *Investment News,* June 7, 2004. <issue.investmentnews.com/ article.cms?articleId=507>

69 "The Equator Principles" [online], [cited July 8, 2004], Equator Principles website. <www.equator-principles.com/principles.shtml>

70 "Equator Principles: Principles, Profits or just PR?" [online], [cited July 8, 2004], BankTrack, June 3, 2004. <www.banktrack.org/fileadmin/user_upload/ documents/0_BT_press_releases/0306_PPP_press_release_01.pdf>

71 "Fact Sheet: Voluntary Principles on Security and Human Rights" [online], [cited July 8, 2004], US Department of State website, February 20, 2001. <www.state.gov/g/drl/rls/2931.htm>

72 "Principles" [online], [cited July 8, 2004], Global Sullivan Principles website. <www.globalsullivanprinciples.org/principles.htm>

73 "Universal Declaration of Human Rights" [online], [cited July 8, 2004], United Nations website. <www.un.org/Overview/rights.html>

74 "Declaration on Fundamental Principles and Rights at Work" [online], [cited July 8, 2004], International Labor Organization website.

75 "Shell Leads International Business Campaign Against UN Human Rights Norms" [online], [cited July 8, 2004], *CEO Info Brief,* March 2004. <www.corporateeurope.org/norms>

76 Thomas P. Lyon, "'Green' Firms Bearing Gifts," *Regulation* 26:3, Fall 2003, p. 36.

77 Roger Crowe, "Business/NGO Partnerships — What's the Payback?" [online], [cited July 19, 2004], "Ethical Corporation", April 2004. <www.greenbiz.com/news/reviews_third.cfm?NewsID=26712>

78 "Who We Are" [online], [cited July 8, 2004], Imagine website. <www.imagine.ca/content/about_imagine/who_we_are.asp?section=about>

79 Jed Emerson, Sheila Bonini, and Kim Brehm, "The Blended Value Map: Tracking the Intersects and Opportunities of Economic, Social, and Environmental Value Creation" [online], [cited July 8, 2004], BlendedValue.org, pp. 1–2. <www.blendedvalue.org/Papers/97.aspx>

80 GlobeScan, "The GlobeScan Survey of Sustainability Experts: 2003–2 Highlights Report," GlobeScan, 2003, p. 6.

81 Paul Muldoon and Ramani Nadarajah, "A Sober Second Look" in *Voluntary Initiatives,* edited by Robert B. Gibson, Broadview Press Ltd., 1999, p. 62.

82 Ibid., p. 56.

83 Robert B. Gibson, "Voluntary Initiatives, Regulations, and Beyond" in *Voluntary Initiatives,* edited by Robert B. Gibson, Broadview Press Ltd., 1999, p. 253.

Chapter 3: First Emerging Driver — A Perfect Storm of Threats

1 Daryl Conner, *Managing at the Speed of Change: How Resilient Managers Succeed and Prosper Where Others Fail,* Villard Books, 1993, p. 93.

2 "Thar She Blows...Literally" [online], [cited July 8, 2004], *Destination Disaster* website. <www.mindspring.com/~emzeman/Disaster10.htm>

3 Thomas Atkins, "Insurer warns of global warming catastrophe" [online], [cited July 8, 2004], Common Dreams News Centre website, March 3, 2004. <www.commondreams.org/headlines04/0303-07.htm>

4 "Ingredients for a Real 'Perfect Storm'" [online], [cited July 8, 2004], *USA Today,* October 30, 2000. <www.usatoday.com/weather/movies/ps/perfectstorm.htm>.

5 "GOES: The Perfect Storm" [online], [cited July 8, 2004], Visible Earth, October 31, 1991. <visibleearth.nasa.gov/cgi-bin/viewrecord?5989>

6 "The Storm" [online], [cited July 8, 2004], Warner Brothers website. <perfectstorm.warnerbros.com/cmp/flash-thestorm-fr.html>

7 Ibid.

8 Bob Willard, *The Sustainability Advantage: Seven Business Case Benefits of a Triple Bottom Line*, New Society Publishers, 2002, pp. 121–138.

9 Paul Gilding, Murray Hogarth, and Don Reed, *Single Bottom Line Sustainability: How a Value Centered Approach to Corporate Sustainability Can Pay Off For Shareholders and Society*, Ecos Corporation, 2002, p. 3.

10 Don S. Doering, Amy Cassara, Christian Layke, Janet Ranganathan, Carmen Revenga, Dan Tunstall, and Wendy Vanasselt, *Tomorrow's Markets: Global Trends and Their Implications for Business*, World Resources Institute, United Nations Environment Programme, World Business Council for Sustainable Development, 2002, p. 4.

11 Ibid, pp. 8–56.

12 "Investors Rate 500 Largest Companies on Climate" [online], [cited July 8, 2004], *GreenBiz.com*, May 19, 2004. <www.greenbiz.com/news/printer.cfm?NewsID=26780>

13 Environment Canada "Online Database" [online], [cited July 8, 2004], Environment Canada website. <www.ec.gc.ca/pdb/ghg/online_data_e.cfm> The six greenhouse gases (GHGs) are carbon dioxide (CO_2), methane (CH_4), nitrous oxide (N_2O), sulphur hexafluoride (SF_6), perfluorocarbons (PFCs), and hydrofluorocarbons (HFCs). The first three are the most prevalent, with methane and nitrous oxide being 23 and 296 times more potent, respectively, than carbon dioxide as greenhouse gases. Using those ratios, greenhouse gas volumes are usually expressed in carbon-dioxide equivalents.

14 "Greenhouse Gas Emissions of the Agriculture and Agri-Food Industry" [online], [cited July 8, 2004], Alberta Agriculture, Food, and Rural Development website. <www.agric.gov.ab.ca/sustain/grnhouse_gas/00032.html#sectors>

15 Joel Makower, "It's the Carbon, Stupid," *The Green Business Letter*, Tilden Press, April 2004, p.8.

16 Martin Whittaker, "Carbon Disclosure Project: Carbon Finance and the Global Equity Market" [online], [cited July 8, 2004], Innovest, 2003). <194.242.156.103/cdproject/downloads/cdp_report.pdf>

17 Ibid., p. 6.

18 Terry Macalister, "Corporates warm to climate change" [online], [cited July 8, 2004], *The Guardian*, May 15, 2004. <www.guardian.co.uk/climatechange/story/0,12374,1217437,00.html>

19 Keith Bradsher, "China's Boom Adds to Global Warming Problem" [online], [cited July 8, 2004], *New York Times,* October 22, 2003. <www.owonder.com/eco/china_nyt_oct22_2003.html>

20 Marq de Villiers, *Water,* Stoddart Publishing, 1999, pp. 112, 113, and 117. Quotes from the chapter "Unnatural Selection." Used by permission of McClelland & Stewart Ltd., The Canadian Publishers.

21 "Nearly 1 in 5 US Counties Have Unhealthy Air — EPA" [online], [cited July 8, 2004], *Planet Ark,* April 16, 2004. <www.planetark.com/ dailynewsstory.cfm/newsid/24729/story.htm>

22 Bernie Fischlowitz-Roberts, "Air Pollution Fatalities Now Exceed Traffic Fatalities by 3 to 1" [online], [cited July 8, 2004], Earth Policy Institute website, September 17, 2002. <www.earth-policy.org/Updates/ Update17.htm>

23 "The Illness Costs of Air Pollution in Ontario: A Summary of Findings" [online], [cited July 8, 2004], Ontario Medical Association (OMA) website, June 2002. <www.oma.org/phealth/icap.htm#summary>

24 Ibid.

25 Doering, et al., *Tomorrow's Markets,* p. 27.

26 Charles O. Holliday Jr., Stephen Schmidheiny, and Philip Watts, *Walking the Talk: The Business Case for Sustainable Development,* Greenleaf Publishing, 2002, pp. 42, 43, 52, and 53.

27 David Korten, *When Corporations Rule the World,* Berrett-Koehler Publishers, 1996, p. 173.

28 "The WTO ... in Brief" [online]. [cited July 8, 2004]. World Trade Organization website. <www.wto.org/english/thewto_e/whatis_e/ inbrief_e/inbr00_e.htm>

29 Korten, *When Corporations Rule the World,* p. 177.

30 Ibid., p. 176.

31 Yves Engler, "Putting the WTO Back in the Spotlight" [online], [cited July 8, 2004], *rabble news,* May 29, 2003. <www.rabble.ca/in_their_own_ words.shtml?x=22108>.

32 Maude Barlow and Tony Clarke, *Global Showdown: How the New Activists Are Fighting Global Corporate Rule,* Stoddart Publishing, 2001, p. 76.

33 Korten, *When Corporations Rule the World,* p. 176.

34 Guy Dauncey with Patrick Mazza, *Stormy Weather: 101 Solutions to Global Climate Change,* New Society Publishers, 2001, p. 198.

35 Ibid.

36 Doering, et al., *Tomorrow's Markets,* p. 25.

37 Charles Arthur, "Oil and gas running out much faster than expected, study says" [online], [cited July 8, 2004], *The Independent,* October 5, 2003.

<news.independent.co.uk/world/environment/story.jsp?story=449053>

38 Greg Ray, "Time Is Running Out For the Age of Oil," *Newcastle Herald*, January 17, 2004.

39 Ross Gelbspan, "Rx for An Ailing Planet" [online], [cited July 8, 2004], *GreenBiz.com*, April 2003. <www.greenbiz.com/news/columns_ third.cfm?NewsID=24524>

40 Dauncey with Mazza, *Stormy Weather*, p. 199.

41 "2004 Edelman Fifth Annual Trust Barometer: Study of Opinion Leaders" [online], [cited October 29, 2004], Edelman website, 2004. <www.edelman.com/image/insights/content/Edelman%202004%20Trust%20B arometer%20Findings.doc>

42 "Climate of Suspicion: Earning Trust in a Turbulent Economy," *Risky Business* 6, PricewaterhouseCoopers, November 2002.

43 "Social Responsibility: Key to Building Reputation and Regaining Trust" [online], [cited July 8, 2004], *The Wirthlin Report* 13:2, April 2004, p. 2. <www.wirthlin.com/pdf/twr0404.pdf>

44 Brian Pearce, *Sustainability and Business Competitiveness: Measuring the Benefit for Business and Competitive Advantage from Social Responsibility and Sustainability*, Forum for the Future and Department of Trade and Industry, 2003) p. 19.

45 "Results of the Survey on Trust" [online], [cited July 8, 2004], World Economic Forum website, November 7, 2002. <www.weforum.org/site/homepublic.nsf/Content/Annual+Meeting+2003%5C Results+of+the+Survey+on+Trust>

46 "Global Survey on Trust: Update 2004" [online], [cited July 8, 2004], World Economic Forum website, April 1, 2004. <www.weforum.org/site/ homepublic.nsf/Content/Survey+on+Trust+2004>

47 "Social Responsibility," *The Wirthlin Report*, p. 2.

48 "Johnson & Johnson Retains 1st Place Rank in Annual Corporate Reputation Survey — But Joins Other Companies in Reputation Decline" [online], [cited July 8, 2004], Harris Interactive website, February 19, 2004. <www.harrisinteractive.com/news/>

49 Ibid.

50 William Baue, "Top Five Social Investing News Stories of 2002" [online], [cited July 8, 2004], *SocialFunds.com*, January 14, 2003. <www.socialfunds.com/news/>

51 "Boycott Brand America" [online], [cited July 8, 2004], *Adbusters*. This was announced by e-mail in March 2003.

52 KPMG, *Beyond Numbers: How Leading Organizations Link Values with Value to Gain Competitive Advantage*, KPMG, 2002, p. 17.

53 David Grayson and Adrian Hodges, *Corporate Social Opportunity! 7 Steps to Make Corporate Social Responsibility Work For Your Business*, Greenleaf Publishing, 2004, p. 36.

54 Carolyn Egri, from notes used in "The Stakeholder Corporation" presentation at York University's Sustainable Enterprise Academy, May 17–20, 2004, York University Executive Learning Centre, Toronto.

55 GlobeScan (formerly Environics International), *The Environmental Monitor 2002*, Environics International, p. 35.

56 Ibid., p. 67.

57 Forest L Reinhardt, *Down to Earth: Applying Business Principles to Environmental Management*, Harvard Business Review Press, 2000, p. 40.

58 John Elkington, *Cannibals With Forks: The Triple Bottom Line of 21st Century Business*, New Society Publishers, 1998, p. 5.

59 Carl Frankel, *In Earth's Company: Business, Environment, and the Challenge of Sustainability*, New Society Publishers, 1998, p. 140. Frankel describes four eras in the history of corporate environmentalism, which are loosely related to the five stages in this continuum.

60 CSR Europe, "Press Release: Investor Interest in Corporate Social Responsibility on the Rise" [online], [cited July 8, 2004], *CSRwire*, March 25, 2003. <www.csrwire.com/article.cgi/1691.html> The press release is about a study by CSR Europe and INSEAD, "Corporate social responsibility and the role of investor relations — from switchboard to catalyst."

61 Interfaith Center on Corporate Responsibility (ICCR), "Press Release: Report: 2003 Proxy Season Expected to Set Records, With CEO Pay and Global Warming Among Top Issues" [online], [cited July 8, 2004], *CSRwire*, February 12, 2003. <www.csrwire.com/article.cgi/1578.html>

62 Ibid.

63 Carolyn Said, "Creating a Corporate Conscience: Foundation Says Doing Good Is Good Business" [online], [cited July 8, 2004], *San Francisco Chronicle*, March 30, 2004. <www.sfgate.com/cgibin/article.cgi?file=/chronicle/archive/2004/03/30/BUGHJ5T3EL1.DTL>

64 Jon Markman, "The Secret Power behind America's Top Companies" [online], [cited July 8, 2004], *MSN Money*, March 10, 2004. <moneycentral.msn.com/content/P75037.asp>

65 Barlow and Clark, *Global Showdown*, pp. 2–5.

66 GlobeScan (formerly Environics International), *The Environmental Monitor 2002*, Environics International, p. 113-115.

67 Barlow and Clark, *Global Showdown*, p. 205.

68 Ibid.

69 David Grayson and Adrian Hodges, *Everybody's Business: Managing Risks and*

Opportunities in Today's Global Society, DK Publishing, 2002, p. 36.

70 William Baue, "Climate Change Litigation Could Affect Companies' Market Value" [online], [cited July 8, 2004], *SocialFunds.com,* July 23, 2003. <www.socialfunds.com/news/article.cgi/article1180.html>

71 Nigel Hunt, "States Sue Federal Government Over Greenhouse Gases" [online], [cited July 8, 2004], *Planet Ark,* October 27, 2003. <www.planetark.org/dailynewsstory.cfm/newsid/22654/story.htm>.

72 Amanda Griscom, "Public Nuisance No. 1" [online]. [cited August 4, 2004]. *Grist Magazine,* July 30, 2004. <www.climatebiz.com/sections/ news_detail.cfm?NewsID=27021>

73 Jeremy Rifkin, "Analysis: A precautionary tale," *The Guardian,* May 12, 2004.

74 "US not interested in CR and SRI says new report," *EC Newsdesk,* March 30, 2004.

75 World Economic Forum, "Values and Value: Communicating the Strategic Importance of Corporate Citizenship to Investors," World Economic Forum, 2004, p. 13.

76 CSR Europe, Deloitte, and Euronext, "Investing in Responsible Business: The 2003 Survey of European Fund Managers, Financial Analysts, and Investment Relations Officers," CSR Europe, 2003, p. 4.

77 Martin Whittaker, for the United Nations Environment Programme (UNEP) Finance Initiatives, "CEO Briefing: Climate Change and the Financial Services Industry," Innovest Strategic Advisors, 2002, pp. 4–7.

78 Martin Whittaker, from charts used in the Environmental Finance course, IES1707, at the University of Toronto, week 11, March 21, 2003. The chart is from Innovest Strategic Value Advisors, Richmond Hill, ON.

79 Laas Turnbull, "The best of all possibilities," *Globe & Mail* "Report on Business," March 2004, p. 11.

80 Environmental Management Initiative, *Clear Advantage: Building Shareholder Value,* 2004, p. 1.

81 *Measures That Matter* [online], [cited July 8, 2004], Ernst & Young, 2000, p. 8. <www.ey.com/GLOBAL/content.nsf/UK/CF_-_Library_-_MTM>

82 Gilding, et al., *Single Bottom Line Sustainability,* pp. 10 and 22.

83 Charles Handy, "What's a Business For?" *Harvard Business Review* December 2002.

84 Michael Porter and Mark Kramer, "The Competitive Advantage of Corporate Philanthropy," *Harvard Business Review,* December 2002.

85 Roger Martin, "The Virtue Matrix: Calculating the Return on Corporate Responsibility," *Harvard Business Review,* March 2002, Reprint R0203E.

86 Ashok Ranchhod, *Marketing Strategies: A Twenty-first Century Approach,* Prentice Hall, 2004, p.60.

87 World Business Council for Sustainable Development, *The Business Case for Sustainable Development: Making a Difference toward the Johannesburg Summit 2002 and beyond*, World Business Council for Sustainable Development, 2001, p. 6.

88 Reprinted by permission of *Harvard Business Review*. From "The Virtue Matrix" by Roger Martin, March 2002, Reprint R0203E, p. 9. Copyright © 2002 by Harvard Business School Publishing Corporation, all rights reserved.

89 Steven Rattner, "Why Companies Pay Less" [online], [cited July 18, 2004], *Washington Post*, May 18, 2004, p. A19. <www.washingtonpost>

90 Warren Buffet, "The Oracle Says: Pay Your Corporate Taxes," *Corporate Knights* 2:4, Spring 2004, pp. 42–43.

91 "Federal Corporate Tax Rate Reductions" [online], [cited July 8, 2004], Canada Department of Finance website, August 2003. <www.fin.gc.ca/toce/2003/taxratered_e.html>

92 "Excerpts from 'Unfair $hares: Corporations and Taxation in Canada,' published by Ontario Coalition for Social Justice and Ontario Federation of Labour, February, 1997, ISBN-1-895998-04-2" [online], [cited July 8, 2004], Flora Community Web. <www.flora.org/library/mai/unfair.html>

93 Jim Stanford, "The Business of Being Ethical" [online], [cited July 8, 2004], Canadian Auto Workers (CAW) website, November 18, 2002. <www.caw.ca/news/factsfromthefringe/issue55.asp>

94 Marjorie Kelly, *The Divine Right of Capital*, Berrett-Koehler Publishers, 2001, p. 129.

95 Korten, *When Corporations Rule the World*, pp. 54–55.

96 Deloitte & Touche, "SD Energy Leaders: Analytical Framework," from a slide deck received by e-mail from Dale Littlejohn, April 2004.

97 "US not interested in CR and SRI says new report," *EC Newsdesk*, March 30, 2004.

98 Ibid.

99 David Ticoll, "The Naked Corporation," from a chart he used in York University's Sustainable Enterprise Academy, May 17–20, 2004, York University Executive Learning Centre, Toronto.

Chapter 4: Second Emerging Driver — Compelling Business Value

1 Sanjay Sharma, "Managerial interpretations and organizational context as predictors of corporate choice of environmental strategy," *Academy of Management Journal* 43:4, August 2000, p. 681.

2 Paul Gilding, Murray Hogarth, and Don Reed, *Single Bottom Line Sustainability: How a Value Centered Approach to Corporate Sustainability*

Can Pay Off For Shareholders and Society, Ecos Corporation, 2002, pp. 3 and 6.

3 Five Winds International and Pollution Probe, "Policy Framework for Environmental Sustainability Project: Summary Report," Five Winds International, 2004, pp. 14–21.

4 Robert Kaplan and David Norton, "The Balanced Scorecard: Measures That Drive Performance," *Harvard Business Review*, January-February 1992, pp. 71–79.

5 Francesco Zingales and Kai Hockerts, "Balanced Scorecard & Sustainability: Examples from Literature and Practice" [online], [cited July 8, 2004], INSEAD, 2003, pp. 5–11. <ged.insead.edu/fichiersti/inseadwp2003/2003-30.pdf>

6 Luk van Wasenhove, Francsco Zingales, and Kai Hockert, "Balanced Scorecard & Sustainability: Blending environmental and social issue in financial control systems" [online], [cited July 8, 2004], *INSEAD Quarterly*, 2003, p. 23. <www.insead.edu/CMER/events/sbsc2003/download/BSS_%20INSEAD_Quarterly.pdf>

7 Marc Epstein and Priscilla Wisner, "Measuring and Managing Social and Environmental Impacts," *Handbook of Cost Management*, 2001 edition, edited by John Shank, WG&L, 2001, pp. 31 and 58.

8 Bob Willard, *The Sustainability Advantage Worksheets*, New Society Publishers, 2002, are available in Excel format from New Society Publishers at <www.newsociety.com>

9 Business in the Community, *Responsibility: Driving Innovation, Inspiring Employees*, Business in the Community, 2003, p. 4.

10 Bob Willard, *The Sustainability Advantage*, New Society Publishers, 2002. The sample company, Sustainable Development or SD Inc., is a composite of IBM, HP, Dell, Compaq, and Xerox, based on 1999 Fortune 500 data and representing 83% to 85% of top ten computer companies.

11 "Corporate recruiters face the 'Enron effect'" [online], [cited July 18, 2004], The Work Foundation press release, December 19, 2002. <www.theworkfoundation.com/newsroom/pressreleases.jsp?ref=79>

12 "Social Responsibility: Key to Building Reputation and Regaining Trust" [online], [cited July 8, 2004], *The Wirthlin Report*, April 2004, 13:2, p. 2. <www.wirthlin.com/pdf/twr0404.pdf>

13 Vicky Kemp, *To Whose Profit? Building a Business Case for Sustainability*, WWF-UK, 2001, p. 16.

14 Conference Board of Canada, "The National Corporate Social Responsibility Report: Managing Risks, Leveraging Opportunities," The Conference Board of Canada, 2004, pp. 11–12.

15 Arthur D. Little, *The Business Case for Corporate Citizenship*, Arthur D. Little, 2002, p. 1.

16 "Stanford Business School Study Finds MBA Graduates Want to Work for Caring and Ethical Employers" [online], [cited July 28, 2004], press release from Stanford Graduate School of Business, *CSRwire,* July 26, 2004. <www.csrwire.com/article.cgi/2910.html>

17 "Corporate recruiters face the 'Enron effect.'"

18 Anne Papmehl, "Accounting for Knowledge" [online], [cited July 8, 2004], *CMA Management,* March 2004 <www.managementmag.com/index.cfm/ci_id/1482/la_id/1>

19 "Expecting Sales Growth, CEOs Cite Worker Retention as Critical to Success" [online], [cited July 8, 2004], PricewaterhouseCoopers Trendsetter Barometer, March 15, 2004.

20 KPMG, "Ethical Business and Sustainable Communities" [online], [cited July 8, 2004], KPMG, 2002, p. 6. <www.erc.org.au/busethics/kpmg_ethical_bus.pdf>

21 "Encouraging Responsible Business" [online], [cited July 16, 2004], Small Business Service website. <www.sbs.gov.uk/content/pdf/sbsbrochure1.pdf>

22 "Corporate recruiters face the 'Enron effect.'"

23 Susan Flynn, "The Retention Dilemma: Keeping Your Best People," Strategic Leadership Forum (Toronto) *Focus on Strategy* 6:1, March 2002, p. 2.

24 Stephan Bevan, Nick Isles, Peter Emery, and Tony Hoskins, *Achieving High Performance: CSR at the Heart of Business,* The Work Foundation, 2004, p. 3.

25 Business in the Community, *Responsibility,* p. 3.

26 Steven Morton, "Business Case for Green Design" [online], [cited July 8, 2004], *Building Operating Management,* November 2002. <www.facilitiesnet.com/bom/Nov02/Nov02environment.shtml>

27 Green Building Council, "Making the Business Case for High Performance Buildings," Green Building Council 2004, p. 4.

28 Corey Griffith, "An Introduction to Biophilia and the Built Environment," *RMI Solutions Newsletter,* Rocky Mountain Institute, 2004, 20:1, Spring 2004, pp. 7–9.

29 Edward O. Wilson, *Biophilia,* Harvard University Press, 1984.

30 Bob Doppelt, *Leading Change Toward Sustainability: A Change-Management Guide for Business, Government and Civil Society,* Greenleaf Publishing, 2003, pp. 16-17.

31 "Xerox Saved $2bn through Eco-Design and Manufacturing" [online], [cited July 8, 2004], *GreenBiz.com,* May 1, 2002. <enn.com/news/enn-stories/2002/05/05012002/s_47053.asp>

32 L. Hunter Lovins, "Can One Person Change the World? You Bet" [online], [cited July 8, 2004], *ClimateBiz,* July 2004. <www.climatebiz.com/sections/news_detail.cfm?NewsID=26897>

318

33 Joel Makower, "E Tu, E2?" *The Green Business Letter*, Tilden Press, June 2004, pp. 1, 5, and 6.

34 "Making the Business Case for High Performance Buildings," pp. 2 and 3.

35 Morton, "Business Case for Green Design."

36 Ibid, p.7.

37 Makower, "E Tu, E2?" p. 1.

38 Anne Papmehl, "Environmental Sustainability through Knowledge Management" in *Emerging Dimensions of Environmental Sustainability: A Canadian Perspective of Innovative Practices*, edited by Anshuman Khare, forthcoming.

39 "More About Pollution Prevention Pays" [online], [cited July 8, 2004], 3M Worldwide website, 2004. <www.3m.com/about3m/sustainability/policies_ehs_tradition_3p.jhtml>

40 "Xerox Employees Mix Innovation, Initiative to Protect the Environment" [online]. [cited July 8, 2004]. *GreenBiz.com*, April 23, 2004. <www.greenbiz.com/news/news_third.cfm?NewsID=26693>

41 Ashok Ranchhod, *Marketing Strategies: A Twenty-first Century Approach*, Prentice Hall, 2004, p. 89. © 2004. Reprinted by permission of Pearson Education, Upper Saddle River, NJ.

42 Environics, "The Millennium Poll on Corporate Social Responsibility," conducted by Environics International Ltd., in cooperation with the Prince of Wales Business Leaders Forum and the Conference Board. The results are accurate to within 3%, 19 times out of 20.

43 Rosalind Oakley and Jason Perks, *The SIGMA Guidelines Toolkit: SIGMA Sustainability Marketing Guide*, The SIGMA Project, 2001, p. 18.

44 "Social Responsibility," *The Wirthlin Report*, p. 2.

45 Stan Maklan and Simon Knox, *CSR at a Crossroads*, Cranfield University School of Management, 2003, p. 10.

46 Brian Pearce, *Sustainability and Business Competitiveness: Measuring the Benefit for Business and Competitive Advantage from Social Responsibility and Sustainability*, Forum for the Future and Department of Trade and Industry, 2003, p. 23.

47 "Business' Contribution Fundamental to Sustainable Development" [online]. [cited July 8, 2004]. World Business Council for Sustainable Development website, July 1, 2004. <www.wbcsd.org/plugins/DocSearch/details.asp?type=DocDet&DocId=NjEzMQ>

48 UNEP Finance Initiative, "The Materiality of Social, Environmental and Corporate Governance Issues to Equity Pricing" [online], [cited July 8, 2004], UNEPFI website. <www.unepfi.net/stocks/CEOMateriality6pp100604.pdf>

49 "CSR Activities Generate Higher Performance — Official" [online], [cited July

8, 2004], The Work Foundation press release, March 25, 2004.
<www.theworkfoundation.com/newsroom/pressreleases.jsp?ref=128>

50 World Economic Forum, "Values and Value: Communicating the Strategic Importance of Corporate Citizenship to Investors," World Economic Forum, 2004, p. 15.

51 Keith O'Brien, "Trust and the Bottom Line" *PR Week*, May 10, 2004.

52 Brian Pearce, Patrick Roche, Nick Chater, and Pensions and Investment Research Consultants (PIRC), *Sustainability Pays*, Co-operative Insurance Society, 2002, Chapter 2.

53 "Dow Jones Sustainability Indexes Monthly Update, July 2004" [online], [cited August 13, 2004], *SAM Indexes*, p. 6. <www.sustainability-indexes.com/djsi_pdf/news/MonthlyUpdates/DJSI_Update_0407.pdf>

54 "Jantzi Social Index Gains 2.34% in June, S&P/TSX 60 gains 2.22%, S&P/TSX Gains 1.73% Over Same Period" [online]. [cited July 18, 2004]. Michael Jantzi Research Associates press release, July 13, 2004. <www.mjra-jsi.com/current_issues.asp?section=4&level_2=13&level_3=0&pr_id=74>

55 "Two thirds of UK investors prepared to invest 'ethically'"[online], [cited July 8, 2004], *Environmental Finance*, July 2, 2004. <www.wbcsd.org/plugins/DocSearch/details.asp?type=DocDet&DocId=6267>

56 Willard, *Sustainability Advantage Worksheets,* available in Excel format from New Society Publishers at <www.newsociety.com>.

57 Travis Engen, "Sustainability: A Critical Component of Successful Business Models in the 21st Century," notes for an address by Travis Engen, president and chief executive officer, Alcan Inc., at Globe 2004, Vancouver, Canada, March 31, 2004 [online], [cited July 8, 2004], Alcan website. <www.alcan.com/web/publishing.nsf/Content/Sustainability:++A+Critical+Component+of+Successful+Business+Models+in+the+21st+Century>

58 Doppelt, *Leading Change Toward Sustainability,* pp. 17–21.

59 Paul Hawken, "Dreams of a livable future" [online], [cited July 8, 2004], *Utne* website, May-June 2003, p. 50. <www.utne.com/pub/2003_117/promo/10489-1.html>

Chapter 5: Objection-Handling Clinic on Inhibiters to Next Wave

1 Stephen R. Covey, *The 7 Habits of Highly Effective People*, Simon & Schuster, Fireside Books, 1989.

2 "More about Pollution Prevention Pays" [online], [cited July 8, 2004], 3M. <www.3m.com/about3m/sustainability/policies_ehs_tradition_3p.jhtml>

3 Deidre A. Kavanagh, "A Multi-Disciplinary Literature Review of Eco-

Labelling Schemes," working paper, prepared for TerraChoice Environmental
Services Inc., York University, Ontario, p. 4.

4   Stratos, in collaboration with Alan Willis & Associates and SustainAbility,
    "Stepping Forward: Corporate Sustainability Reporting in Canada, 2001,"
    [online], [cited July 8, 2004] Stratos website, p. 3. <www.stratos-sts.com/
    sts_files/stratos.full.report.pdf>

5   Roger Crowe, *Risk Returns and Responsibility*, Association of British Insurers,
    2004, p. 10.

6   SustainAbility Ltd. and the United Nations Environment Programme (UNEP),
    "Trust Us: The Global Reporters 2002 Survey of Corporate Sustainability
    Reporting," UNEP and Sustainability, 2002, p. 12.

7   Ray C. Anderson, *Mid-Course Correction*, Peregrinzilla Press, 1999, p. 79.

8   James C. Collins and Jerry I. Porras, *Built To Last: Successful Habits of Visionary
    Companies*, HarperBusiness, 1994, p. 9.

9   "Whistling in the Dark" [online], [cited July 8, 2004], *Corporate Responsibility*,
    2003. <www.corporateresponsibility.nl/index.htm>

10 "CSR and corporate governance: two sides of the same coin?" [online], [cited
    July 8, 2004], EurActiv.com, February 18, 2004. <www.wbcsd.org/plugins/
    DocSearch/details.asp?type=DocDet&DocId=4076>

11 Hill & Knowlton and Korn/Ferry International, "2003 Corporate Reputation
    Watch Survey," [online], [cited July 8, 2004], Hill & Knowlton, 2003.

12 Paul Drissen, "Back to Petroleum" [online], [cited July 8, 2004], Center for the
    Defense of Free Enterprise website, March 2003. <www.cdfe.org/
    back_to_petroleum.htm>

13 Tobias Webb, "World News: Shell Attacked for Alleged Environmental 'Double
    Standards' by Campaign Group" [online], [cited July 8, 2004], *Ethical
    Corporation Online,* June 24, 2004. <www.ethicalcorp.com/
    content.asp?ContentID=2251>

14 "Partnership for Sustainable Development" [online], [cited July 8, 2004],
    United Nations Department of Economic and Social Affairs website.
    <www.un.org/esa/sustdev/partnerships/partnerships.htm>

15 Business for Social Responsibility (BSR), "Illustrative List of Companies"
    [online], [cited July 8, 2004], Business for Social Responsibility (BSR) website.
    <www.bsr.org/Meta/MemberList.cfm>

16 Trudy Heller and Jeanne Mroczko, "Information Disclosure in Environmental
    Policy and the Development of Secretly Environmentally Friendly Products" in
    *Research in Corporate Sustainability: The Evolving Theory and Practice of
    Organizations in the Natural Environment,* edited by Mark Starik and Sanjay
    Sharma, Edward Elgar Publishing, 2002, pp. 8–14.

17 "Green Range and Fleet Average" [online], [cited July 8, 2004], Electrolux website. <ir.electrolux.com/html/environmentalreport2002/index_16.phtml>

18 "2002 Sustainability Survey Report" [online], [cited July 8, 2004], PricewaterhouseCoopers website, unnumbered Key Statistics page. <www.pwcglobal.com/fas/pdfs/sustainability%20survey%20report.pdf>

19 "Corporate Citizenship Programs Gaining More Attention Among CEOs and Top Managers" [online], [cited July 8, 2004], Conference Board press release, August 15, 2002. <www.csrwire.com/article.cgi/1257.html>

20 "More about Pollution Prevention Pays," <www.3m.com/about3m/sustainability/policies_ehs_tradition_3p.jhtml>

21 Friends of the Earth, Taxpayers for Common Sense, and US Public Interest Research Group, *Green Scissors 2002*, Friends of the Earth, 2002, p. 1.

22 Bob Willard, *The Sustainability Advantage: Seven Business Case Benefits of a Triple Bottom Line*, New Society Publishers, 2002, pp. 56–59.

23 Ibid., p. 82.

24 Bob Willard, *The Sustainability Advantage Worksheets*, New Society Publishers, 2002, are available in Excel format from New Society Publishers at <www.newsociety.com>

25 Don S. Doering, Amy Cassara, Christian Layke, Janet Ranganathan, Carmen Revenga, Dan Tunstall, and Wendy Vanasselt, *Tomorrow's Markets: Global Trends and Their Implications for Business*, World Resources Institute, United Nations Environment Programme, World Business Council for Sustainable Development, 2002.

26 Chris Argyris, "Teaching Smart People How to Learn," *Harvard Business Review*, May-June 1991.

27 Gregory W. Lester, "Why Bad Beliefs Don't Die" [online], [cited July 8, 2004], *Skeptical Inquirer*, November 2000. <www.csicop.org/si/2000-11/beliefs.html>

28 Bjorn Lomborg, *The Skeptical Environmentalist: Measuring the Real State of the World*, Cambridge University Press, 2001.

29 Danish Committees on Scientific Dishonesty, "Decision Regarding Complaints against Bjorn Lomborg," [online], [cited July 8, 2004], Danish Research Agency, 2003. <uk.cambridge.org/economics/lomborg/files/DRA_Decision.pdf>

30 Union of Concerned Scientists, "World Scientists' Warning to Humanity" [online], [cited July 8, 2004], Union of Concerned Scientists, 1992. <www.ucsusa.org/ucs/about/page.cfm?pageID=1009>

31 Adapted from "The Trail of Galileo: A Chronology" [online], [cited July 8, 2004], Famous Trials website. <www.law.umkc.edu/faculty/projects/ftrials/galileo/galileochronology.html>

NEW SOCIETY PUBLISHERS

P.O. Box 189

Gabriola Island,

B.C. V0R 1X0

Canada

BOOKS TO BUILD A NEW SOCIETY

Our books provide positive solutions for people who want to make a difference.

For a copy of our catalog, please mail this card to us.

If you are Internet-capable, save postage by signing up for more information this way:

http://driveit.clickspace.com/subscribe/1000124

We specialize in the following please indicate your area/s of interest:

☐ Activism
☐ Globalization
☐ Ecological Design & Planning
☐ Environment & Economy

☐ Conscientious Commerce
☐ Sustainable Living
☐ Environmental Education
☐ Education & Parenting
☐ Progressive Leadership

☐ Conflict Education
☐ Storytelling
☐ Natural Building & Renewable Energy
☐ Making a Difference

Name

Address/City/Province

Postal Code/Zip _____ Email Address

800-567-6772

NEW SOCIETY PUBLISHERS

www.newsociety.com

32 David Henderson, "Misguided Virtue: False Notions of Corporate Social Responsibility" [online], [cited July 8, 2004], New Zealand Business Roundtable, 2001, pp. xi–xiv. <www.nzbr.org.nz/documents/publications/publications-2001/misguided_virtue.pdf>

33 Dr. Gary Dirks, "CSR — A view from BP." Speech by Dr. Gary Dirks, president of BP China, at the CSR Forum, held at the School of Economics and Management, Tsinghua University, Beijing, China, April 24, 2004 [online], [cited July 8, 2004], World Business Council for Sustainable Development website. <www.wbcsd.org/plugins/DocSearch/details.asp?type=DocDet&DocId=5974>

34 "Two-Faced Capitalism" [online], [cited July 8, 2004], *The Economist*, January 22, 2004. <www.economist.com/business/displayStory.cfm?story_id=2369912>

35 "The Road to Corporate Serfdom," *Financial Post*, March 10, 2004, p. FP19.

36 Ibid.

37 "Arguments Against Corporate Social Responsibility" [online], [cited July 8, 2004], Mallen Baker website, April 2001. <www.mallenbaker.net/csr/CSRfiles/against.html>

38 Memuna Forna, "Could do better! Must try harder! Survey shows that CEOs have been slow to learn the lessons of Enron and Tyco" [online], [cited July 8, 2004], The Work Foundation website, February 20, 2003. <www.theworkfoundation.com/newsroom/pressreleases.jsp?ref=84>

39 Evan Mills, Eugene Lecomte, and Andrew Peara, "US Insurance Industry Perspectives on Global Climate Change," [online], [cited July 8, 2004], Lawrence Berkeley National Laboratory, 2001, p. 19. <eetd.lbl.gov/EMills/PUBS/PDF/Climate_report.pdf>

40 The Aspen Institute and World Resources Institute, "Beyond Grey Pinstripes 2003," [online], [cited July 8, 2004], WRI Sustainable Enterprise Program, 2003). <www.beyondgreypinstripes.org/results/index.cfm>

41 Ron Willingham, *The Best Seller! The New Psychology of Selling and Persuading People*, Prentice-Hall, 1984, p. 55–57.

42 Brian Pearce, *Sustainability and Business Competitiveness: Measuring the Benefit for Business and Competitive Advantage from Social Responsibility and Sustainability*, Forum for the Future and Department of Trade and Industry, 2003, p. 23.

Chapter 6: Conclusion

1 "Interview with Sir David King" [online], [cited July 13, 2004], The Climate Group website, 2004. <www.theclimategroup.org/455.php>

2 Eric Reguly, "A warm welcome to the attitude change on global climate change" [online], [cited July 13, 2004], *The Globe and Mail*, July 8, 2004, p. B2.

<www.theglobeandmail.com/servlet/ArticleNews/TPStory/LAC/
20040708/RREGUL08/?query=reguly>

3   Don Reed and Rick Humphries, "Climate Change Business Drivers: Their
    Development and Current Status" [online], [cited July 8, 2004], Ecos
    Corporation website, 2004, section 1.2. <www.ecoscorporation.com/think/>

4   Sonia Labatt and Rodney White, *Environmental Finance: A Guide to
    Environmental Risk Assessment and Financial Products*, John Wiley & Sons,
    2002, p. 285.

5   Steve Connor, "US Climate Policy Bigger Threat to the World than
    Terrorism" [online], [cited July 8, 2004], *The Independent*, January 9, 2004.
    <news.independent.co.uk/low_res/story.jsp?story=479418&host=3&dir=507>

6   David Stipp, "The Pentagon's Weather Nightmare" [online], [cited July 8,
    2004], *Fortune*, January 26, 2004. <www.fortune.com/fortune/technology/
    articles/0,15114,582584,00.html>

7   "World Must Combat Climate Change" [online], [cited July 9, 2004], Press
    Association, July 9, 2004. <www.wbcsd.org/plugins/DocSearch/
    details.asp?type=DocDet&DocId=6231>

8   Sir John Browne, "Beyond Kyoto." Speech by Sir John Browne, group chief
    executive, BP, at the Council on Foreign Relations, New York, United States,
    June 24, 2004 [online], [cited July 8, 2004], Council on Foreign Relations
    website. <www.cfr.org/pub7148/john_browne/beyond_kyoto.php>

9   "Looking beyond Kyoto" [online], [cited July 9, 2004], *Australian
    Financial Review*, July 9, 2004. <www.wbcsd.org/plugins/DocSearch/
    details.asp?type=DocDet&DocId=6277>

10 Alister Doyle, "Global Warming: The Quadrillion Dollar Question" [online],
    [cited July 8, 2004], *Planet Ark*, October 29, 2003. <www.planetark.com/
    dailynewsstory.cfm/newsid/22680/story.htm>

11 Alister Doyle, "160,000 Said Dying Yearly from Global Warming" [online],
    [cited July 8, 2004], *Planet Ark*, September 30, 2003. <www.planetark.org/
    dailynewsstory.cfm/newsid/22420/story.htm>

12 Allison Jackson, "Premiums up? Blame global warming" [online], [cited July
    8, 2004], *Sydney Morning Herald*, September 27, 2003. <www.smh.com.au/
    articles/2003/09/26/1064083194606.html?from=storyrhs>

13 "FAQ" [online], [cited July 8, 2004], Environment Canada website.
    <www.ec.gc.ca/pdb/ghg/faq_e.cfm#reduce>

14 Martin Whittaker, "Carbon Disclosure Project: Carbon Finance and the
    Global Equity Market," [online], [cited July 8, 2004], Innovest, 2003, pp. 10
    and 11. <194.242.156.103/cdproject/downloads/cdp_report.pdf>

15 Mindy Lubber, "Global Warming's Bottom Line" [online], [cited July 8,
    2004], *Boston Globe*, May 4, 2004. <www.boston.com/news/globe/

editorial_opinion/oped/articles/2004/05/04/global_warmings_bottom_line/>

16 Thomas Homer-Dixon, "Cold Truths about Global Warming" [online], [cited July 8, 2004], *Globe and Mail,* February 16, 2004. <www.globetechnology.com/servlet/story/RTGAM.20040216.gtcotad16/BNStory/Technology/>

17 Ibid.

18 Stipp, "The Pentagon's Weather Nightmare."

19 Innovest Strategic Value Advisors, "Value at Risk: Climate Change and the Future of Governance," CERES Sustainable Governance Project, 2002, p. 12.

20 Katharine Q. Seelye, "Environmental Groups Gain as Companies Vote on Issues" [online], [cited July 8, 2004], *New York Times,* May 28, 2003. <www.globalpolicy.org/socecon/envronmt/2003/0528companics.htm>

21 Sarah Murray, "Environmental Risk: Investors Demand Action on Climate Change," *Financial Times,* January 16, 2004.

22 Joel Makower, "Briefing," *The Green Business Letter*, Tilden Press, February 2003, p. 2.

23 "Climate Change: Shareholders Act To Cut Emissions," *Financial Director,* May 2, 2004.

24 Don Reed and Rick Humphries, "Climate Change Business Drivers: Their Development and Current Status" [online], [cited July 8, 2004], Ecos Corporation website, 2004, section 4.2. <www.ecoscorporation.com/think/>

25 Ibid.

26 Lubber, "Global Warming's Bottom Line."

27 William Baue, "Thirteen Pension Funds Call on SEC to Require Disclosure on Climate Change Risk" [online], [cited July 8, 2004], *SocialFunds.com,* April 16, 2004. <www.socialfunds.com/news/article.cgi/1396.html>

28 Labatt and White, *Environmental Finance,* pp. 205 and 207. Reprinted with permission of John Wiley & Sons, Inc.

29 "Chicago Climate Exchange® Reaches Volume Milestone of 1 Million Tons of Carbon Dioxide Traded" [online], [cited July 8, 2004], Chicago Climate Exchange website, July 1, 2004. <www.chicagoclimateexchange.com/news/CCXPressRelease_040701.html>

30 "Emissions Trading in the European Union" [online], [cited July 8, 2004], Climate Action Network Europe website, 2004. <www.climnet.org/EUenergy/ET.html#ITheDirective>

31 CO2e.com, *Greenhouse Gas Market Overview* [online], [cited July 8, 2004], CO2e.com, 2001, p. 4. <www.co2e.com/images/Trading%20Today%20and%20FAQs.pdf>

32 Alison Arnot, "The Triple Bottom Line" [online], [cited July 8, 2004], *CGA Magazine,* January/February 2004. <www.cga-canada.org/eng/magazine/jan-

feb04/triple_line_e.htm>

33 "GAO Identifies Financial Downside of Underreporting Environmental Risks" [online], [cited August 23, 2004], WRI Features. <www.greenbiz.com/news/news_third.cfm?NewsID=27069>

34 SustainAbility Ltd. and the United Nations Environment Programme (UNEP), "Trust Us: The Global Reporters 2002 Survey of Corporate Sustainability Reporting," UNEP and Sustainability, 2002, pp. 10–11.

35 Ibid., p. 2.

36 "Survey: NGOs More Likely to Believe CSR Reports That Admit Fault" [online], [cited July 8, 2004], *GreenBiz.com*, November 26, 2003. <www.greenbiz.com/news/news_third.cfm?NewsID=26079>

37 William Baue, "AccountAbility Launches Assurance Standard for Corporate Social Responsibility" [online], [cited July 8, 2004], *SocialFunds.com*, March 26, 2003. <www.socialfunds.com/news/article.cgi/article1074.html>

38 Social Accountability International, "SA8000 Overview" [online], [cited July 8, 2004], Social Accountability International website. <www.sa-intl.org/SA8000/SA8000.htm>

39 SustainAbility and UNEP, "Trust Us," pp. 10 and 11.

40 Ibid., p. 14.

41 Paul Hohnen, "Letters to the Editor: From GRI with Regard to Our Recent Article on GRI Reporters" [online], [cited July 8, 2004], Ethical Corporation website, June 27, 2004. <www.ethicalcorp.com/content.asp?ContentID=2285>

42 Joel Makower, "Reporting on Reporting," *The Green Business Letter*, Tilden Press, January 2004, p. 5.

43 William Baue, "Auditing Sustainability Reporting" [online], [cited July 18, 2004], *SocialFunds.com*, June 21, 2004. <www.socialfunds.com/news/article.cgi/1443.html>.

44 Stan Maklan and Simon Knox, *CSR at a Crossroads*, Cranfield University School of Management, 2003, p. 23.

45 "About OneReportTM: How it Works" [online], [cited July 8, 2004], OneReport website. <www.one-report.com/about_onereportB.html>

46 Ethical Corporation, "New Corporate Responsibility Exchange Set to Reduce 'Survey Fatigue'" [online], [cited August 23, 2004], Ethical Corporation. <www.greenbiz.com/news/news_third.cfm?NewsID=27071>

47 "A Solution to CSR Reporting Complexity and 'Questionnaire Fatigue'" [online], [cited July 8, 2004], Future 500 website. <www.future500.org/audit.php>.

48 Vicky Kemp, *To Whose Profit? Building a Business Case for Sustainability*, WWF-UK, 2001, p. 13.

49 Stella Rice, "Greening the Mainstream" [online], [cited July 8, 2004], British Overseas NGOs for Devlopment (BOND) website, June 2003. <www.bond.org.uk/networker/june03/invest.htm>

50 "Corporate Responsibility — Social Security," *Retail Week,* April 9, 2004.

51 Alison Maitland, "Business Put under Pressure to Disclose Ethical Risks," *Financial Times,* February 26, 2004.

52 "Kraft Foods Inc. Financial Terminology and Acronym Dictionary" [online], [cited July 8, 2004], Kraft Foods website, directed to this site by Google search for a definition of "material information," June 12, 2004. <www.kraft.com/investors/definitions.html>

53 "Corporate Reporting" [online], [cited July 8, 2004], Business in the Community website, 2004. <www.bitc.org.uk/programmes/programme_directory/reporting_learning_network/>

54 Conference Board of Canada, "The National Corporate Social Responsibility Report: Managing Risks, Leveraging Opportunities," The Conference Board of Canada, 2004, p. 18.

55 SustainAbility, United Nations Environment Programme (UNEP), and Standard & Poors, *Risk and Opportunity: Best Practice in Non-Financial Reporting,* SustainAbility, 2004, p. 4.

56 "Media Advisory — Companies Lag behind on Verification; Better at Full Sustainability Reporting: KPMG LLP" [online], [cited July 8, 2004], Canada News Wire, July 16, 2002. <www.newswire.ca/en/releases/archive/July2002/16/c5155.html>

57 William Baue, "A Brief History of Sustainability Reporting" and "Trends in Sustainability Reporting" [online], [cited July 11, 2004], SocialFunds.com, June 2, 2004. <http://www.socialfunds.com/news/article.cgi/article1459.html> and <http://www.socialfunds.com/news/article.cgi/article1460.html>

58 "PWC Barometer Survey Results on Triple Bottom Line Reporting" [online], [cited July 8, 2004], SRiMedia website, September 26, 2002. <www.srimedia.com/artman/publish/article_169.shtml>

59 "Brief on proposed new corporate governance requirements" [online], [cited July 8, 2004], Social Investment Organization (SIO) website, May 2004. <www.socialinvestment.ca/policy&advocacy.htm>

60 Stratos, in collaboration with Alan Willis and Associates, *Building Confidence: Corporate Sustainability Reporting in Canada,* Stratos, 2003, p. 2.

61 Conference Board of Canada, "The National Corporate Social Responsibility Report," p. i.

62 The Conference Board, "Does It Pay To Be Good?" *Across the Board,* Jan/Feb 2003, p. 17.

63 Malcolm Gladwell, *The Tipping Point: How Little Things Can Make a Big*

Difference, Little, Brown and Company, 2002, pp. 7–9.

64 "Investors Rate 500 Largest Companies on Climate" [online], [cited July 8, 2004], *GreenBiz.com*, May 19, 2004. <www.greenbiz.com/news/printer.cfm?NewsID=26780>

65 Carbon Disclosure Project [online], [cited July 8, 2004],

66 Blair Feltmate, Brian Schofield, and Ron Yachnin, "Sustainable Development, Value Creation and the Capital Markets, Report 324-01," Conference Board of Canada, 2001, p. i–ii. The seven funds examined were Domini Social Equity Index (US), EcoValue 21 (US), Dow Jones Sustainability Group Index (international), Storebrand Scudder Environmental Value Fund (European), the Jantzi Social Index (Canadian), Ethical Funds (North American), and Sustainable Value Pension Fund (Canadian).

67 Shaun Mays and the BT Financial Group, "Corporate Sustainability — An Investor Perspective: The Mays Report," Australian Department of Environment and Heritage, 2003, p. 6.

68 Stephan Bevan, Nick Isles, Peter Emery, and Tony Hoskins, *Achieving High Performance: CSR at the Heart of Business*, The Work Foundation, 2004, p. 8.

69 Laas Turnbull, "The best of all possibilities," *Globe & Mail* "Report on Business," March 2004, p. 11.

70 "Social Responsibility: Key to Building Reputation and Regaining Trust" [online], [cited July 8, 2004], *The Wirthlin Report*, April 2004, 13:2, p. 2. <www.wirthlin.com/pdf/twr0404.pdf>

71 William Baue, "A Brief History of and Trends in Sustainability Reporting" and "Trends in Sustainability Reporting."

72 Glen Emerson Morris, "Nike: Free Speech or Truth or Consequences" [online], [cited July 8, 2004], *Advertising and Marketing Review*. <www.ad-mkt-review.com/public_html/air/ai200304.html>

73 "About Beyond Grey Pinstripes" [online], [cited July 13, 2004], Beyond Grey Pinstripes website. <www.beyondgreypinstripes.org/results/about/executive_summary.cfm>

74 Ibid.

75 Ibid.

76 Ibid.

77 Alison Weeks, "Training a New Generation of Business Leaders" [online], [cited July 26, 2004], *GreenMoneyJournal.com*, Summer 2004. <www.greenbiz.com/news/reviews_third.cfm?NewsID=26973>

78 Net Impact website.

79 "Stanford Business School Study Finds MBA Graduates Want to Work for Caring and Ethical Employers" [online], [cited July 28, 2004], Press release by Stanford Graduate School of Business, July 26, 2004.

<www.csrwire.com/article.cgi/2910.html>

80 "ISO to go ahead with guidelines for social responsibility" [online], [cited July 8, 2004], ISO website, June 29, 2004. <www.iso.org/iso/en/commcentre/pressreleases/2004/Ref924.html>

81 "Social Concerns Drive Purchases of 68 Million US Consumers, Says Study" [online], [cited July 8, 2004], *GreenBiz.com,* June 16, 2003. <www.greenbiz.com/news/news_third.cfm?NewsID=25003&CFID=13816613&CFTOKEN=55135221>

82 Paul H. Ray and Sherry Ruth Anderson, *The Cultural Creatives: How 50 Million People Are Changing the World,* Three Rivers Press, 2000.

83 Ashok Ranchhod, *Marketing Strategies: A Twenty-first Century Approach,* Prentice Hall, 2004, p. 89.

84 Jon Henley, "France launches radical green tax on bigger cars" [online], [cited July 13, 2004], *The Guardian,* June 23, 2004. <www.guardian.co.uk/international/story/0,3604,1245100,00.html>

85 Ibid.

86 Dr. Gary Dirks, "CSR — A view from BP." Speech by Dr. Gary Dirks, president of BP China, at the CSR Forum, held at the School of Economics and Management, Tsinghua University, Beijing, China, April 24, 2004 [online], [cited July 8, 2004], World Business Council for Sustainable Development website. <www.wbcsd.org/plugins/DocSearch/details.asp?type=DocDet&DocId=5974>

87 Adrian Loader, "Putting Principles into Practice." Notes for an address by Adrian Loader, director, strategic planning, sustainable development and external affairs, Royal Dutch/Shell Group, at the Singapore/UK: Developing Corporate Social Responsibility seminar, Singapore, February 23, 2004 [online], [cited July 8, 2004], World Business Council for Sustainable Development website. <www.wbcsd.org/plugins/DocSearch/details.asp?type=DocDet&DocId=6040>

88 James C. Collins and Jerry I. Porras, *Built To Last: Successful Habits of Visionary Companies,* HarperBusiness, 1994, pp. 90–114.

89 Ira A. Jackson and Jane Nelson, *Profits With Principles: Seven Strategies for Delivering Value with Values,* Currency, 2004, pp. 17–19.

Appendix A: SME-Relevant Business Case

1 Lynn Johannson, "ISO 14001: One For All, Or Just For Some?" *ISO Management Systems,* September-October, 2002, p. 51.

2 Richard Starkey and the Centre for Corporate Environmental Management, *Environmental Management for SMEs: A Handbook,* European Environmental Agency, 1998, pp. 8 and 9.

3 "Appendix C: Small and Medium-Sized Enterprises (SMEs) Definitions. Table

46 SME Definitions" [online], [cited October 31, 2004], Cultural Affairs Canada website. <www.pch.gc.ca/progs/ac-ca/pubs/profile/15_e.cfm>

4 Canadian Federation of Independent Business, "Small Business — Big Picture," [online], [cited October 31, 2004], Canadian Federation of Independent Business, 2004) p. 1. <www.cfib.ca/research/reports/ Cda_big_picture_e.pdf>

5 Ibid.

6 "Frequently Asked Questions" [online], [cited July 8, 2004], US Small Business Administration website, May 13, 2002. <app1.sba.gov/faqs/ faqindex.cfm?areaID=24>

7 Five Winds International and Pollution Probe, "Policy Framework for Environmental Sustainability Project: Summary Report," Five Winds International, 2004, p. 6.

8 European Multistakeholder Forum, "Report of the Roundtable on 'Fostering CSR Among SMEs'" [online], [cited July 15, 2004], European Multistakeholder Forum CSR website, May 2004, p. 9. <forum.europa.eu.int/irc/empl/csr_eu_multi_stakeholder_forum/info/ data/en/CSR%20Forum%20RT%20report%20SME.pdf>

9 Starkey and CCEM, *Environmental Management for SMEs,* pp. 9 and 10.

10 "Engaging SMEs in Community and Social Issues" [online], [cited July 15, 2004], Business in the Community website, 2002. <www.bitc.org.uk/docs/ SMEs_1.pdf>

11 "Report of the Roundtable on 'Fostering CSR Among SMEs,'" p. 8.

12 "Corporate Social Responsibility: Commission Launches European Multi-Stakeholder Forum" [online], [cited July 15, 2004], Europa website, October 16, 2002. <europa.eu.int/rapid/pressReleasesAction.do?reference =IP/02/1487&format=HTML&aged=0&language=EN&guiLanguage=en>

13 "Report of the Roundtable on 'Fostering CSR Among SMEs,'" p. 7.

14 Canadian Federation of Independent Business (CFIB), *SMEs: The Natural Facts,* Canadian Federation of Independent Business, 2001, p. 4.

15 Ibid., p. 3.

16 NetRegs, *SME-nvironment 2003* [online], [cited July 8, 2004], NetRegs, 2003, p. 5. <www.getf.org/file/toolmanager/CustomO16C45F42827.pdf>

17 Subhasis Ray, ICFAI Knowledge Centre, Hyderabad, India, from an e-conference on the possibilities and challenges of corporate social responsibility among small and medium enterprises, sponsored by the World Bank, February 4, 2004.

18 European Commission, "SMEs in Focus: Main Results from the 2002 Observatory of European SMEs" [online], [cited July 8, 2004], Enterprise Publications, 2002, p. 16. <europa.eu.int/comm/enterprise/

enterprise_policy/analysis/doc/execsum_2002_en.pdf>

19 CFIB, *SMEs: The Natural Facts,* p. 5.

20 Ibid., p. 3.

21 Canadian Business for Social Responsibility, *Engaging Small Business in Corporate Social Responsibility: A Canadian Small Business Perspective on CSR,* Canadian Business for Social Responsibility, 2003, pp. 13 and 17.

22 CFIB, *SMEs: The Natural Facts,* p. 3.

23 Starkey and CCEM, *Environmental Management for SMEs,* p. 34.

24 Lynn Johannson, e-mail message to author, December 2, 2003.

25 CBSR, *Engaging Small Business in Corporate Social Responsibility,* p. 17.

26 NetRegs, "SME-nvironment 2003," p. 5.

27 "Winslow Green Growth Fund Finishes 2003 Among Small-Cap Growth Leaders" [online], [cited July 8, 2004], Winslow Management Company website, January 8, 2004. <winslowgreen.com/docs/press_releases/ Q4%2003%20WGGF%20peformance%20Press%20Release.pdf>

28 Envirowise, *Increase Your Profit with Environmental Management Systems,* Envirowise, 2002, p. 10.

29 Daryl W. Ditz, Janet Ranganathan, and R. Darryl Banks, *Green Ledgers: Case studies in corporate environmental accounting,* World Resources Institute, 1995.

30 Lynn Johannson, e-mail message to author, December 2, 2003.

31 Envirowise, *Increase Your Profit with Environmental Management Systems,* p. 5.

32 Marc Epstein and Priscilla Wisner, "Measuring and Managing Social and Environmental Impacts," *Handbook of Cost Management,* 2001edition, edited by John Shank, WG&L, 2001, p. 3.

33 Envirowise, *Increase Your Profit with Environmental Management Systems,* p. 5.

34 Greenest City and Upper Village Business Improvement Area, *Greening the Small Retail Sector,* Clean Air Foundation Cool Shops Program, 2004, p. 4.

35 Ibid.

36 Ibid.

37 Ibid., p. 5.

38 Ibid.

39 Envirowise, *Increase Your Profit With Environmental Management Systems,* p. 12.

40 Greenest City and Upper Village Business Improvement Area, *Greening the Small Retail Sector,* p. 5.

41 Ibid., p. 10.

42 Ibid.

43 United Nations Environment Programme (UNEP), "The Efficient Entrepreneur Calendar Assistant," UNEP Division of Technology, Industry, and Economics, and Wuppertal, Germany: Wuppertal Institute, 2001, p. 23.

44 Envirowise, *Increase Your Profit With Environmental Management Systems,* p. 14.

45 Ibid., p. 26.

46 Kill-a-watt meters are available from numerous sources, such as Safe Home Products. <www.safehomeproducts.com/SHP/SM/Electricity_Monitor.asp>

47 Envirowise, *Increase Your Profit With Environmental Management Systems*, p. 26.

48 Ibid., p. 12.

49 UNEP, "The Efficient Entrepreneur Calendar Assistant", p. 23.

50 Envirowise, *Increase Your Profit With Environmental Management Systems*, p. 26.

51 Greenest City and Upper Village Business Improvement Area, "Greening the Small Retail Sector," pp. 6–9.

52 UNEP, *The Efficient Entrepreneur Calendar Assistant*, p. 23.

53 Greenest City and Upper Village Business Improvement Area, "Greening the Small Retail Sector," p. 11.

54 Envirowise, *Increase Your Profit With Environmental Management Systems*, p. 26.

55 The Sustainable Business Network and the New Zealand Ministry of the Environment, *Enterprise3: Your Business and the Triple Bottom Line*, Sustainable Business Network, 2003, p. 13.

56 Envirowise, *Increase Your Profit With Environmental Management Systems*, p. 14.

57 Greenest City and Upper Village Business Improvement Area, *Greening the Small Retail Sector*, p. 11.

58 UNEP, "The Efficient Entrepreneur Calendar Assistant," p. 32.

59 The Sustainable Business Network and the New Zealand Ministry of the Environment, *Enterprise3*, p. 14.

60 Cameron Smith, "A Potent Way To Heat Portables," *Toronto Star*, February 20, 1999, B6.

61 Envirowise, *Increase Your Profit With Environmental Management Systems*, p. 11.

62 Ibid., p. 25.

63 Epstein and Wisner, "Measuring and Managing Social and Environmental Impacts," pp. 16–17.

64 Alameda County Waste Management Authority and Source Reduction and Recycling Board, *Re-Think Your Bottom Line: A Resource Guide for Alameda County Business to Reduce, Reuse and Recycle* [online], [cited July 8, 2004], <www.stopwaste.org/b-guide.html>

65 "Report of the Roundtable on 'Fostering CSR Among SMEs,'" p. 10.

66 "Finding the Formula for Responsible Small Companies," *Business Respect — CSR Dispatches* 74, May 23, 2004. <www.mallenbaker.net/csr/nl/74.html>

67 "Engaging SMEs in Community and Social Issues," p. 15. <www.bitc.org.uk/docs/SMEs_1.pdf>

68 Deborah Doane and Alex MacGillivray, *Economic Sustainability: The Business of Staying in Business*, The Sigma Project, 2001, p. 0.5.

69 "About the Small Business Consortium" [online], [cited July 8, 2004], Small Business Journey website. <www.smallbusinessjourney.com/output/page45.asp>

70 "Socially responsible small and medium-sized enterprises — unlock your potential..." [online], [cited July 8, 2004], SME Key website. <www.smekey.org/english_lan/default.aspx>

71 "SME Program" [online], [cited July 15, 2004], Canadian Business for Social Responsibility website. <www.cbsr.bc.ca/cbsrsupport/sme.htm>

BIBLIOGRAPHY

I have read hundreds of books, articles, and reports on sustainability and related issues. None of the books compete directly with my book, which is why I felt it needed to be written. Instead, they provide excellent background context and supportive evidence for the arguments I propose. My book describes traditional and emerging drivers of corporate commitment to sustainability and uses a sales call framework to help sustainability champions more effectively convince a critical mass of corporate executives to transform their companies to sustainability leaders.

My book pulls together practical ideas from these and other sources, reframes them as useful tips for sustainability champions, and suggests effective sales call techniques to use when trying to convince hard-nosed executives to embrace sustainable practices. That is what makes my book unique.

I collect books — I read with a highlighter (which is not a good approach to use with library books). I have categorized more than 90 books in my personal library, which are most relevant to this research, into four themes.

- Books about deterioration of environment and society
- Books about corporate contributions to environmental and social problems
- Books about Stage 4 and Stage 5 companies
- Books about benefits of moving from Stage 3 to Stage 4

Books about Deterioration of Environment and Society

Books like the following catalog distressing environmental and social trends and raise alarms that they are not abating.

Brown, Lester, Michael Renner, and Brian Halwell, *Vital Signs 1999: The Environmental Trends That Are Shaping Our Future*, W.W. Norton & Company, 1999.

Christianson, Gale E., *Greenhouse: The 200-Year Story of Global Warming*, Greystone Books, 1999.

Colborn,Theo, Dianne Dumanoski, and John Peterson Meyers, *Our Stolen Future: Are We Threatening Our Fertility, Intelligence, and Survival? — A Scientific Detective Story*, Plume Books, 1997.

de Villiers, Marq, *Water*, Stoddart Publishing Company, 1999.

Flavin, Christopher, Hilary French, and Gary Gardner, *State of the World 2002: A Worldwatch Institute Report on Progress Toward a Sustainable Society*, W.W. Norton & Company, 2002.

Gordon, Anita, and David Suzuki, *It's a Matter of Survival*, Stoddart Publishing, 1990.

Homer-Dixon, Thomas, *The Ingenuity Gap*, Alfred A. Knopf, 2000.

Hunter, Robert, *2030: Confronting Thermageddon in Our Lifetime*, McClelland & Stewart, 2002.

Mackenzie, Fred T., *Our Changing Planet: An Introduction to Earth System Science and Global Environmental Change*, Prentice Hall, 1998.

Meadows, Donella, Dennis Meadows, and Jorgen Randers, *Beyond the Limits: Confronting Global Collapse, Envisioning a Sustainable Future*, Chelsea Green Publishing, 1992.

Ponting, Clive, *A Green History of the World: The Environment and the Collapse of Great Civilizations*, Penguin Books, 1992.

Suzuki, David, *The Sacred Balance: Rediscovering Our Place in Nature*, Prometheus Books, 1998.

Wackernagel, Mathis, and William Rees, *Our Ecological Footprint: Reducing Human Impact on the Earth*, New Society Publishers, 1996.

Countering these claims are a couple of books that say things are not really as bad as environmentalists say they are.

Huber, Peter, *Hard Green: Saving the Environment from the Environmentalists — A Conservative Manifesto*, Basic Books, Perseus Book Group, 1999.

Lomborg, Bjorn, *The Skeptical Environmentalist: Measuring the Real State of the World*, Cambridge University Press, 1998.

Other books show how activist stakeholders can be part of the solution so that we collectively help reverse the current environmental trends as citizens, investors, and activists.

Abbey, Deb, *Global Profit and Global Justice: Using Your Money to Change the World*, New Society Publishers, 2004.

Bornstein, David, *How to Change the World: Social Entrepreneurs and the Power of New Ideas*, Oxford University Press, 2004.

Dauncey, Guy, *Stormy Weather: 101 Solutions to Global Climate Change*, New Society Publishers, 2001.

Day, Paul H., and Sherry Ruth Anderson, *The Cultural Creatives: How 50 Million People Are Changing the World*, Three Rivers Press, 2000.

Dressel, Holly, and David Suzuki, *Good News for a Change: Hope for a Troubled Planet*, Stoddart Publishing, 2002.

MacKenzie Mohr, Doug, and William Smith, *Fostering Sustainable Behavior: An Introduction to Community-Based Social Marketing*, New Society Publishers, 1999.

Svendsen, Ann, *The Stakeholder Strategy: Profiting From Collaborative Business Relationships*, Berrett-Koehler Publishers, 1998.

Books about Corporate Contributions to Environmental and Social Problems

Some authors not only say the environment and society are suffering; they also point the finger of blame at corporations. They accuse companies of being the culprits at the root of ecological problems.

Bakan, Joel, *The Corporation: The Pathological Pursuit of Profit and Power*, Viking Canada, 2004.

Barlow, Maude, and Tony Clarke, *Global Showdown: How The New Activists Are Fighting Global Corporate Rule*, Stoddart Publishing, 2001.

Beder, Sharon, *Global Spin: The Corporate Assault on Environmentalism*, Chelsea Green Publishing, 1997.

Casten, Thomas R., *Turning Off the Heat: Why America Must Double Energy Efficiency To Save Money And Reduce Global Warming*, Prometheus Books, 1998.

Dobbin, Murray, *The Myth of the Good Corporate Citizen: Democracy Under the Rule Of Big Business*, Stoddart Publishing, 1998.

Douthwaite, Richard, *The Growth Illusion: How Economic Growth Has Enriched the Few, Impoverished the Many, and Endangered the Planet*, New Society Publishers, 1999.

Fagin, Dan, Marianne Lavelle, and the Center for Public Integrity, *Toxic Deception: How the Chemical Industry Manipulates Science, Bends the Law, and Endangers Your Health*, Common Courage Press, 1999.

Hammond, Alan, *Which World? Scenarios for the 21st Century*, Shearwater Books, Island Press, 1998.

Kelly, Marjorie, *The Divine Right of Capital: Dethroning the Corporate Aristocracy*, Berrett-Koehler Publishers, 2001.

Klein, Naomi, *No Logo: Taking Aim at the Brand Bullies*, Vintage Canada, Random House, 2000.

Korten, David C., *When Corporations Rule the World*, Kumarian Press and, Berrett-Koehler Publishers, 1995.

Rowell, Andrew, *Green Backlash: Global Subversion of the Environment Movement*, Routledge, 1996.

Other authors go further and claim that corporations are deliberately or ignorantly colluding in the decline of environment and society. They suggest a new economic model is required to change that behavior.

Brown, Lester R., *Eco-Economy: Building an Economy for the Earth*, W.W. Norton & Company, 2001.

Daly, Herman E., and John B. Cobb, Jr., *For the Common Good: Redirecting the Economy toward Community, the Environment, and a Sustainable Future*, Beacon Press, 1989.

Henderson, Hazel, for the New Economics Foundation, *Beyond Civilization: Shaping a Sustainable Global Economy*, Kumarian Press, 1999.

Jacobs, Jane, *Systems of Survival: A Dialogue on the Moral Foundations of Commerce and Politics*, Vintage Canada, Random House books, 1994.

Jacobs, Jane, *The Nature of Economics*, Vintage Canada, Random House Books, 2001.

Korten, David, *The Post-Corporate World: Life after Capitalism*, Berrett-Koehler Publishers, and Kumarian Press, 1999.

Milani, Brian, *Designing the Green Economy: The Post-Industrial Alternative to Corporate Globalization*, Rowan & Littlefield Publishers, 2000.

Books about Stage 4 and Stage 5 Companies

Some authors describe case studies of publicly owned Stage 4 companies that have incorporated sustainability considerations into strategic business decisions to benefit their shareholders.

Nattrass, Brian, and Mary Altomare, *The Natural Step for Business: Wealth, Ecology and The Evolutionary Corporation*, New Society Publishers, 1999.

Nattrass, Brian, and Mary Altomare, *Dancing With the Tiger: Learning Sustainability Step by Natural Step*, New Society Publishers, 2002.

Rowledge, Lorinda R., Russell S. Barton, and Kevin S. Brady, *Mapping The Journey: Case Studies In Strategy And Action Toward Sustainable Development*, Greenleaf Publishing, 1999.

Company founders or CEOs who have a personal, values-based passion for sustainability can give their organizations a mandate to mitigate environmental and social problems, even if such initiatives detract somewhat from the bottom line. Books about these Stage 5 companies, operating with a mission to improve world conditions, help reinforce that it is possible to do well while doing good.

Anderson, Ray C., *Mid-Course Correction — Toward A Sustainable Enterprise: The Interface Model*, Peregrinzella Press, 1998.

Chappell, Tom, *The Soul of a Business: Managing for Profit and the Common Good*, Bantam Books, 1993.

Cohen, Ben, and Jerry Greenfield, *Ben & Jerry's Double Dip: How to Run a Values-Led Business and Make Money, Too*, Fireside Books, Simon & Schuster, 1997.

Hollender, Jeffery, and Stephen Fenichell, *What Matters Most: How a Small Group of Pioneers Is Teaching Social Responsibility to Big Business, and Why Big Business Is Listening*, Basic Books, Perseus Books, 2004.

Books about Benefits of Moving from Stage 3 to Stage 4

The largest group of books is about how and why companies that are not yet at Stage 4 can and should undertake the transformation. Authors outline business benefits of sustainability agendas and quantify them to various degrees.

Arnold, Matthew B., and Robert M. Day, *The Next Bottom Line: Making Sustainable Development Tangible*, World Resources Institute, 1998.

DeSimone, Livio D., and Frank Popoff, with the World Business Council for Sustainable Development, *Eco-Efficiency: The Business Link to Sustainable Development*, The MIT Press, 1997.

Doppelt, Bob, *Leading Change toward Sustainability: A Change-Management Guide for Business, Government and Civil Society*, Greenleaf Publishing, 2003.

Elkington, John, *Cannibals with Forks: The Triple Bottom Line of 21st Century Business*, New Society Publishers, 1998.

Elkington, John, *The Chrysalis Economy: How Citizen CEOs and Corporations Can Fuse Values and Value Creation*, Capstone Publishing, John Wiley & Sons, 2001.

Frankel, Carl, *In Earth's Company: Business, Environment, and the Challenge of Sustainability*, New Society Publishers, 1998.

Gibson, Robert B., editor, *Voluntary Initiatives: The New Politics of Corporate Greening*, Broadview Press, 1999.

Gordon, Pamela J., *Lean and Green: Profit for Your Workplace and the Environment*, Berrett-Koehler Publishers, 2001.

Grayson, David, and Adrian Hodges, *Everybody's Business: Managing Risks and Opportunities in Today's Global Society*, DK Publishing, 2002.

Hawken, Paul, *The Ecology of Commerce: A Declaration of Sustainability*, HarperBusiness, 1993.

Hawken, Paul, Amory B. Lovins, and L. Hunter Lovins, *Natural Capitalism: Creating the Next Industrial Revolution*, Little Brown and Company, 1999.

Hoffman, Andrew J., *Competitive Environmental Strategy: A Guide to the Changing Business Landscape*, Island Press, 1988.

Holliday, Charles O., Stephan Schmidheiny, and Philip Watts, *Walking the Talk: The Business Case for Sustainable Development*, Greenleaf Publishing, 2000.

Jeucken, Marcel, *Sustainable Finance and Banking: The Financial Sector and the Future of the Planet*, Earthscan Publications, 2001.

Labatt, Sonia, and Rodney R.White, *Environmental Finance: A Guide to Environmental Risk Management and Financial Products*, John Wiley & Sons, 2002.

Laszlo, Chris, *The Sustainable Company: How to Create Lasting Value through Social and Environmental Performance*, Island Press, 2003.

Lowe, Ernest A., John L. Warren, and Stephen R. Moran, *Discovering Industrial Ecology: An Executive Briefing and Sourcebook*, Battelle Press, 1997.

Makower, Joel, *The E-Factor: The Bottom-Line Approach to Environmentally Responsible Business*, Plume, Penguin Books, 1994.

McDonough, William, and Michael Braungart, *Cradle to Cradle: Remaking the Way We Make Things*, North Point Press, 2002.

Quarter, Jack, *Beyond the Bottom Line: Socially Innovative Business Owners*, Quorum Books, 2000.

Ranchhod, Ashok, *Marketing Strategies: A Twenty-First Century Approach*, Pearson Education, 2004.

Reinhardt, Forest L., *Down To Earth: Applying Business Principles to Environmental Management*, Harvard Business Press, 2000.

Repetto, Robert, and Duncan Austin, *Pure Profit: The Financial Implications Of Environmental Performance*, World Resources Institute, 2000.

Robert, Karl-Henrik, *The Natural Step Story: Seeding a Quiet Revolution*, New Society Publishers, 2002.

Rocky Mountain Institute, *Green Development: Integrating Ecology and Real Estate*, John Wiley & Sons, 1998.

Romm, Joseph J., *Cool Companies: How The Best Businesses Boost Profits And Productivity By Cutting Greenhouse Gas Emissions*, Island Press, 1999.

Schmidheiny, Stephan, with the Business Council for Sustainable Development, *Changing Course: A Global Perspective on Development and the Environment*, The MIT Press, 1992.

Seiler-Hausmann, Jan-Dirk, Christa Liedtke, and Ernst Ulrich von Weizsacker, eds., *Eco-Efficiency and Beyond: Toward the Sustainable Enterprise*, Greenleaf Publishing, 2004.

Starkey, Richard, and Richard Welford, eds., *The Earthscan Reader in Business and Sustainable Development*, Earthscan Publications, 2001.

Tapscott, Don, and David Ticoll, *The Naked Corporation: How the Age of Transparency Will Revolutionize Business*, Viking Canada, 2003.

von Weizacker, Ernst, Amory B. Lovins, and L. Hunter Lovins, *Factor Four: Doubling Wealth — Halving Resource Use: The New Report To The Club Of Rome*, Earthscan, 1997.

Wagge, Sissel, ed., *Ants, Galileo, & Gandhi: Designing the Future of Business through Nature, Genius, and Compassion*, Greenleaf Publishing, 2003.

Willard, Bob, *The Sustainability Advantage: Seven Business Case Benefits of a Triple Bottom Line*, New Society Publishers, 2002.

INDEX

ABOUT THE AUTHOR

BOB IS THE AUTHOR OF *The Sustainability Advantage: Seven Business Case Benefits of a Triple Bottom Line* (New Society Publishers, 2002). He is a leading expert on the business value of corporate sustainability strategies and in the last three years has given over 120 keynote presentations to corporations, consultants, academics, and nongovernmental organizations.

During his 34-year IBM career, Bob held leadership positions in marketing, technical support, education, and human resources, including 20 years in management. Between 1990 and 2000, Bob led leadership development for IBM's 2,000 managers and executives in Canada. Since taking early retirement in 2000, he has worked full time on applying his business and leadership development experience to engage the business community in proactively avoiding risks and capturing opportunities associated with sustainability.

Bob recently served on the boards of Eco-Energy Durham and the Ontario Sustainable Energy Association (OSEA). He currently serves on the advisory boards of The Natural Step, Canada, and the Certificate in Adult Training and Development at OISE/University of Toronto.

A resident of Ontario, he is a delighted owner of one of the first Honda Civic hybrid-electric cars sold in Canada.

More information about Bob and his books can be found at www.sustainabilityadvantage.com. He can be reached at bobwillard@sympatico.ca.

If you have enjoyed *The Next Sustainability Wave,*
you might also enjoy other

BOOKS TO BUILD A NEW SOCIETY

Our books provide positive solutions for people who want
to make a difference. We specialize in:

**Environment and Justice • Conscientious Commerce
Sustainable Living • Ecological Design and Planning
Natural Building & Appropriate Technology • New Forestry
Educational and Parenting Resources • Nonviolence
Progressive Leadership • Resistance and Community**

New Society Publishers

ENVIRONMENTAL BENEFITS STATEMENT

New Society Publishers has chosen to produce this book on recycled paper made with
100% post consumer waste, processed chlorine free, and old growth free.

For every 5,000 books printed, New Society saves the following resources:[1]

47	Trees
4,218	Pounds of Solid Waste
4,641	Gallons of Water
6,054	Kilowatt Hours of Electricity
7,668	Pounds of Greenhouse Gases
33	Pounds of HAPs, VOCs, and AOX Combined
12	Cubic Yards of Landfill Space

---

[1]Environmental benefits are calculated based on research done by the Environmental Defense Fund and
other members of the Paper Task Force who study the environmental impacts of the paper industry.

For a full list of NSP's titles, please call **1-800-567-6772** *or check out our web site at:*

www.newsociety.com

NEW SOCIETY PUBLISHERS